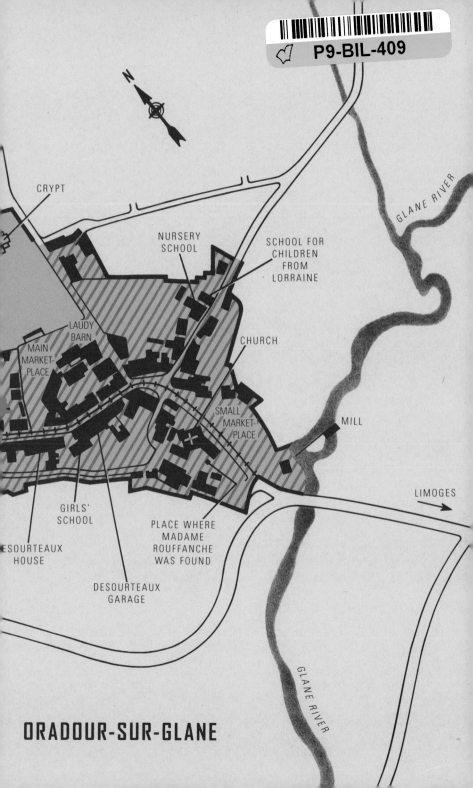

N

CRYPT

NURSERY SCHOOL

SCHOOL FOR CHILDREN FROM LORRAINE

GLANE RIVER

LAUDY BARN

MAIN MARKET-PLACE

CHURCH

SMALL MARKET-PLACE

MILL

LIMOGES

GIRLS' SCHOOL

PLACE WHERE MADAME ROUFFANCHE WAS FOUND

ESOURTEAUX HOUSE

DESOURTEAUX GARAGE

GLANE RIVER

ORADOUR-SUR-GLANE

MARTYRED VILLAGE

MARTYRED VILLAGE

Commemorating the 1944 Massacre
at Oradour-sur-Glane

SARAH FARMER

University of California Press   Berkeley   Los Angeles   London

University of California Press
Berkeley and Los Angeles, California

University of California Press, Ltd.
London, England

This work has appeared in different form as *Oradour: Arrêt sur mémoire*, © 1994 by Editions Calmann-Lévy. Parts of chapter 2 have appeared in *French Historical Studies* 14, no. 1 (Spring 1985). Parts of Chapter 4 have appeared in *French Historical Studies* 19, no. 1 (Spring 1995), © 1995 by Duke University Press; *Parolechiave* 9 (1995), © 1995 Donzelli editore; *Eikon* 14/15 (1995) © 1995 Turia and Kant Verlag.

Library of Congress Cataloging-in-Publication Data

Farmer, Sarah Bennett.
  Martyred village : commemorating the 1944 massacre
  at Oradour-sur-Glane / Sarah Farmer.
    p.   cm.
  Includes bibliographical references and index.
    ISBN 0-520-21186-3
    1. Oradour-sur-Glane Massacre, 1944.   2. World War,
  1939–1945—Atrocities.   3. Massacres—France—
  Oradour-sur-Glane.   4. Oradour-sur-Glane (France)—
  History.   I. Title.
  D804.G4F2913   1999
  940.54′05′094466—dc21   98-29646
                                                      CIP

Printed in the United States of America
9 8 7 6 5 4 3 2 1

CONTENTS

ILLUSTRATIONS

ABBREVIATIONS

ADEIF   Association des Evadés et Incorporés de Force

ADHV   Archives Départementales de la Haute-Vienne

ADP   Archives de la Direction du Patrimoine

AN   Archives Nationales

ANFM   Association Nationale des Familles des Martyrs d'Oradour-sur-Glane

FFI   Forces Françaises de l'Intérieur

FTPF   Francs-Tireurs et Partisans Français

GPRF   Gouvernement Provisoire de la République Française

IHTP   Institut d'Histoire du Temps Présent

MRP   Mouvement Républicain Populaire

MUR   Mouvements Unis de la Résistance

PCF   Parti Communiste Français

RPF   Rassemblement du Peuple Français

SFIO   Section Française de l'Internationale Ouvrière

STO   Service du Travail Obligatoire

PREFACE

This book really began in 1978 when I worked for seven months on a sheep farm in the Limousin region of west central France. I came to French history through love of the language and of that place. My experiences during the spring lambing season taught me not only about the intricacies of ovine birthing but also about the influence of the recent past and the role of memory in current French politics and society.

One day when we had ducked into a barn to take refuge from a sudden storm, Marcel Lajarige, the shepherd with whom I worked, discussed the upcoming legislative elections. In that regard, he referred to the war years in the Limousin and to Communist-led resistance to the Nazis. To my surprise, events of that period still moved him and—though he had been a small child during the war—shaped his present-day political loyalties.

Lajarige mentioned the most traumatic wartime event in the region: the massacre of the women, children, and men of the town of Oradour-sur-Glane by SS soldiers on 10 June 1944. A seven-year-old at the time, Lajarige remembered seeing smoke in the western sky and being told that Oradour was burning. I learned that the remains of the town had been preserved as an emblem and reminder of that epoch. The next summer, when I returned to the Limousin to conduct historical research on the Communist Resistance there, I also went to see Oradour. I walked through the ruins of the town and, in the burned-out church, listened to the guide tell the story of the massacre. Finding the place eerie and horrible, I left quickly.

Six years later, when I began doctoral studies in history at the University of California, Berkeley, Professor Susanna Barrows encouraged my interest in twentieth-century French history. When the time came to choose a thesis topic, she suggested that I explore the period of the Second World War in France through the history of memory—a subject of renewed interest among French scholars who had rediscovered Maurice Halbwachs's path-breaking work on the sociology of memory.[1] Historians had become fascinated with the study of memory as a historical object—in particular, with the evolution of different commemorative practices that have the purpose of representing the past so as to shape and maintain the cultural tradition and political identity of a certain group or the society as a whole.

In France I found that, with the fortieth anniversary of the Allied landings in Normandy and the approaching bicentennial of the French Revolution, the subject of commemoration was receiving much attention in the press and in the publishing world. At the Institut d'Histoire du Temps Présent (IHTP) in Paris, historians of twentieth-century France had come to reflect on the history of memory by way of methodological concerns about the uses of oral history.[2] At the IHTP, Dominique Veillon guided me to the most recent scholarly works on the subject.[3]

I attended Pierre Nora's seminar at the Ecole des Hautes Etudes en Sciences Sociales, the atelier for his multivolume collection of historical scholarship on the "national memory" of France, *Les Lieux de mémoire*. In Nora's estimation, France's sense of national history is rooted in *lieux de mémoire*: "specific objects that codify, condense, anchor France's national memory." They can take many forms:

> These can be monuments (the *château* of Versailles or the cathedral of Strasbourg); emblems, commemorations, and symbols (the tricolor of the French flag, the Fourteenth of July, the Marseillaise); rituals (the coronation of the kings at Reims) as well as monuments (such as the *monuments aux morts* in every French village or the Pantheon); manuals (a textbook used by all French children, a dictionary); basic texts (the Declaration of the Rights of Man or the *Code civil*); or mottoes (for example, "Liberté, Egalité, Fraternité").[4]

Nora's definition is notably broad and abstract: "*Les lieux de mémoire* are not *what* one remembers, but the places *where* memory works; not the [historical] tradition itself, but its laboratory."[5] This book, on the other hand, is specifically concerned with *lieux de mémoire* that are essentially material and have been imbued with symbolic significance—not monuments as such, but places one can walk through, places where the landscape has been inscribed with memory. In this pursuit, I have relied on the work of cultural geographers, historians, and philosophers with a particular interest in landscape.[6]

Most broadly, this study grows out of recent work in the history and sociology of memory, literary and film testimony about remembrance of the Second World War and of the Holocaust, and general postmodern interests in the presentation of the past. The writings of Primo Levi and the scholarly work of James E. Young, Shoshanna Felman, and Lawrence L. Langer are particularly enlightening on questions of testimony and the afterlife of events as expressed in narrative.[7] James Young's most recent work on Holocaust memorials is a model for the interpretation of memorials and their meanings in light of national myths, ideals, and politics.[8] The documentary films of Marcel Ophuls (*The Sorrow and the Pity, Memory of Justice, Hotel Terminus: The Life and Times of Klaus Barbie*) and Claude Lanzmann (*Shoah*) are invaluable sources for any historian of the Second World War in Europe.

In the course of my research, I became personally involved in questions of film and testimony and their intersection with the writing of history. At the start of my work on Oradour-sur-Glane I met Marc Wilmart, a journalist from the French television network FR3, and Michel Follin, an independent film director, who were planning a documentary about Oradour. I joined their team as an informal collaborator and historical advisor. When filming began, I provided commentary on camera. Many of the interviews on which sections of this book are based were done in the course of working on the film, which was first aired in France in June 1989.[9]

My work on Oradour has had several incarnations: as a doctoral thesis in 1992, as a book published in France by Editions Calmann-Lévy in 1994, and now as this English-language book.

I have many people to thank, in France and America, for intellectual guidance and friendship without which I could not have completed these projects.

At Berkeley, Susanna Barrows and Thomas Laqueur were enormously generous with their time and critical insights. They helped me to specify the problems I had in mind and to pursue them as relentlessly as possible. During the eighteen months spent writing in Berkeley, members of Susanna Barrows's dissertation group provided a lively intellectual community and careful readings of chapter drafts: David Barnes, Marjorie Beale, Michael Bess, Avi Chomsky, Joshua Cole, Jeff Ravel, Sylvia Schafer, Regina Sweeney, Matt Truesdell, and Jeffrey Verhey. Vanessa Schwartz led me to think more creatively about my own work as relating to broader issues concerning French history and culture. After I left Berkeley, Randolph Starn gave me detailed and careful advice on the introduction to my French-language book.

My parents, Thomas Farmer and Elizabeth Midgley, my brother, Daniel, and my grandfather, Merle Curti, all encouraged me to push ahead. My twin sister, Elspeth, offered a sounding board for my ideas. My friend Martha Weiss holds a special place in this project. In Berkeley we discussed our respective work in botany and history at lunch and dinner, while running in Tilden Park, and in daily phone calls.

The Center for European Studies at Harvard University generously granted me a fellowship year in 1992–1993, which provided the time and place to prepare the manuscript published in France. I have Abby Collins, Guido Goldman, and Stanley Hoffmann to thank for all they do to make CES an extraordinary resource for scholars of contemporary Europe.

Since joining the faculty at the University of Iowa, the university has generously granted me two summer fellowships to conduct further research. While working through this new material I depended on the advice of my colleague and friend Ken Cmiel. At the University of California Press I have been fortunate to have Sheila Levine, Dore Brown, Evan Camfield, and Laura Driussi to guide me in preparing this work for an American audience.

There are at least as many people to thank in France: Dominique Veillon at the Institut d'Histoire du Temps Présent, Pierre Nora and Patrick Fridenson at the Ecole des Hautes Etudes en Sciences Sociales, Alain Corbin at the Sorbonne, Freddy Raphael at the University of Strasbourg, Chantal Tourtier-Bonazzi at the Archives Nationales, Françoise Bercé at the Bibliothèque du Patrimoine, Jean Luquet at the Mission auprès des Archives Nationales, Ministère de l'Equipement et du Logement, and Patrick Weil at the Institut d'Etudes Politiques. Christian Jouhaud at the Ecole des Hautes Etudes first encouraged me to publish my work in France. Robert Paxton took time during research trips to Paris to offer his wisdom about modern France as well as practical advice on how to shape this project. Charles-Constantin de Toulouse-Lautrec was the best confidant one could ever hope for.

Since 1994 I have benefitted from the generous assistance of the Director of the Departmental Archives of the Haute-Vienne, Pierre Channu, and his colleagues Françoise Mirouse and Véronique Mercier. Marc Wilmart of FR3 Limoges, Michel Follin, and the entire crew who worked on the documentary *Oradour* made research more fun than I ever would have expected. At Oradour-sur-Glane I am particularly grateful to

Lucette Bichaud, André Desourteaux, Dr. Robert Lapuelle, and Amélie Lebraud. At the farm of L'Essart near Roussac, there is Miranda de Toulouse-Lautrec, who first brought me to the Limousin and to whose home and friendship I have returned over the years. She and Marcel and Annie Lajarige made the Limousin a second home for me. At Le Mas Grenoux, Laurie McGraw and Gilles Couturaud extended their friendship and open-ended hospitality.

In so many ways this book is bound up with friends; although perhaps unrecognizable to them, their contributions appear in these pages: Jean-Michel Helvig, Simon Hirschhorn, Sheryl Kroen, Anne Lilensztein, Susanne Lowenthal, James Markham, Lilianna Sardelli, Debbie Seward, Li Schorr, Beate Thewalt, Glenn Voloshin.

It is a great sadness to me that a number of the people who counted so much during my involvement in this project have died: Gilles Coutureaud, Merle Curti, Marcel Lajarige and Charles-Constantin de Toulouse-Lautrec. I think of them often.

MARTYRED VILLAGE

INTRODUCTION

Among German crimes of the Second World War, the massacre of 642 women, children, and men of Oradour-sur-Glane by SS soldiers on 10 June 1944 is one of the most notorious. On that Saturday afternoon, four days after the Allied landings in Normandy, SS troops encircled the town of Oradour in the rolling farm country of the Limousin and rounded up its inhabitants. In the marketplace they divided the men from the women and children. The men were marched off to barns nearby and shot. The soldiers locked the women and children in the church, shot them, and set the building (and then the rest of the town) on fire. Those residents of Oradour who had been away for the day, or had managed to escape the roundup, returned to a blackened scene of horror, carnage, and devastation.

In 1946 the French state expropriated and preserved the entire ruins of Oradour. The forty acres of crumbling houses, farms, and shops became France's *village martyr* (martyred village), a testament to French suffering under the German Occupation. The absence of any resistance activity in Oradour facilitated efforts to universalize the meaning of the event, allowing it to stand for the ultimate victimization of innocent French people. Today, those who make the journey to the ruins of Oradour hear a commemorative narrative of an ideal French village that, through no fault of its own, became the target of Nazi barbarism.

The particular events of 10 June 1944 have been recounted in extensive detail in numerous books. This study investigates the prominence of the massacre in French understanding of the national experience under German domination. How and why, in the aftermath of the war, did this particular story emerge from the myriad possible stories that could be told? What political factors led to the choice of Oradour for national commemoration as a "martyred village"? How has commemoration of the massacre, in particular the preservation of the physical traces of destruction, influenced the afterlife of the event? This book explores how the French shaped their sense of the national past through the meanings attributed to the massacre and the transformation of the ruins of Oradour into a national monument. It tells of the postwar trial of some of the perpetrators, which had a significant impact on the memory and commemoration of the massacre at Oradour. My study of the community of survivors at Oradour addresses the personal and private ways in which, through remembrance, these people have sought to come to terms with their enormous loss.

In the last decade, scholars across a range of fields in the humanities and social sciences have used concepts of memory to explore a variety of concerns and topics: the traditional arts of memory, the concept of "modern memory," the relationship between history and memory, participation in memorial practices that refer to a historical past, the survival of oral traditions, the writing of memoirs and oral testimony, memories of childhood as the foundation for Freudian psychoanalysis and other forms of psychotherapy (and in that regard the notion of repressed memory, as well as attacks on that notion), and individual and collective responses to political torture, natural catastrophes, and mass murder on the scale of genocide. Increasingly memory provides the moral dimension to discussions of what makes up the individual, to quests for political justice, and to the desire to insure a better future.[1]

It has seemed useful to me, particularly in a work of history, to pare back on the use of the general term "memory" in order to distinguish between recollection of past experience, invocation of the experience of others, and historical or cultural tradition (often referred to as cultural or historical memory). Although I, like many others, am indebted to the work of Maurice Halbwachs, I have become increasingly skeptical of the concept of "collective memory," largely because it leaves unexamined the possibility of autonomy for the individual in relation to the shared memories of groups to which he or she belongs.[2] This does nothing to diminish or contradict Halbwachs's key insight that remembering is a social act and practice (because we need others to remember), and that such remembering is a major element in constituting group identities. This book is concerned with a particular aspect of social memory: commemoration, defined here as the act of remembering and memorializing past events, in public, as a member of a group.[3]

Commemoration reveals much about a society's relationship to its past because it mediates between individual testimony and collective remembrance; between the often conflicting perspectives of participating groups (survivors, the families of those touched by the events being memorialized, associations, government authorities, political parties); between past, present, and future; between remembered experience and the written works of professional historians; between remembering and forgetting. Groups that organize around maintaining and communicating a common memory, or public authorities that erect memorials or mark anniversaries, seek to gather others to their view of the events being recalled and thereby to influence public understanding of the past. Yet these commemorative efforts are often punctuated as much by conflict as by consensus. This certainly holds true for French commemoration of the complex and divisive period of the Second World War.

Incorporating recent history into the fabric of the remembered past posed particularly acute problems for the French after the Second World War. The other Allied victors—the United States, Britain, Canada, and the Soviet Union—could refer to the Second World War in uncomplicated terms like "the good war." France too had great themes to celebrate: the activity of the Resistance and the battles of the Liberation have been officially commemorated with pride since the end of the war. Yet the experience of the Occupation created deep and lasting animosities in France equal to those of the *guerres franco-françaises* of the French Revolution, the Commune of 1871, or the Dreyfus affair in the 1890s. As damaging to French society as the defeat in 1940 and the German Occupation that followed were the French dealings with each other during those years. The Allied invasion of June unleashed a bitter settling of accounts and summary executions that lasted into the fall of 1944, when the provisional French government established administrative control of the country and the courts assumed the thorny task of purging collaborators. The widespread enthusiasm for General de Gaulle at the Liberation glossed over only briefly the divisions created by the Occupation and the Vichy regime, which splintered the French in every conceivable way. The historian Robert Frank put it neatly: "The defeat of 1940, the occupation, the Vichy regime, the civil war are very much present in the memory of the French. But that which is sadly memorable is not easily commemorable."[4]

The war had split the French along geographical as well as ideological lines. The terms of the armistice in 1940 divided France into the German-occupied north and west and the so-called "free zone" administered from Vichy. Another new border, established along the Somme river, cut off the departments of the Nord and the Pas-de-Calais from the rest of France. The eastern departments of the Bas-Rhin, the Haut-Rhin, and the Moselle were annexed de facto into the Third Reich. The Italian military occupied the southern Alpine departments from November 1942 to September 1943. These new internal boundaries, along with other conditions of the Occupation such as a censored press, restricted domestic travel, and food rationing constricted the lives and narrowed the world of many French people. In areas where the Occupation proved particularly harsh, or where there was active resistance, a particularly intense regional sensibility developed, which has imbued people's memories to this day. This regionalism also contributed to the difficulty in France of creating a cohesive sense of the national past for the period 1940–1944.

The problems the French have faced in commemorating the Second World War come more clearly into focus when placed against the commemorative culture for the years 1914–1918. For the Great War, November 11 served as the single national holiday; the *monument aux morts* stood as the unifying symbol of the enormous losses in the trenches; in the Tomb of the Unknown Soldier, one body represented all the losses.

The *monument aux morts* in the town square became the focal point of First World War commemoration in France. Hardly a village in France did not raise a *monument aux morts* inscribed with the names of the local war dead. The initiative to erect monuments was a truly popular movement emanating from the communes, indicating an overwhelming desire to remember those who died in the trenches and a general consensus about the physical form the remembrance should take.[5] Despite richness and diversity in their style and symbolism, there is a consistency among the *monuments aux morts*. They possess a visual coherence; these structures have become almost as common a feature in the French landscape as the village church. They enabled each commune to participate in the mourning of the nation, while the list of names of the dead symbolically brought home men whose bodies often lay hundreds of kilometers away.[6]

In 1945, General de Gaulle sought to mobilize the feelings of unity and pride that the French had experienced in November 1918. A master of constructing "mobilizing myths," de Gaulle joined the two wars into one, consciously seeking to subsume the shame of defeat, occupation, and collaboration into a seamless, heroic, historical narrative of French victory over German aggression.[7] For the first national celebration to mark the end of the war, de Gaulle celebrated the armistice of 1918 and the 1945 victory in Europe in one grandiose ritual.[8] On the eve of 11 November 1945, fifteen coffins containing the bodies of people who had died in the most recent conflict were brought into Paris by cortege. The next morning, hearses solemnly transported the catafalques to the Arc de Triomphe, and soldiers laid them around the Tomb of the Unknown Soldier. Here de Gaulle gave a speech that called up the image of one long battle—a "thirty years' war."[9] That night the fifteen bodies were interred at the Mont Valérien, the site of execution of thousands of prisoners during the Occupation, and the place where a national monument would be established in the honor of the *morts pour la France* of the Second World War.[10]

Despite its elaborate use of the sites and symbols of the First World War, even in its formal aspects this ceremony could only partially conceal the fractures of the Second World War. Whereas one unnamed solider's body under the Arc de Triomphe officially represented all the dead of the Great War, the Council of Ministers chose fifteen named bodies to represent the war of 1939–1945. There were two resisters (a man and a woman from the metropolitan Resistance), two political deportees (also a man and a woman), one member of the Forces Françaises de l'Intérieur (FFI), a prisoner of war killed trying to escape, and nine soldiers from France and the colonies. Their names adorned their catafalques and their circumstances of death were made public.[11]

After 1945, the emphasis in European memorialization increasingly shifted from the traditional cult of the war dead to an unprecedented effort to mark and preserve the sites and traces of destruction.[12] Indicating the places of important events took priority over erecting traditional monuments. In France, for example, commemorative plaques denote the locations where victims and combatants died: battle sites of the Resistance, the places of atrocities against civilians, and the exact spots where people were shot down.

The preservation of sites and increased recourse to notions of martyrdom were due in part to changes in the nature of warfare. The Occupation, the exodus of refugees to the south, the expulsions from Alsace and Lorraine, the deportation of laborers to Germany, the extermination of Jews, mass killings in concentration camps, food shortages, bombings, the guerrilla tactics of the Resistance—all blurred the distinction between home and front. Many of the French losses for 1939–1945 were civilians who died under widely varying circumstances, sometimes at the hands of their own compatriots. Memorializing these deaths posed an entirely different task than the commemoration of soldiers who died in the trenches during the First World War. While the French commonly appended the comparatively few names of those who died in uniform during the Second World War to the *monuments aux morts* of the First, they could not be claimed to represent an experience shared by many.[13]

The particular geography of the war and Occupation also played a part in the shift toward marking sites. The fighting and the physical damage of 1914–1918 had been largely restricted to the front-line areas of the northeast; the *monuments aux morts* of the First World War had symbolically brought the war from the front back to the soldiers' home towns. During the Second World War, however, the Occupation and its disruptions spread across the entire country. Guerrilla warfare and the battles of the Liberation left physical scars across entire regions. In 1945, the war did not have to be brought home with a statue or a stele; it had already been there, in all its moral and political complexities. The preservation of the ruins of Oradour as a *village mar-*

tyr in the heart of France speaks to this new pattern of commemoration.

Other countries also maintained physical signs of destruction. The Germans and the English gave particular attention to preserving ruined churches as war memorials. The Frauenkirche in Dresden, the St. Nikolaikirche in Hamburg, and the St. Aegidienkirche in Hannover were purposely left in ruins.[14] Fragments of ruins were incorporated into the designs for rebuilding the Kaiser-Wilhelm-Gedächtniskirche in Berlin and Coventry Cathedral in England. The bombed remains of two churches in London were turned into garden-ruins as memorials to the Blitz.[15]

In a more radical move, whole portions of landscapes where people had been killed were set aside, as in the "martyred villages" of Oradour and Lidice (Czech Republic); the sites of the American landings on the beaches of Normandy; the key battle sites of the Resistance on the plateau of the Vercors in eastern France; and concentration camp sites in East and West Germany, Austria, and Poland.[16] After the First World War, people throughout France had mourned the dead and organized public tribute to their sacrifices. After the Second World War, the sense that Nazi crimes had been of unprecedented moral depravity spurred the survivors to gather evidence for the effort to make those responsible pay for their deeds. The initial commemorative concern of the societies that had come under Nazi domination was to establish the criminal nature of the Nazi regime and to reinforce their own legitimacy by preserving the scene of the crime. A martyred village or a concentration camp site served not so much to symbolize loss as to provide unmediated testimony of the destruction of entire communities of people. The ruins at Oradour and the barracks at Auschwitz were preserved as bare facts that speak for themselves.

These memorials carried a message different from that of traditional war monuments. In France, the nation as victim and martyr took on new importance as a theme of commemoration. Though the nation had long been represented as sacred, the increased use of the term "martyr" in commemoration reflected, in part, the enormous importance of ideology in the Second World War; the struggle against Nazism had greater moral stakes than the fight against Germany's nationalist ambitions in 1870 or 1914.

At least as important, the representation of the particular victims as martyrs ennobled the humiliating experience of the French defeat in 1940 and French passivity during the Occupation. The story of innocent villagers massacred by the Nazis implicitly gave the message that, regardless of their political choices or wartime loyalties, every French person was at risk and potentially a martyr. The Resistance has received the most attention in official remembrance of the Second World War, but Oradour provides an alternative, symbolizing the victimization of unengaged French people rather than those who opposed the oppressor. The martyred village presents a vision of the French as powerless in the face of the Nazis. In this respect, the symbol of Oradour may have distracted from the brutal policies of the Vichy authorities.

Those who preserved the ruins of Oradour decided to freeze a particular moment in time—10 June 1944—after the town's destruction. The account offered here will illustrate the inherent impossibility of arresting time and memory. Over time, rain has washed white the blackened remains of Oradour, and the jagged walls have crumbled under the impact of frost and thaw. Though workmen repair the ruins and cut back ivy and nettles, decay and new growth threaten to change Oradour from a scene of horror into a melancholy, even romantic vista. Just as memory is continually reworked and reorganized, memorial sites never stand still. Oradour has its own life story, entangled with political forces, the forms of memory, and aesthetic concerns that have been brought to bear on the memorial site.

Chapter One

THE MASSACRE

The ruins of the town of Oradour-sur-Glane lie twenty-two kilometers northwest of Limoges in the Limousin region of west central France. Made up of the departments of the Creuse, the Corrèze, and the Haute-Vienne, the Limousin is, for the most part, rural, poor, and sparsely populated. The upland country of the Limousin is, for many of the French, a backward area one passes through on the way between the Paris region and the south. The region has never been prosperous and has produced few of the cultural riches that attract outsiders. The appeal of the Limousin is in its verdant fields, rolling landscape, and a way of life that is slow to change.

Some three hundred thousand people a year turn off the main highway and make their way along smaller country roads of the Haute-Vienne to reach the crumbling vestiges of the *village martyr*. Almost all (89 percent) of the visitors are French, usually stopping off on their way to or from vacation. Of the foreigners,

53 percent are English and 40 percent Dutch, many of whom continue south to vacation in the Dordogne. A third of the yearly visitors come in August.[1]

On the warm days of August, throngs of families with young children, groups of friends, and couples stroll down the main street, peering into the gutted houses and filing in and out of the church where the women and children of Oradour were closed in and burned to death. The rusted tramlines running through the town, the handsome carved stone lettering on the façade of the old post office, the gaping shopfronts, and the plaques that list the names and professions of the people who once lived here conjure up a vitality of rural life that has vanished from the France of today, a time when the streets of Oradour were full of activity.

Before its destruction, Oradour was a bourg: a compact market town, set between the wild hills of the Monts de Blond and the valley of the Vienne, that served a large surrounding agricultural community. The census of 1936, the last taken before the war, indicates that 330 people lived in the town proper—most of them artisans and shopkeepers. The local notables (a notary, two doctors, a pharmacist, a postal receiver, and a priest) also resided in the bourg.[2] The rest of the commune's 1,574 residents were spread out in the fifty-three hamlets and small farms that lay clustered around the town.[3]

Greater social contrasts existed within the bourg than in the countryside. In town there were a few bourgeois families that, over generations, had accumulated power and material security. The Desourteaux family, for example, had family members in the professions and commerce. Dr. Paul Desourteaux ran a medical

FIGURE 1

Postcard views of Oradour-sur-Glane between the wars.
Top, general view. Bottom, view from the bridge.

practice with his son Jacques and lived in an imposing stone house on the main street—the rue Emile Desourteaux, named after his grandfather who had been mayor from 1892 to 1906. His three other sons, Hubert, Paul, Etienne, were, respectively, proprietor of a garage, a grocer, and the secretary in the mayor's office.

In the interwar period, Oradour was also a lively center of sociability. There were numerous cafés, three musical clubs, a soccer team, and two veterans' associations from the Great War. On Sundays, clubs from Limoges would come by tram to spend the day on the banks of the Glane, where they organized fishing contests.[4] Commercial and social connections created a tightly knit extended community. Local farmers came into Oradour to conduct all manner of business. Their wives ventured into town less frequently but could be seen on the semimonthly market days going to the local grocer, or sometimes stopping at the fabric shop of Monsieur Dupic in the main street. The commune's elementary schools were in town, so many children from outlying hamlets walked into Oradour to go to school. In 1944, 64 boys and 106 girls from the commune were enrolled in Oradour's schools. The smallest children attended the nursery school.

In the early summer of 1944, Oradour-sur-Glane was a prosperous, tranquil haven, largely protected from the deprivations of war. The biggest disturbance to family life was the absence of men who had been drafted to work in Germany or were still prisoners of war after being captured during the short campaign of 1939–1940.[5] All in all, people lived well here; there was no shortage of food and the German occupation of Limoges seemed far away. When asked in 1988 if in Oradour one had had the feeling of being at war, a survivor of the massacre, Marcel Darthout, responded: "Not that much. Yes and no, but in general not that

FIGURE 2

Members of a local musical society.

much. One eats well in the country. One finds what one wants. One finds poultry. Then bread, that's a big problem. We got bread that wasn't very good, but one managed to find white flour. It wasn't bad. It was a very agreeable life."[6] The Germans occupied the southern part of France starting in November 1942. Their presence was less obtrusive there than in Paris and the cities of the north. Today, people of Oradour claim that until the massacre no German, at least none in uniform, had been seen in wartime Oradour.

During the war, banking on the relative isolation of the spot, many well-to-do residents of Limoges stored their cars in barns in Oradour to hide them from the Germans. One resident of Oradour, recalling his family's perceptions at the time, captured the prevailing mood: "Really, we sort of thought that we were— that we weren't part of the war. We thought that we wouldn't be concerned by the war—anyway, not a lot. . . ."[7]

The apparent safety and obvious comfort of Oradour had already attracted refugees. In 1939, twenty-six Spanish loyalists fleeing the civil war settled in Oradour. The Second World War brought more outsiders: in September 1939, the French government evacuated 380,000 residents—for the most part women, children, and young people—from the department of the Bas-Rhin in Alsace and sent them to the Limousin, Dordogne, Périgord, and the Charente. Oradour was designated to host residents of the town of Schiltigheim, an industrial suburb of Strasbourg.[8]

For the Alsatians, as well as residents of "the interior," this encounter proved difficult. Eighty percent of the Alsatians did not speak French. They were often viewed with suspicion and disdain by their hosts, who, imitating the Alsatian word for "yes," referred to them as *les ya-ya*. In addition, Alsace was a devoutly

Catholic region in which, alone among the regions of France, religious instruction was offered in school. (When Alsace rejoined
France in 1918, after having been annexed by Germany in 1871,
it was allowed to keep the religious instruction in schools that
the French parliament had abolished in 1905.) When Alsatian
refugees sought religious instruction for their children, it did not
sit well in the radical, secular, leftist regions of the Limousin and
Périgord.[9]

Fleeing the German advance in May 1940, millions of French
and Belgians poured into southern France. The Haute-Vienne
received the fourth largest number of refugees of any department.[10] One month later, eighty-four expellees came to Oradour
from the Lorraine towns of Charly and Montois-Flauville near
Metz. By 1943, approximately one hundred refugees from the
different areas of France had settled in the community.[11] In addition to the Lorrains, women and children from the Paris region,
Montpellier, and Avignon boarded with local families or rented
rooms in Oradour's hotels and inns. Some of these refugees had
been born in eastern Europe and were probably Jewish. It is difficult to know exactly how many people resided in the town of
Oradour on the eve of the massacre. The commune as a whole
counted at least 1,664 residents.[12]

Oradour also received local visitors. Five trams a day ran in
each direction from Limoges to St-Junien, with a stop in
Oradour. The trip from Limoges to Oradour took a little over an
hour. On Saturdays during the war years, residents of Limoges
came by tram to provision themselves with meat and other items
that were in short supply in the city. The Limogeauds often
made the trip into a day's outing, spending the morning shop-
ping and then taking the afternoon to picnic or fish on the banks

of Glane, which passed under a bridge at the southern entrance to the town.

Arriving at Oradour from Limoges, the tram stopped before the bridge at the edge of town. This was the stop for the hamlets of Les Bordes, Le Mas du Puy, and Laplaud. The tram then continued across the bridge and up the main road, passing, on the left, the impressive village church with its twelfth-century romanesque vaulted chancel and fifteenth-century nave and side chapels. The Church had progressively lost ground in the region since the French Revolution, but Oradour once was an important local religious center; the name is believed to derive from the Limousin word *ouradour,* which comes from the Latin *oratorium,* or place of prayer. *Ouradours* were generally rudimentary square chapels at the intersection of important roads.[13]

A small marketplace and the Café/Hôtel Milord faced the church. A few yards up, the road to the hamlet of Les Bordes branched off to the right. On its journey up the main road, the tram passed shops, barns, a garage, workshops, private dwellings, the girls' school, and the entrance to the large marketplace. Across the street from this marketplace stood the house of Dr. Paul Desourteaux, the wartime mayor of Oradour.[14] As the tram approached the north end of town, it stopped at the little station next to the post office and across from the town hall before continuing out of Oradour toward Javerdat and the small city of St-Junien, thirteen kilometers to the southwest.

10 June 1944

Saturdays were often busy in Oradour and this one—four days after the Allied invasion of Normandy—was no exception. Saturday afternoon was a time for running errands, getting a haircut at the Café Duchêne, or chatting with neighbors. For the young men who often took a few hours to socialize in town on Saturday, there was the added attraction of the afternoon distribution of the tobacco ration. On this Saturday, school attendance was good because a medical check was scheduled for the afternoon.

At approximately two o'clock the midday calm was shattered by the appearance of German troops at the southeastern entrance to the village. The soldiers quickly blocked the entrances to Oradour. Sentinels fanned out and encircled the town and some of the neighboring farms. These 120 soldiers were members of the Der Führer regiment of the Waffen SS tank division Das Reich, which had been sent toward Limoges a few days before to fight the Resistance. As soldiers went from house to house, the Germans sent the town crier through the streets to call the population to assemble in the central marketplace. Meanwhile, soldiers in armored cars rounded up men working in nearby farms and fields.

According to survivors' accounts, most of Oradour's inhabitants obeyed the orders, believing they had nothing more to fear than a routine check of identity papers. Some, mostly men who feared being deported to Germany, concealed themselves in barns, attics, and basements. Martial Brissaud, for example, a nineteen-year-old whose family lived at the western edge of town, hid in the attic while the Germans searched the house. Later he sneaked into the garden, where he lay flat on the ground until he could escape to the woods beyond town.

The SS soldiers moved quickly through town, hunting people out of their houses and driving them toward the market square. When soldiers came to the makeshift school for refugee children from the Lorraine, eight-year-old Roger Godfrin fled out the back door of the school building. He hid for a while in a field of tall grass and then ran on toward the Glane. Though shot at by German soldiers, he made it across the river to safety.[15] He was the only schoolchild in Oradour to survive. One other little boy survived, André Pinède, who was not attending school.[16]

Within an hour the Germans had gathered the townspeople in the marketplace. Dr. Jacques Desourteaux, who had been out on a house call in a neighboring hamlet, was stopped as he drove back into town and ordered to join the crowd. At about three o'clock, the soldiers separated the women and children from the crowd, herded them to the church, and shut them in. Speaking through an interpreter, an officer addressed the 200 to 250 men remaining in the square. He announced that the SS knew of a cache of arms and munitions at Oradour and demanded that all those who possessed guns step forward. When nothing came of this, the officer turned to the mayor, Paul Desourteaux, and instructed him to designate hostages from among the townspeople.[17] The mayor refused, offering himself and his sons instead. After taking Desourteaux back to the town hall for discussion, the Germans apparently changed their minds about singling out captives. Mayor Desourteaux returned to the crowd, and the officer announced that his men were going to search the town.

Following a signal from the commander, the SS soldiers then divided the men into groups and hustled them off to various barns and garages around the marketplace. The only ones to survive what was about to happen were six young men from the group of sixty-two shut into the Laudy barn.[18] While the men stood in the barn, talking nervously among themselves, an SS solider set up a machine gun on a tripod. Other soldiers stood guard. They waited. Then, from outside, came the sound of a detonation: the signal to fire. Someone shouted a command, and bullets mowed down the Frenchmen. Soldiers came forward to give a coup de grâce to those who might still be alive. The Germans then covered the bodies with straw, kindling, and phosphorous and set fire to the building. The six who survived had been standing near the front of the group; they were protected by the bodies that fell on them. One, Marcel Darthout, described the moment: "We felt the bullets, which brought me down. I dove . . . everyone was on top of me. And they were still firing. And there was shouting. And crying. I had a friend who was lying on top of me and who was moaning. And then it was over. No more shots. And they came at us, stepping on us. And with a rifle they finished us off. They finished off the buddy who was on top of me. I felt it when he died."[19]

As smoke filled the barn, the survivors groped their way through a small door that led into another barn. Three of them hid in the loft, the others behind a woodpile. When that refuge was set on fire, they crawled outdoors and surreptitiously worked their way over walls and gardens toward the edge of town. Only five made it: Pierre-Henri Poutaraud was killed on the way by a sentinel. By seven in the evening the others had reached safety. Behind them, Oradour burned. In the late afternoon the SS soldiers had gone through the streets pillaging houses and shops, systematically setting Oradour on fire and shooting people forced out of hiding by the flames.

While the Germans were killing the men of Oradour, the women had been locked in the church. At approximately five o'clock, two soldiers came in and placed a large chest on the altar. They retreated, laying out a long fuse, which they lit before shutting the door. Moments later the chest exploded, releasing clouds of suffocating smoke and blowing out some of the church windows. In the ensuing chaos, the soldiers opened the door and sprayed the group with gunfire. They piled flammable material on some of the bodies, set a bonfire with the church pews, and abandoned the building.

Only one person managed to save herself from the conflagration. Marguerite Rouffanche, a forty-seven-year-old woman, had been part of a group that pushed back into the sacristy in search of fresh air. As the church burned, she crawled behind the altar and found a stool used for lighting candles. She managed to climb up and out the window. She dropped three meters to the ground below. Looking up, Madame Rouffanche saw that she had been followed by a young woman with a baby. The young woman handed down her baby before jumping, but all three were caught in a hail of machine-gun fire. Mother and child were killed; wounded, Madame Rouffanche was able to crawl into the garden of the presbytery, where she hid among rows of peas.

In the early evening of 10 June, the Germans stopped the last tram from Limoges as it approached Oradour. SS soldiers forced twenty-two residents of the commune of Oradour to step off the tram before sending it back to Limoges. The passengers were held for two hours and then released with no explanation. Terrified, they took refuge in nearby hamlets or spent the night in the woods.

On the morning of 11 June, all that remained of Oradour was a smoldering mass of burnt farms, shops, and houses.[20] Six hundred forty-two people had died.[21] The losses included 393 people living in Oradour (longtime residents and 84 refugees), 167 people from the villages and hamlets of the commune, 33 people from Limoges, and 25 others from different parts of the Haute-Vienne.[22] Roughly 80 residents of Oradour survived in one way or another: the men from the Laudy barn, Roger Godfrin, Marguerite Rouffanche, 28 who hid from the roundup and managed to escape the encircled town, and approximately 36 others who happened to be away for the day, like the butcher Desvignes, who had gone to the market in St-Victurnien, and the postman, Gabriel Senon, who had been out on his rounds. Twelve other men were away as prisoners of war, working in Germany as part of Vichy's compulsory labor service, the Service du Travail Obligatoire (STO); or enrolled in the *chantiers de jeunesse*, Vichy's youth camps.[23]

The massacre blighted outlying areas as well. The hamlets remained physically intact, but they lost their young children who had been in the school at Oradour. The village of Le Mas du Puy is typical. Of the forty-four people recorded in the census of 1936 as living in this settlement, fourteen died in Oradour, among them four mothers and eight children between the ages of five and ten. The mothers, concerned that their children had not come home from school, had gone to town looking for them. They died with them in the church.[24]

News of a disaster in Oradour spread quickly in the immediate vicinity. Albert Valade, a fourteen-year-old boy at the time, had been tending his uncle's cows outside of town on the afternoon of 10 June. As he stood in a small green field cut by the Glane in the late afternoon, something dark floated to the ground and caught his eye. It was a burned page of paper on which he could read the words of the catechism.[25]

André Desourteaux, the twenty-year-old grandson of the mayor, worked for the postal service in Limoges during the

FIGURE 3

Aerial view of the ruins of Oradour-sur-Glane. The
cemetery is located in the upper left. The map in the
endpapers is oriented to this view.

week. On the weekends he would return home to Oradour, where his parents ran a grocery store in the rue Emile Desourteaux. On Sunday morning, 11 June, Desourteaux took his bicycle on the train as far as St-Victurnien and then rode toward Oradour. As he entered the town, he encountered his friend Martial Brissaud, who told him that everyone was dead. Desourteaux had lost his parents, two sisters, three uncles, and both grandfathers.[26]

That day, survivors of the massacre and peasants from outlying villages came into Oradour, on foot and by bicycle, to search the burning village for relatives and friends. Madame Rouffanche was discovered, wounded but alive, lying behind the church. Smoke from the burning town could be seen as far away as St-Victurnien, Limoges, and Bellac.

The terror was not yet over. In the early hours of Monday a group of German soldiers, possibly sent from Limoges, entered the ruined village and set about burying bodies. They hastily dug shallow graves behind barns, next to the church, and in various gardens throughout the village. They removed some half-burned corpses from the church. They piled bodies in the basement and covered them with debris and the twisted remains of baby carriages. After a few hours, unable to dispose completely of the mass of bodies, they withdrew from Oradour—now a city of the dead.

Chapter Two

FRAMING THE STORY

The facts of the atrocity recounted in the previous chapter form the heart of the commemorative narrative as it emerged in the aftermath of the war. The story of the horrific events of 10 June was recounted to visitors to the ruins and to French children at school, and reported in newspapers throughout the country on the anniversary of the massacre. It became a set piece. Going back to the days and months just after the massacre permits one to appreciate the complexity of the historical context that, over time, was pared away to produce a simple tale of French innocence violated by Nazi barbarism.

Aftermath

By Sunday afternoon, 11 June, Vichy's prefect for the Limousin region, Marc-Paul Freund-Valade, had heard rumors of the massacre. (Telephone communications in the region had been interrupted.)

The German Occupation authorities refused to grant him a pass to travel until Tuesday, 13 June, when he went to Oradour accompanied by the bishop of Limoges, the delegate prefect, and the subprefect from Rochechouart.

On 14 June, the first rescue teams from St-Junien and St-Victurnien arrived at the scene. They began to exhume bodies the Germans had rapidly buried and to transport cadavers to the cemetery, which was the only part of town undisturbed by the massacre. The next day a special tram brought a health inspector and 148 more workers from Limoges: a team from the International Red Cross, a crew from the Limoges Office of Civil Defense, technical help from the Department of Roads and Bridges, and seminarians to oversee the burials.[1] For five days they worked to recover bodies, bury dead animals, and sanitize the town. They returned to Limoges every evening, bringing back details of the carnage.[2]

News of the massacre had already spread horror and fear in Limoges. On 16 June, an agent of the Service de Renseignements Généraux, France's domestic security service, reported:

> It was not until Monday, the twelfth of June, that one learned
> that on Saturday the tenth, in the course of the afternoon,
> the entire bourg of Oradour had been prey to fire and that
> the whole population had been shot and burned following
> police operations undertaken by the occupying authorities.
> Emotion gave way to horror and consternation when one
> knew with certainty that many women and children died a
> horrible death in the burning of the church.

The intelligence report concludes with an image of a populace cowed by such brutality and fearing more violence from either the Germans or the Resistance: "One can sum up the attitude of the population by saying that it is stupefied and is expecting the worst, fearful that further rash acts perpetrated by foreign agents or terrorists will drag them into an unprecedented catastrophe."[3]

On 15 June, Freund-Valade sent a long report to the government in Vichy, describing the massacre in detail and stating that both he and the bishop had protested personally to the chief of the Occupation forces, General Gleiniger. Freund-Valade wrote that he had complained about "such methods of repression, which are against all laws of war and whose atrocity raises indignation and horror in the whole region."[4] Bishop Rastouil took a strictly religious stand, describing his "sorrowful indignation on learning that the church of Oradour-sur-Glane has been sullied by the execution within its walls of hundreds of women, young girls, and children and profaned by the destruction of the tabernacle and the consecrated ciborium [receptacle for holding the consecrated wafers of the Eucharist]."[5]

In Limoges, though public outrage and disgust were muted by fear, clergymen spoke out against the massacre. On 18 June the Protestant minister of Limoges, Albert Chaudier, gave a sermon in which he briefly described the massacre and spoke out against "inexpiable misdeeds, inexcusable crimes" and underscored "the solemn, the heart-rending, the necessary protest of the Church of Jesus Christ, in the face of this insane massacre that plunges us into consternation and mourning." Bishop Rastouil announced a funeral mass for the victims of Oradour, to be held in the cathedral of Limoges on the morning of 21 June. Journalist Pierre Poitevin depicted the event as

a day of mourning invested with the character of a grandiose manifestation of sympathy to honor the martyrs of Oradour, and at the same time a protest against Teutonic barbarism. All the stores and cafés were closed. The buildings of the public administration and the newspaper *Le Courrier du centre* [Poitevin's paper] had brought out their flags, which flew at half mast and were tied with crêpe. And despite the fear and terror that the Germans inspired . . . an enormous crowd appeared that Wednesday morning at the cathedral. . . .

Poitevin estimated the crowd, which overflowed the cathedral, at twenty thousand.[6]

In the face of the outcry about the massacre, German and Vichy authorities in Limoges tried to limit public discussion of the event. On the morning of 19 June, the head of the German censorship service held a meeting with representatives of the French censorship office and the directors of Limoges newspapers. According to Poitevin, he "deemed it preferable for the press to be silent about this 'affair.' " Soon after this meeting, the Agence Havas, France's largest advertising group, now run by Occupation authorities, received an order to stop publishing the funerary notices requested by families of the victims.[7]

Still, the Vichy government thought of paying a visit of condolence. In a letter on 29 June, a representative for Marshal Pétain informed the regional prefect of the "deep emotion" with which the marshal had learned of "the cruel and inhumane treatment imposed on the commune of Oradour-sur-Glane." Pétain proposed, "as soon as circumstances permitted," to send a cabinet member to Oradour "to bow, in his name, on the spot where so many innocent victims . . . died such an atrocious death."[8] This visit never took place. In any case, it is unlikely that his representative would have been welcome. The Resistance had already capitalized on public feeling with a tract entitled "Le

Crime horrible des hitlériens à Oradour-sur-Glane" and signed by the Communist Resistance organization, the Francs-Tireurs et Partisans Français (FTPF). Found in mailboxes in the neighborhood of the city hall in Limoges on 20 June, the tract rejected in advance any placating gestures from Vichy: "Pétain better not come bow in front of the burnt remains of the children and women of Oradour. . . ."[9]

Since 1940 the Vichy proponents of collaboration, Pierre Laval and his followers, had justified their policy by claiming that it protected the French from the worst aspects of Nazi occupation. The massacre of Oradour represented the bankruptcy of "the policy of the lesser evil." The fact that Freund-Valade, as he related in his report, was prohibited from going to Oradour before 13 June only underscored the impotence of Vichy authorities in their relations with the Germans.

Not surprisingly, the Resistance used Oradour to attack Vichy, which by this time had seen its support reduced to little more than the diehards of the extreme right. Local Resistance groups—the FTPF and groups aligned with de Gaulle, such as the Mouvements Unis de la Résistance (MUR)—broadcast news of the massacre as part of their call for support of the Allied invasion: "The French know their duty. In order to avoid that all of France experience such crimes, by the thousands they rise up in the liberating fight. Limousins, against the terror of the Nazi hordes, against the traitors of the Milice in the service of the Boches, join the ranks of the fighters without delay. . . ."[10]

News of the massacre of Oradour-sur-Glane spread through the region and then abroad before being reported in the French national press. On 12 June, Gaston Hyllaire, one of local leaders of MUR, visited the ruins and sent a report of the massacre to

London.[11] It was two weeks later that the event was reported throughout France.

During the war, especially during the final months, constraints on communication and travel, and censorship of the press, made it common for some parts of France to enjoy communication abroad while remaining isolated from each other. Such patterns had been established in the period from 1940 to 1942, when the country was cut up by all kinds of internal boundaries that made travel difficult and dangerous for resisters and inconvenient for others. The line of demarcation that divided the northern zone from Vichy France was not abolished after the total occupation of France in November 1942; in 1944 one was still required to show identity papers when crossing, and surveillance of the line was increased after the Allied landings.[12] Railway connections and telephone links were often cut for days at a time. By June 1944, the Germans had prohibited travel outside of cities surrounded by the partisan groups, known in French as the *maquis*.[13] Limoges was such a city. Most underground newspapers, if they appeared regularly at all, came out only once a month.

On 15 June, the same day that Prefect Freund-Valade reported to Vichy, the Swiss consular agent at Limoges informed the head of the Swiss legation in Vichy about the massacre.[14] On 26 June, the journalist Pierre Limagne noted that "the English radio begins to speak of the affair of Oradour-sur-Glane, but taken from the Swiss press; the latter certainly borrowed their information from unreliable Vichy sources; hence numerous errors."[15] Two days later, Radio Algiers reported news of the massacre.[16]

Not until July did the story of atrocities in Oradour reach a larger French audience, through the clandestine press of the Resistance. Resistance newspapers of all kinds (*Libération*, *Résistance*, *La Marseillaise*, to name a few) publicized the massacre of Oradour. On 1 August, *Les Lettres françaises*, a clandestine newspaper created by resisters from the literary world, put out a special issue on Oradour.[17] The centerpiece of this edition was the testimony of a Monsieur Paillet, an engineer with the French railway who had gone to Oradour on the evening of 10 June to visit his family, who were refugees there. He was held at the edge of town with the group from the tram and then, like them, released. Paillet spent the night in Les Bordes and entered Oradour the next morning to find that his wife and children were dead. His testimony, published under the headline "Amidst the Ruins of Morality: Oradour-sur-Glane," described all he saw before returning directly to Paris. *Les Lettres françaises* printed twenty thousand copies of this tract.[18]

Once Limoges and Paris were liberated (on 22 and 25 August, respectively), many newspapers and radio stations either emerged from concealment or began to publish and broadcast again after having been shut down during the Occupation. The Liberation also saw the birth of hundreds of new newspapers. Papers that had collaborated were closed down, and the Resistance press moved into their offices. In this first burst of freedom the massacre of Oradour-sur-Glane was widely discussed, particularly in the regional press. The timing of the massacre played a role in its instant notoriety, as other incidents of August and September were lost in the shuffle during the culmination of the Liberation, but the outrage seems to have been all the more intense because until Oradour the Germans had not engaged in widespread killing of French civilians. A front-page article on 24 August in

Le Centre libre expressed this shock: " 'Exterminate'? We did not know exactly what that meant. Here now in the heart of France in the middle of the Limousin countryside, Hitler's extermination swept through."[19]

Comparing German behavior in France during the two world wars, Richard Cobb has noted:

> In World War I, relations between civilian and military went in reverse order to what was to happen in the Second World War. The longer the Occupation lasted, the closer became French civilians and German military. Most of the atrocities and signal brutalities had been committed, in the full flood of early military successes, in August/September 1914. In 1944, the German forces proved themselves the most ferocious while in retreat from the Southwest of France, where, previously, they had little contact with the local population.[20]

Indeed, in many areas of the southern zone, the Germans were seen only briefly in 1940, when they conquered the country. They then pulled back to the north. Occupation of all France came after the Allied landings in North Africa in 1942, but even then it took the form of occupation of cities and garrisoned towns and was not generally obtrusive. Most of the German troops stationed in and around Lyon, for example, were training for the Russian front and were never seen in central Lyon.[21] The population in rural areas did not have day-to-day contact with the Germans, as they did in the more urbanized north. The exceptions were centers of resistance, such as the Limousin and the Dordogne. These areas had already been punished in the spring of 1944, when German troops had been sent in to fight the growing bands of *maquisards*.

The Context of Resistance

The story of Oradour, in the book published by the Association Nationale des Familles des Martyrs d'Oradour-sur-Glane (ANFM), as told by the guides to the ruins, and as shown in the preservation and presentation of the ruins, is paradigmatic of ultimate victimization—a peaceful French town, uninvolved in any resistance activity, destroyed on a beautiful summer day. In much of the literature on the subject, in discussions with the mayor of Oradour and members of the ANFM, one notes great insistence on the fact that there had been no resistance in Oradour, and that no reason is known why this town was singled out for destruction. Yet if one widens the lens only slightly, it is evident that the massacre took place in the context of punishment and reprisal. That is, in fact, the way it was described in Resistance papers in the final months of the war and the early days of the provisional government,[22] as one in a constellation of acts of reprisal aimed at intimidating the Resistance.

Throughout the war the Resistance press, seeking to rally people to its cause, reported assassinations, executions, and hangings of resisters. In the summer and fall of 1944, the Resistance papers all recorded the same cluster of incidents—most of which had occurred before the massacre at Oradour in June 1944. In newspaper accounts and in pamphlets published in 1944 and 1945, these events were often listed and discussed together. Just a few days before the Liberation of Paris, *Ce Soir* printed a front page article entitled "Frenchmen, never forget: Ascq/ Châteaubriant/Oradour-sur-Glane":

> For four years we have all lived in horror, we have all been
> used to hearing in low voices in our families, among friends,

the sinister news of prisoners shot, whole buildings where inhabitants, chosen at random as hostages, have been savagely
slaughtered, farms and their inhabitants burned: it was our
daily news. Nonetheless, certain dreadful massacres which go
beyond the Occupier's habitual savagery have sorrowfully
made several French villages famous. The names of
Châteaubriant, Oradour-sur-Glane, Ascq are on all lips.[23]

In the paragraphs that followed, the editors gave equal space and
equal attention to these three incidents.

The massacre at Châteaubriant had been the first execution
of hostages to receive widespread notoriety in France. On 22
October 1941, in reprisal for attacks on German officers in the
western port city of Nantes, the Germans took twenty-seven
prisoners from an internment camp at nearby Châteaubriant (in
the department of the Loire-Atlantique) and shot them in a
quarry, along with twenty-one inmates of the Nantes prison. Of
the twenty-seven hostages from Châteaubriant, all but six were
Communists. As they were taken from their barracks, they sang
the *Marseillaise*. Other inmates echoed their song. As they were
driven, still singing, through Châteaubriant, people in the streets
uncovered their heads in respect. According to Henri Noguères,
a historian of the Resistance, although the victims of Châteaubriant were not the first French hostages to be shot, their martyrdom "remains, more than any other, engraved in the people's
memory. It was this [martyrdom] which, from now on, would
evoke, in an exemplary fashion, all massacres of hostages."[24]

The massacre at Ascq occurred three years later, near the railway station of this dreary working-class town eight kilometers
east of the northern industrial city of Lille. Many of the three
thousand citizens of Ascq were employees of the railway, known

in France as *cheminots.* Throughout France, the *cheminots* were among the most active resisters, engaging in sabotage of the railway lines and the gathering and passing on of intelligence.[25] At a quarter to eleven on the night of 1 April 1944, a train carrying a convoy of SS troops and equipment was derailed by an explosion as it entered the Ascq train station. Moments later, an officer and SS soldiers burst into the station and shot the station chief and his assistant. Troops spread out in the surrounding neighborhood. They dragged sixty men at random from their houses, lined them up along the railway track, and shot them. Twenty-six others—including the local priest—were shot in their homes.

Word of this brutality spread immediately to railway workers in Lille and Paris. By dawn the following day, fliers had been posted calling for a work stoppage from 11:30 until noon and urging mass attendance at the funeral for the victims of Ascq.[26] The *cheminots* throughout the northern railway system stopped work for one hour. Workers in the Landy depot at the Gare du Nord in Paris paraded in front of a *monument aux morts* near the station.[27] It was too late for news of events at Ascq to make the April issues of the Resistance papers, but the May issues of *L'Humanité, Les Lettres françaises, Combat, Le Franc-Tireur,* and *Résistance* all ran front-page stories on the massacre. Nor was Ascq forgotten after the war. In 1948, on the fourth anniversary of the massacre, President Vincent Auriol laid the foundation stone for a monument to the victims of Ascq on the site where they had been shot.[28]

In the late spring and summer of 1944, the major reports of atrocities were the March hanging of hostages in Nîmes (Gard) and the June massacres by Das Reich of civilians in Tulle (Corrèze) and Oradour-sur-Glane. In Nîmes on 2 March, the SS stopped traffic in the center of town and publicly hanged fifteen hostages and three resisters in reprisal for the death of twenty-five German soldiers in a skirmish between the *maquis* and the Wehrmacht. Both the April edition of *Le Franc-Tireur* (Edition Sud) and the May edition of *Les Lettres françaises* gave detailed accounts of the events in order to illustrate "to what ferocious beasts the cowards of Vichy had knowingly delivered France."[29] During the summer months of 1944, clandestine newspapers in both the northern and southern zones presented these events, including the massacre at Oradour, as a series of Nazi reprisals for activities of the Resistance.

Vichy, too, linked the atrocities to the Resistance, blaming the incidents on provocation by French citizens disloyal to Pétain. By 27 July, the massacre at Oradour had caused such indignation that Xavier Vallat, the spokesman of the Vichy government, made it the subject of a radio editorial. In response to a letter from a *lycée* student whose schoolteacher had been a victim at Oradour, Vallat replied:

> This young sensitive child wants to know what I think of German reprisals. . . . I'll tell him: the death of his great friend is a horrible thing, and the hearts of all the French, whoever they may be, are wrenched by the unmerciful rigor of certain reprisals. But what is even more grave is to think that it is the French who are morally responsible for the death of this woman and a lot of others. In the village . . . there had not been any Germans before 8 November 1942, and moreover there would not be any there today if at that time French people in North Africa, disobeying the Marshal, had not provoked the occupation of the southern zone. And if later in this village, other French, they too disobeying the

advice and orders of the Marshal, had not, in the name of
false patriotism, caused serious trouble, German soldiers
would not have been led to make the innocent population
endure the consequences of the misdeeds of a few bandits.[30]

Even at this late date, with Allied victory imminent, Vallat was
reminding his listeners of the connection between Resistance
and reprisal.

The connection was real. The spring of 1943 had marked a
turning point for the Resistance in France, as well as the involvement of local populations in the conflict. Communist militants, acting independently of Party leadership, had organized
the first *maquis* in the Limousin and the Puy-de-Dôme in the
spring of 1942; but when, on 16 February 1943, Prime Minister
Pierre Laval initiated the STO, he provided an incentive for
young men to take to the hills. A volunteer program announced
on 22 June 1942 to send skilled workers to Germany in exchange for the release of French prisoners of war had failed to
produce enough manpower. The German invasion of the southern zone in November 1942 further increased Occupation demands on the French economy and workforce.[31] When young
men from the town and country evaded the forced labor program, older resisters formed *maquis* out of the need to organize
and protect the young, inexperienced *réfractaires*, as well as anti-
fascist refugees from Central Europe and Italy, and immigrant
Jews who had avoided the first deportations that began in the
summer of 1942.[32]

Réfractaires who came to the Limousin found Communist networks already in place, especially in the southwestern part of the
department of the Haute-Vienne, where the Parti Communiste

Français (PCF) had established its regional stronghold in the 1930s.[33] Throughout France, Communists had already become practiced in operating underground; the leadership had instructed militants to build secret party cells and networks when the Party was outlawed in September 1939 for supporting the Hitler-Stalin Pact. When the Vichy police stepped up their campaign of anti-Communist harassment, Party militants responded by strengthening the clandestine networks. Structures for resistance were already in place once the Germans invaded Russia in June 1941 and the PCF called for an all-out fight against the German occupation.

The most active *maquis* in the Limousin were those organized and led by the Communist militant Georges Guingouin in the hills of the southwestern Haute-Vienne and the northern Corrèze.[34] Because the *maquis* did not receive arms until late in the war, their method of resisting was sabotage. It should be noted that rural resistance was not limited to guerrilla activities and that the quieter, though by no means less dangerous, activity of aiding resisters, refugees, immigrants, Jews, and others threatened by the Vichy and German authorities was also at the heart of the Resistance. It was in these areas that women played a central role.

In the spring of 1943, Guingouin organized a campaign against German requisitions in the region. In the summer he moved on transport and communication networks. Bridges, telephone lines, and railways were especially vulnerable; because of their length they were unguarded and could be attacked with little risk.[35] In July 1943, his *maquis* attacked telephone lines vital to the Germans. In the spring and summer of 1944, the *maquis* of the Limousin proved themselves to be fierce fighters against Vichy and German authorities.

Though the Socialists were the strongest political party in the Limousin, the Communists surpassed them in resistance activity. The Socialist Party had disbanded in accordance with the edict of the National Assembly at Vichy, which had outlawed party politics on 10 July 1940. The clandestine Communist cells gave great political advantage to the PCF. Once the Communists joined the Resistance in full force, their actions were identifiable as PCF-directed. Socialists, on the other hand, blended into the movements that rallied behind de Gaulle in the second half of the war.[36] Though the Socialist leadership did not organize resistance in the party's name, it did not discourage individuals from acting on their own or joining whatever resistance groups were available.[37]

The Communists disparaged as fence-sitters those resistance groups that chose to wait for the best moment to attack.[38] The PCF strategy was to exploit every possible means and opportunity to strike against Vichy and the German Occupation. One goal was to create a climate of insecurity for enemy troops. The Communists also believed that such attacks would produce a favorable effect on the French population by proving that resistance was indeed possible. By engaging the general population in the struggle, they hoped to build an atmosphere of popular insurrection, which, once the Allies invaded, would lead to mass participation in the final struggle.[39]

De Gaulle and most of his entourage in London saw a role for guerrilla warfare only when linked to a general plan, conceived, outlined, and directed by his resistance organization: the Free French.[40] De Gaulle's people doubted the effectiveness of guerrilla tactics, believing that isolated, limited actions would have a minimal effect on the German war machine and that civilians would pay disproportionate penalties.[41] There were few places in France where guerrilla warfare could be conducted far enough away from settlements that the Germans would retaliate with military operations against the *maquisards* rather than with reprisals against civilians.[42] Direct attacks on the Germans therefore tended to be left to the activist, Communist-led FTPF. This was certainly true in the Limousin.[43]

The threat of reprisal, from the Germans or the French authorities, haunted all relations between the *maquis* and the local population. The survival and success of the *maquis* depended on the support of country folk; the *maquis* needed the food and the protective silence that only the local inhabitants could provide. Those involved in provisioning the *maquis* exposed themselves to extreme danger.

In March 1944, the Germans began a campaign of repression throughout France in response to increased activity by the *maquis*. Until this time, the Germans had been able to keep open lines of communication and transport. As the Liberation approached, however, the *maquis* posed a threat not just to the social order but also to the German Occupation forces. As the numbers of *maquisards* increased through the winter and spring of 1944, the Germans were no longer content to leave the job of "maintaining order" to their French subordinates.[44]

Aided by members of the French Milice, the Germans led a campaign to wipe out the *maquis* in three centers of resistance in the southern zone. Their sweep penetrated the departments of Jura, Ain, Savoie, Haute-Savoie, Gard, Lozère, Ardèche, Dordogne, Corrèze and Haute-Vienne.[45] Reprisals against civilians were an integral part of their tactics. This marked the first time the Germans subjected the civilian population to measures of systematic repression. Henri Amouroux tells us: "It is in the first weeks of 1944 that the Germans systematically undertook actions of collective reprisal, acting not only against hostages taken from concentration camps but against villagers and city folk rounded up by chance."[46] Well aware that the *maquis* could not survive without the complicity of the local population, the Germans sought to cut the *maquisards'* lifeline by terrorizing the local populations.

In a report to Vichy written on 15 April 1944, the prefect of the Corrèze, Pierre Trouillé, described the "bloody week" of 31 March–7 April, when German troops came in to wipe out the *maquis:*

> [The repression] took the form of a devastation that came crashing down on towns and villages whose inhabitants were affected much more than the partisans spread out in the woods. One had the distinct feeling that the Occupier wanted to strike fear into the population and change their opinion by showing them that the evils they were suffering were the direct consequence of the existence of the *maquis* and that they had made the mistake of tolerating them.[47]

Three thousand people were arrested, of whom fifty-five were shot and 1,500 detained. Houses and farms were burned. Trouillé cited the commune of Lonzac, where seventeen people were shot and twenty-three houses burned. Three hundred *réfractaires* were captured and deported to Germany.[48] According to Trouillé, the impact on public opinion was tremendous: "If the occupation authorities wanted to strike a fierce psychological blow, they unquestionably succeeded. Until then, the population had lived as neighbors with the *maquis*, often mixing with them, totally unaware of the future."

It seems that German reprisals achieved their objectives, at least for a time. Henri Amouroux reports a similar reaction for another area of active *maquis* resistance: the plateau of the Vercors, east of Grenoble. A note written by someone in the Resistance after the German attack on the Vercors in July 1944 indicated that "public sentiment . . . had weakened after the first hard blow." The author complained that the *maquis* "go after the Boches, kill some, and then take off. And when the Gestapo came . . . they were able to operate in complete tranquility. The *maquis* were quite careful not to show themselves."[49]

There is insufficient evidence on which to judge the results of the German policy. Although some people were undoubtedly frightened into submission and made resentful of the *maquis*, a significant portion of the population may have been shocked into hatred of the Nazis, and some turned to active support of the Resistance. In his study of the Puy-de-Dôme, a department bordering the Limousin, John Sweets concluded that the local population generally supported the Resistance but resented its more reckless exploits, which put them in danger.[50]

Once the Allies landed in Normandy on 6 June, all forces of the Resistance, in the Limousin as elsewhere, threw themselves into the uprising. On the night of 5 June, following the decision of General Eisenhower, the BBC sent out coded messages to Resistance forces prepared to execute sabotage. By setting off operations throughout the country, Eisenhower hoped to keep the Germans confused about the actual place of the landing and give the Allied forces longer to establish a beachhead on the Normandy coast. On 6 June, General de Gaulle followed with his call for nationwide mobilization: "It is the battle of France and it is France's battle. All sons of France, wherever they are, whoever they are, have the simple and sacred duty to combat the enemy by all the means at their disposal." There was an immediate response in the Limousin, which was part of the region that had been dubbed "little Russia" by the German troops stationed there.[51] According to Henri Noguères, in the Corrèze, the Haute-Vienne, the Creuse, and the Indre, all sabotage plans were carried out immediately. Railway and telephone lines were severed, and *maquis* groups engaged in "veritable military operations" against the Germans.[52]

German garrisons in towns all over central France reported the pandemonium. German Army headquarters for the southern zone received this message from Bordeaux: "The departments of Dordogne and Corrèze are held by terrorists. Part of the departments of the Indre and the town of Tulle are dominated by gangs. The city of Limoges is besieged. Périgueux and Brive are expecting attacks by gangs."[53] The German High Command, misjudging the significance of the Allied attack, did not decide to immediately send all combat forces available to hold the Normandy Front. It sent units to guerrilla strongholds to fight the *maquis*.

On 6 June, a part of the Second Armored Division of the SS unit Das Reich moved from Montauban into the Massif Central to attack the *maquis*.[54] On 8 June, Field Marshal von Rundstedt, Supreme Commander of German forces on the Western Front, ordered the rest of Das Reich to leave its garrison in Montauban and proceed through central France to Normandy. The coastal route, by way of Bordeaux, would have been faster and more secure, but an integral part of Das Reich's mission was to wipe out the *maquis*, intimidate the local population, and regain control of large tracts of south central France. Von Rundstedt informed his officers, "Limited success in such operations is useless."[55] He ordered brutal measures: "It is necessary to crush resistance forces by means of rapid, encircling attacks. For the reestablishment of order and security, the most energetic measures must be taken in order to frighten the inhabitants of this infested region, whom we have to make give up the taste for welcoming resistance groups and letting themselves be controlled by them. This will serve as a warning to the entire population."[56] The officers of the division had plenty of experience in this sort of operation. Das Reich had fought on the Eastern Front against partisans as well as the Russian military. The name of General Heinz Lammerding, who took command of Das Reich at the end of 1943, had appeared on documents ordering the total destruction of entire villages and towns that were thought to have helped partisans.[57] Of the group that had withdrawn to southwest France in April 1944 to train for fighting in Europe, only 2,500 were survivors of the original battle group. The ranks of Das Reich were filled for the most part by nine thousand seventeen- and eighteen-year-old boys—many of them ethnic Germans drafted from Hungary, Romania, and Alsace. Yet, according to Max Hastings, a historian of Das Reich, "the overwhelming majority of Das Reich's regimental officers and NCOs were experienced, battle-hardened veterans."[58] On 8 June, about fifteen thousand men moved north with 209 tanks and self-propelled guns.[59] They fanned out into a three-pronged advance through the Dordogne and Limousin.

Resistance leaders in the Limousin were unaware of these movements. The Communist Party was impatient to liberate territory where the FTPF controlled the majority of Resistance forces.[60] Their push for political power in the Limousin focused on the liberation of Limoges and Tulle, the administrative capitals of the Haute-Vienne and the Corrèze, respectively. To ensure themselves a strong position before the anticipated Allied landing, the clandestine secretariat of the PCF in Paris ordered simultaneous attacks on these cities. The local leadership decided against an immediate attack on Limoges, judging it unfeasible,[61] but a higher officer who directed the FTPF for the departments of the Haute-Vienne, Creuse, Corrèze, and Dordogne agreed to direct an attack on Tulle. The unhappy coincidence of this action with the surprise Allied invasion of Normandy had tragic consequences for the citizens of Tulle.

On 7 June, the *maquis* of the Corrèze led an attack on a German garrison at Tulle that turned into a major skirmish. The German high command for France ordered Das Reich to head for the Tulle-Limoges area, where its chief, General Lammerding, was to place himself under the orders of the 56th Reserve Corps (headquartered in Clermont-Ferrand), the unit in charge of fighting terrorists in central France. The regiments of Das Reich closest to Tulle received orders to rescue the beleaguered Wehrmacht. Their arrival in Tulle on the evening of 8 June put an end to the fighting. The *maquis*, completely unprepared and unequipped to take on such a formidable adversary, were forced to retreat. German losses were considerable; they reported thirty-seven dead, twenty-five wounded, and thirty-five missing.[62] The next afternoon, in reprisal, the SS hanged ninety-nine men of the town from the balconies, trees, and bridges along the main street. Another 149 were deported to Germany.[63]

The next day, a different unit of the same division committed the massacre at Oradour-sur-Glane. The precise reason why this town was chosen is still unclear. There had been no resistance in

Oradour itself. The nearest *maquis* was in the hills of the Monts de Blond, approximately twelve kilometers away. It was hoped that the military trial in 1953 of a group of soldiers who participated in the massacre would provide an answer to this question, but the defendants in the case were all common soldiers with little information on the origin of the orders. None of the officers responsible were present. Major Otto Dickmann, who led the operation, was killed in Normandy in August 1944. General Lammerding made it back to his home in Düsseldorf and was never tried. The 1983 trial in East Berlin of a junior officer, Heinz Barth, shed no new light on the question.

Other Contenders

After the war, other sites and other incidents contended with Oradour for a place in public memory. In addition to Tulle, many villages in France suffered in ways that could have suited them to be portrayed as the massacre at Oradour later was: as representative of France's suffering and uniquely horrible. From 1944 to 1946, private publishing houses and government agencies produced books and pamphlets about German atrocities. In some accounts, the story of Oradour was mixed with tales of suffering in other places. The booklet *Récits d'atrocités nazies,* for example, published in 1944, catalogued the treatment of Jewish families in the Paris region, the hangings in Nîmes, the sufferings of a deportee who made it back to France, German raids in the Jura in spring 1944, life in a concentration camp in Silesia, and the massacre at Oradour-sur-Glane.[64] The stories of Tulle and Oradour tended to be lumped together, but the fact that almost the entire population of Oradour was killed, the massacre of women and children in the church, and the burning of the town overshadowed what had happened at Tulle.[65]

The years 1944 and 1945 saw a flurry of popular accounts of such *villages martyrs* as Mussidan and Mouleydier in the Dordogne, Dortan in the Jura, La Bresse in the Vosges, and Maillé in the Touraine. These places, spread out through France, represented a spectrum of the circumstances and forms of civilian suffering. In all cases, civilians were caught in the crossfire of events beyond their control as the war entered into its final phase.

In the case of Mouleydier, *maquis* responding to orders from the leadership of the Forces Françaises de l'Intérieur (FFI) had come out of the woods on 8 June to take control of a bridge over the Dordogne as well as of all roads that ran parallel to the river. The inhabitants of Mouleydier emerged from their houses in the morning to find the town in the hands of the *maquis*. Three days later, the German Army broke through a resistance barricade near the town, killing twenty *maquisards*. On 21 June, a German armored column skirmished with the FFI and shot six *maquisards*. A few hours later, German troops entered the town, pillaged, and then systematically set the town on fire. They executed twelve people suspected of resistance and shot four bystanders as well. In all, the Germans killed twenty-two people and burned 202 houses and farms in and around Mouleydier. In the city of Mussidan, also in the Dordogne, the FTPF attacked an armored train on 11 June as it stood in the train station. In retaliation, the Germans shot fifty-two hostages, including the mayor.[66]

Today neither Mouleydier nor Mussidan are known outside of the region as *villages martyrs*, though in 1947 Mussidan did ask for recognition by the government. That year, on the occasion of an official visit by President Vincent Auriol to Oradour-sur-Glane to commemorate the massacre of 10 June, the mayor of Mussidan asked Auriol to come there: "The municipality of Mussidan would be particularly happy if you could also attend the ceremony that will take place on 11 June in the city of Mussidan. We have the sad privilege of commemorating the largest massacre in the department of the Dordogne; a department which, as you know, suffered particularly and which has the honor of being one of the premier French departments in terms of Interior Resistance."[67] A visit to Mussidan was not added to the President's itinerary.

The east of France also produced its tales of civilian suffering. For ten days in July 1944, a detachment of five thousand German soldiers took over the town of Dortan, in the Jura mountains near the French-Swiss border. Between 12 and 21 July they raped women, pillaged the town, desecrated the church, and killed twenty-six people, including the local priest. As they left, the Germans set Dortan on fire and reduced it to a ruin. A small book published in 1944 evoked Dortan as an archetypical French village: "It was a French village . . . a village like all other villages of France, with its welcoming face, its closely packed houses through which wound the road, its century-old church, its factories, its flowing river, and its bridge; its fields and woods, its spread-out farms and its grouping of hamlets. . . . It was a French village like all villages . . . of France, with its deep and mysterious soul. . . ."[68] The author, a writer from Lyon, had a vision of Dortan not unlike that to be realized in the commemoration of Oradour: the vision of a quintessential French village that found itself, unluckily, in the destructive path of German barbarism.

La Bresse, a small industrial city in the Vosges mountains near Epinal, endured a whole array of afflictions during the months of September to November 1944: forced labor for the Germans, requisitions by German troops, a September attack on the local *maquis* in which seventy *maquisards* (fifty-one of them local boys) and nine civilians were killed, the deportation of four hundred men, and finally, in November, evacuation and burning of the town. La Bresse counted among its victims 59 *morts pour la France* (that is, those later honored as having died "for the country"), 42 civilians, 12 executed, 483 deportees, 330 prisoners of war, and 77 sent to Germany as STO workers.[69]

Of all the martyred villages, the town of Maillé, in the Touraine, suffered a massacre most closely resembling the one at Oradour. On the morning of 25 August 1944, SS troops retreating from France encircled this village of 480 inhabitants. They entered the town and for three hours massacred men, women, and children with grenades and machine guns. In the afternoon they shelled. The death toll reached 124. Though there was guerrilla fighting around Maillé, there was no particular reason why this town should have been singled out. The Touraine had not been a region of *maquisard* resistance during the war, but partisan groups had sprung up during the summer of 1944.[70] In August, the FFI and American forces attacked German troops retreating through the Loire valley. According to the authoritative work on the Liberation in the Touraine, these attacks caused civilians to suffer because "the Germans did not recognize the FFI and the FTP as soldiers, and often took revenge by attacks on the civilian population."[71] In an account of the massacre, the priest of Maillé characterized the attack as a reprisal for an ambush, on the outskirts of Maillé, of two cars driven by German soldiers.[72] The prefect of the Indre-et-Loire corroborated the story and reported a German claim that one of their officers had been mortally wounded. But, he added, since no body was ever produced, in his judgment "nothing could be known for certain."[73]

Like other chroniclers of the destruction of particular towns, the author of *Un village martyr, Maillé* saw the pain inflicted on his town as somehow exemplary of the brutality France experienced at the hands of the Germans: "Certainly there is not a region that did not suffer, that does not suffer the war in its children and in its blood [*dans ses enfants et dans son sang*]. But here more than elsewhere, man can contemplate, with horror, the depths of misery where the spirit of violence and primacy of force have cast him."[74] A place like Maillé could have qualified as France's preeminent example of a martyred village. But that did not happen. Maillé was rebuilt, and in 1947 the townspeople contented themselves with a local monument commemorating the massacre.[75]

These examples of other sites of civilian suffering suggest that there was nothing about the events at Oradour that made them necessarily more memorable than other incidents. Tulle, Mouleydier, La Bresse, Maillé, Dortan—all have some of the elements found in the story of Oradour: the death of women and children, the burning of the town, the desecration of the church. In all cases, clashes between the Germans and the Resistance were involved.

Nonetheless, the cumulative power of contingent facts poised Oradour for notoriety. Other martyred villages seem to have recognized these claims. Many of the booklets about martyred villages mentioned or compared themselves to Oradour, which seemed, by 1945, to have already become the standard against which suffering was measured. This lends weight to the common-sense argument that what put Oradour first in the public mind and made it commemorable were the facts of the massacre and the presence of material remains. In places where only part of the population died, such as in the towns of the Vercors, survivors often preferred to rebuild and carry on; but the annihilation of most of the population of Oradour did away with advocates of rebuilding on the old site.

Although such specific features may have predisposed Oradour for fame, they cannot explain what this monument came to stand for or its success in attracting the interest of the French public. Nor are any of the facts of the massacre, in and of themselves, sufficient to confer particular meaning to the site. They provided the frame for the story that would be told. The ruined town's rise to national prominence as the preeminent example of innocence violated was neither automatic or "natural." The events of the massacre had to be removed from their historical context and dramatized, visually and in narrative, to be rendered suitable for telling the archetypical story of innocence and victimization.

Immediately after the war, however, the massacres at villages such as Oradour were spoken of in the context of the Resistance. The government itself put out a booklet, *Terreur en France*, which discussed Oradour in a chapter on punitive expeditions by the German Army and the Waffen-SS. The opening line of the book drew a clear connection between resistance and reprisals: "To retrace the history of repression in France is also, consequently, to write the history of the Resistance."[76] A history of SS activity in the Limousin and Périgord supports this claim with facts and figures.[77] Indeed, one of these many reprisals took place within eleven kilometers of Oradour, at St-Victurnien, on 27 June 1944—less than two weeks after the massacre at Oradour.[78]

The official guide by the ANFM, the association of families of the Oradour victims, that was written in 1946, placed Oradour in the context of the Resistance. In the preface Pierre Boursicot, the Commissioner of the Republic (one of eighteen "super prefects" named by de Gaulle in 1944 to replace Vichy's Regional Prefect and establish the general's authority), referred to the repression that preceded the massacre at Oradour: "For months, in the region, a bloody fury had been given free rein. It was horror raised to the level of policy, with the aim of terrorizing the French who had risen up against the invader. . . ."[79] Works by such respected historians as Henri Noguères and Henri Amouroux make this point as well. So does the more recent *Petite Histoire d'Oradour-Sur-Glane* by Albert Hivernaud, a small book sold at the ruins.

In much of what is written and said about Oradour, one notes a palpable tension between the desire to clarify the cause of what happened and an imperative that it remain unexplained. Even accounts that attempt a plausible explanation often undermine the authority of their own conclusions. A typical example is that of Hivernaud, who writes in the *Petite Histoire:* "Still today, despite the efforts of investigators and historians, all that we know for certain is the identity of the troops who carried out the massacre."[80]

It is in the commemorative accounts of the massacre that Oradour is detached from its historical context. While the Vercors, for example, retained its original significance as a symbol of *maquisard* sacrifice, Oradour became decoupled from the context of reprisal related to Resistance. The commemoration of Oradour perpetuates the memory of a random massacre of French civilians uninvolved in any resistance activity.

Historical analysis provides a different perspective. In 1968, when Jacques Delarue presented the first detailed, highly researched account of the activity of Das Reich, he framed reprisals in the context of the suppression of the Resistance. He also remarked on the phenomenon of this context being lost:

> The drama of Oradour eclipsed all the other crimes of the "Das Reich" Division. The name of the martyred Limousin village became a symbol, the image of crime and of suffering, and that is understandable. But this attitude, in isolating the crime from its general context, that is to say the wave of crimes that surrounded it, the long succession of murders, assassinations, arson, and destruction, which this account has tried to reconstruct, has caused one to forget all these other crimes and made of Oradour an exceptional event, an involuntary excess due to the war, when it was only the application, more total and complete, of the daily methods of the "Das Reich" Division.[81]

Delarue articulated a persistent tension in the ways Oradour is talked about: a tension between historical facts, context, and the commemorative message.

Immediate political concerns of the postwar period played a critical role. Oradour seems to have been decontextualized as part of an attempt to diminish the divisiveness of the activities of the *maquis*. The *maquisards* were controversial for both their leftist political leanings and the dangers they posed for the local population. This is precisely why Tulle was never deemed suitable for national commemoration, or even commemoration in conjunction with Oradour.[82]

Taking Oradour out of context was made easier by the lack of reliable information about why Oradour was picked as a target. Thus the commemoration of Oradour permitted avoidance of uncomfortable political tensions and accentuated the idea of French innocence and victimization, blurring the distinction between resisters and bystanders by giving the message that *everyone* was at risk. Oradour provided an interesting corollary to the notion of France as a nation of resisters: that of France as a nation of victims, martyred regardless of political choice or wartime activity.

Commemorative accounts of the massacre dwell on personal experience of horror, not on the war or the Occupation. The history of the commemoration of Oradour-sur-Glane is, to a large extent, the story of how this incident was emptied of its political particularities in order to become universalized as the ultimate victimization—an archetypical atrocity that could stand as a symbol for the suffering of France.

Chapter Three

CREATING THE MONUMENT

In March 1945, Charles de Gaulle, now president of the French Republic, made a solemn tour of the ruins of Oradour as part of an official trip through the Limousin and the Périgord. Accompanied by the subprefect, Guy Pauchou, and a group of survivors, President de Gaulle walked what has now become the traditional route through the ruins: past the barns where the men were shot and down the main street to the church. De Gaulle's visit assured the success of local efforts to preserve the town in its ruined state; spurred by the General's attention to Oradour, the Ministry of National Education expropriated the site and appointed a member of its elite corps of architects to take charge of the ruins. In 1946, the National Assembly passed special legislation designating Oradour a historic monument and authorizing construction of a new town. One year later, Vincent Auriol, the first president of the newly formed Fourth Republic, attended the ceremony marking the third anniversary of the massacre and laid the foundation stone of the first house in the new town. In just a few years Oradour had been transformed from a chaotic scene of destruction to a historic monument owned and administered by the French state.

The initial efforts to commemorate the massacre of Oradour-sur-Glane took place in the context of a nationwide desire to take public notice of the events of the recent past. This public notice took two forms: the first was a call to bring collaborators and perpetrators of wartime crimes to quick justice. The second entailed establishing monuments and commemorative rituals in the interest of shaping memory for the long term. In some cases the two forms of remembering were intertwined; Oradour is a case in point. The desire to find and punish the perpetrators of the massacre became a chief motivation of the families of the victims. And the ruins of Oradour were meant to serve for eternity as a silent condemnation of "Nazi barbarism." The passion for revenge has softened over the years, but at the moment the monument was being established, there was both a call for immediate justice and a desire to perpetuate the memory of the massacre for all time.

At the Liberation, after four years of repression, fear, and censorship, memories and resentments that had been harbored privately could be voiced and physically expressed. German crimes and atrocities were obviously a subject of bitter recollection, but there was also hatred for each other among the French, and a desire by some to avenge the wrongs committed by the Vichy regime and its supporters. By the end of the war, the Vichy government, with the help of a mass of informers, had interned seventy thousand "suspects," many of them refugees from Central Europe.[1] Thirty-five thousand civil servants had been removed from their jobs. As part of the STO, the Vichy government had sent 650,000 French men to work in Germany. The French administration had helped the Germans to deport 200,000 people, of whom only 50,000 had survived. Of the 76,000 French and foreign Jews who were deported, only three percent made it back from the camps.

In the spring of 1943, as Vichy and the Milice mounted full-scale attacks on the Resistance, life in parts of southern France took on aspects of a civil war. The Resistance also resorted to violence against collaborators and black marketeers. The most reliable estimates available suggest that, during the war years, between 5,200 and 6,700 French people were killed by their compatriots before the Allied invasion of Normandy on 6 June 1944.[2] When the war ended, formal justice took on the task of settling scores. But long before the tide turned against the Nazis, a consensus had formed among the resistance movements that when they came into their own, they would make collaborators and Nazis pay a heavy price. These words, written after the massacre at Ascq, are a typical expression of the desire of resisters and their sympathizers to be vigilant about both justice and memory: "One day scores will be settled. The hour of punishment will come and we will not forget the Darnands, the Phillipe Henriots, and other *miliciens* who extol the chivalrous spirit of the SS and the military honor of the men of the lordly race."[3]

The call for retributive justice began in late autumn of 1943, when underground newspapers of the metropolitan resistance began to blacklist informers and provocateurs as well as collaborationist shopkeepers. A resistance newspaper from the southeast made its intentions eminently clear: "Under this rubric we will regularly publish the names of traitors and collaborators, individuals of ill repute, who respect neither law nor religion, opportunists or servants of the 'vilest of Judases' who collaborated with the German or his Vichy 'Gauleiter.' . . . The hour of justice is imminent and implacable justice awaits them. We will exact it and it will be vengeance."[4] The issue of remembering had a specific purpose: to intimidate the adversary and to insure that once the war was over, justice would be done. But for the Resistance vengeance was not to be an end in itself. It would be part of the larger task of renewing France by sweeping out the corruption of the Third Republic, redeeming the country from the sins of collaboration, and enacting complete social reform.

The Liberation unleashed a period of social and political upheaval in which those who had opposed Vichy and the Germans called their enemies to account—enemies both inside and outside the country. Though the Resistance press often mixed accusations against Germans and French collaborators, the accusations had very different implications and consequences for the two groups. Once the Germans had retreated, they were beyond the reach of French civilians, and any reckoning could only be carried out across the border by the French occupiers of Germany and the international war crimes trials. French collaborators, on the other hand, were vulnerable to their enemies; they had nowhere to go.

From the moment the Allies landed in Normandy on 6 June, the French who had sided with the Resistance set in motion what became known as *l'épuration:* the purge. The purge was the first, short-lived effort by the French government to face the negative aspects of the Vichy past. But it did not initiate any widespread examination of French behavior during the war.

The purge had two distinct phases. The first lasted from 6 June until September 1944, when de Gaulle's Commissioners of the Republic established administrative and judicial control of the central government. This was the period of popular summary justice. Though violence was quickly controlled, the most reliable estimates suggest that "at least four and a half thousand summary executions took place in France in the months following the Liberation."[5] Most of the violence occurred south of the Loire, an area that was liberated not by Allied troops but by the French themselves. On 15 August, American and French troops landed in Provence and drove up the Rhône valley to meet General Patton's troops in Dijon on 11 September. The Germans occupying the southwest raced northeast to avoid the Allied trap, leaving to the Resistance the huge area from the Pyrénées to the Loire and the Atlantic to the Rhône.

Hardest hit by summary justice were agricultural workers, small farmers, and artisans.[6] Also among the victims were *gendarmes*, policemen, and accomplices of the Nazis against whom resisters had been pursuing a campaign since 1943.[7] In small towns and the countryside where everyone knew each other, the political and personal intertwined in a particularly explosive mix. An example of this potential appears in Marcel Ophuls's film documentary *The Sorrow and the Pity* during an interview with the *résistant* Grave brothers. Alexis Grave tells that he knows which neighbor denounced him to the police—an act that resulted in Grave's deportation to Buchenwald. Fortunately, not all such situations degenerated into reprisals; Grave decided not to settle this score when he returned home at the end of the war.[8]

The second, courtroom phase of the *épuration* began belatedly, in the opinion of those who sympathized with the Resistance. Technical obstacles to a swift purge proved enormous. Before any trials could take place, for example, the judiciary itself had to be purged, as nearly all Third Republic judges had remained at their posts during the Occupation.[9] Though the first trials began in October, de Gaulle waited until 18 November 1944 to establish a high court with jurisdiction over the cases of Pétain and his prime minister, cabinet officers, and colonial governors.

In the end, official Liberation justice proved quite moderate.[10] President de Gaulle pardoned women, minors, and small fry. Out of the total of 124,751 cases heard, the court pronounced 2,853 death sentences in the presence of the accused. Of these, only 767 sentences were actually carried out. The court pronounced an additional 3,910 death sentences in absentia. The most common sentence—deprivation of rights—broke down as follows: 2,702 people sentenced to life at hard labor, 10,637 to terms of hard labor, 2,044 to sentences of solitary confinement, and 22,883 to terms in prison.[11] The judgment of "civic unworthiness" (*l'indignité nationale*) was pronounced in the cases of 49,723 individuals who were sentenced to forms of "national degradation."[12] All in all, postwar justice was not harsh. In the assessment of Charles de Gaulle: "Considering the mass of collaboration evidence and the number of atrocities committed against the resistance fighters, and recalling the torrent of rage which spread in all directions once the enemy began to withdraw, it can be said that the judgments of the courts of justice were rendered with as much indulgence as possible."[13]

The purge did not rid the administration of collaborators. Rather, as scholars have convincingly argued, the *lampiste*—the fall guy—was punished disproportionately:

> The most severely punished were the unimportant and the
> poor. The wealthy and influential could employ the best

lawyers, drag out the proceedings, get their case transferred to another *département*, find favourable witnesses, and invoke in their defence secret help given to the Resistance, help made all the more valuable of course by virtue of their social position. . . . Indeed, all the evidence available today confirms that far from being the brutal application of a socially inspired "People's Justice," the *épuration* was in fact more indulgent towards the notables than the underlings, and less hard on the well-established members of society than on the young.[14]

When the principal purge courts closed down in 1947, few of the French were satisfied with the outcome. In the view of many resisters, the procedures lacked the rigor necessary for postwar justice to become the cornerstone of a France "pur et dur." On the opposite end of the spectrum, unreconstructed proponents of Vichy denounced the trials as a gross injustice orchestrated by their political enemies.[15]

The purge had captured public attention, but vigilance soon faded. Though some individuals were punished, the process produced no deep reflection about collective responsibility for collaboration. Leniency was granted in the interest of national unity. In the judgment of historian Jean-Pierre Rioux, "The end to the *épuration* was imposed by necessity: that of survival and reconstruction. It was the priority of getting the nation back to work and consolidating the State which brought a general pardon for the errors of the past."[16] Many believed this required putting aside the most unpleasant and divisive aspects of the Vichy period. It was in this context of a general desire for consensus that the first moves took place to commemorate the massacre at Oradour-sur-Glane.

Only a handful of people knew Oradour immediately after the massacre and were privy to the effort to preserve the ruins. Present-day inhabitants of Oradour—even the older ones—know little about how Oradour was made into France's "martyred village." They are familiar only with the barest outline of the steps leading to the preservation of the ruins and the building of the new town of Oradour.

This can be attributed in part to the fact that after the massacre most survivors went to Limoges or to relatives in other towns. Robert Hébras and André Desourteaux recall that in the first days after the massacre they banded together with other young people who had also lost their families. At the end of June the two young men joined the *maquis*, and after the Liberation of Limoges on 22 August 1944 they enlisted in the French Army. They did not return to the region until the war was over. During the year following the massacre, only two people remained in the immediate vicinity: Martial Machefer, whose house had sustained limited damage, and Hubert Desourteaux, who lived at the family farm just beyond the edge of town. When survivors slowly returned, they were more concerned with resolving their personal tragedies than engaging in or following the process that led to memorialization. They were largely absorbed by mourning their dead, starting new lives, and seeking retribution against those responsible for the crime.

The preservation of Oradour originated in the initiatives of a few local people, who acted almost immediately after the massacre, and soon reached out for national support. Oradour's rapid ascension to official status as a *monument historique* testified to local achievement in pressing the state to become involved in commemorating the massacre.

Only four months after the massacre, the first steps were taken to found an association dedicated to making a monument from the vestiges of Oradour. On 2 October 1944, the mayor of Oradour submitted to the prefect of the Haute-Vienne a list of possible members for "a Comité Provisoire [provisional committee] for the protection of the ruins and the creation of a sanctuary at Oradour-sur-Glane."[17] Meanwhile, others were organizing in Limoges. Georges Frugier-Laverine, a Limogeaud with old family ties to Oradour, laid out their goals to the prefect: to commemorate the massacre each year on its anniversary; to organize a fundraising campaign to finance the building of an ossuary for the ashes of the victims; to aid survivors and defend their rights; to inform the French and the world of the atrocity; and to preserve for the future Oradour's "halo of glory" made from "the blood of her martyrs."[18] The two groups from Oradour and Limoges pursued their common goals as the Comité du Souvenir.[19] Only four people from Oradour proper appeared as members of the Comité du Souvenir: Mayor Louis Moreau, Hubert Desourteaux, M. Besson, and Martial Machefer, an artisan from Oradour. Marcel Darthout, a survivor from the Laudy barn, and Jeannette Montazeaud, the daughter of the notary public, helped out as secretaries.[20]

In the meantime, yet another group had formed to address the material needs of survivors: the Association des Sinistrés et Rescapés (Association of the Victims and Survivors).[21] In February 1945, the Comité du Souvenir and the Association des Sinistrés united as the Association Nationale des Familles des Martyrs d'Oradour-sur-Glane (ANFM).[22] The ANFM continues today as the sole representative of the victims of the massacre and their families.[23]

FIGURE 4

Oradour-sur-Glane, November 1944.

The nature of the event—the killing of almost all the towns-people and the departure of the survivors—meant that the massacre had to be memorialized largely by outsiders. The work of setting up the commemorative site took place when Oradour was a ghost town. In fact, an examination of the minutes of the Comité du Souvenir, administrative records, and interviews with people in Oradour today indicate that townspeople played a minor role in the initial efforts to make Oradour a monument. It was not until the spring of 1945, with the formation of the ANFM, the construction of wooden barracks to house survivors, and the first visits of the government architect to plan construction of a new town, that people from Oradour took charge. By that time the major decisions concerning the physical shape of the commemorative site were a fait accompli.

Dr. Pierre Masfrand, not an Oradour survivor but a Limousin notable from the town of Rochechouart, thirteen kilometers to the southwest, and the subprefect, Guy Pauchou, first articulated a vision for Oradour based on preserving the vestiges of the destroyed town.[24] On 10 October, Dr. Masfrand made the first request for official action: "The ruins of what was still yesterday a cheerful little town eloquently symbolize heinous Nazi barbarism. We should assure their conservation so that they can serve to instruct future generations. It is in this spirit that I have the honor of requesting their classification as a historical monument."[25]

Pauchou and Masfrand gathered an impressive array of regional political and religious figures, as well as representatives of the administration who could be helpful in the conservation effort. Members of the acting committee included the priest serving Oradour, a canon of the diocese of Limoges, a delegate to the commission on religious art from Limoges, the health inspector who had overseen the clearing of the ruins, and the departmental architect. At the request of the prefect, representatives of the "movements of the Liberation and of the National Front" (in other words, men who had been active in or in some capacity connected to the Resistance) had been invited to participate.[26]

The leaders of the Comité du Souvenir were the first to formulate a vision for Oradour as a monument. The Comité held its first meeting on the afternoon of 21 October in a damaged house serving temporarily as Oradour's town hall. Two representatives of the Fine Arts Administration also attended: M. de Chalup, Regional Inspector of Sites, and Jean Creuzot, a Chief Architect of Historic Monuments.[27] This meeting was the start of a long, and later difficult, partnership between the central administration and the people at Oradour.

In this forum, Dr. Masfrand formally presented the Comité's radical plan for the future of Oradour. The centerpiece of the proposal was the designation of the ruins as a historic monument and the creation of a new town near the ruins of the old. For Dr. Masfrand it was out of the question that a new town be built on the old site: "We must incontestably conserve the ruins of Oradour-sur-Glane for the pious remembrance of future generations."[28] The minutes of the Comité's meeting indicate that large numbers of people from the region and surrounding departments were, in fact, already visiting the ruins. Dr. Masfrand described how guides would receive visitors and lead them in groups to key spots, "to the church, to houses, in particular to the tragic barns [*granges tragiques*], and finally to the cemetery. . . ." He had clear ideas not only about what visitors should see in Oradour, but also how they should comport themselves: "Visitors on their own should not enter the houses and cause damage by gathering objects they find useful or by collecting souvenirs. Neither is it fitting that they should settle down to eat or to chat on the steps, which are the thresholds of the houses and should be treated with the same respect as tombs."[29] At its next meeting, on 14 November, the Comité chose a repatriated prisoner of war to act as a guide.[30]

The unifying theme of Masfrand's plan was the conviction that creating an emotional impact was the best guarantee of making a lasting impression on the visitor to Oradour. "The visitor will remember," explained Dr. Masfrand, "all the more to the extent that he will have been moved and he will have been given [the opportunity] to feel the invisible presence of the houses' inhabitants." This could be best achieved by the presentation of "certain houses in the state in which they were found right after the conflagration." Rather than just the preservation of the shells of the buildings, he envisaged a whole mise en scène designed to evoke the domestic life of the families the Nazis had destroyed. "An object that the visitor will find in its proper place, for example, a pot on the hearth, . . . will often make the deepest impression." Dr. Masfrand was well aware that creating the proper effect would require careful restoration of the surroundings:

> In many dwellings where all the furnishings were destroyed, our work will necessarily be limited to preserving the walls. But in many others, in particular in certain garages where there are automobiles, trucks, bicycles, and metal objects that survived the fire, it is fitting (except if their disorder gives them a particularly striking character) to remove the vehicles from the accumulated debris and to present them, as well as other objects, in the places they used to occupy, in order to piously and faithfully show the spot as it was at the moment of the fire.

In some cases, vigorous intervention would be necessary since the interiors of the ruined houses had been disturbed by search crews, scavengers, and souvenir hunters.[31] Dr. Masfrand proposed nothing less than recreating a moment in time—at the moment of the fire—and then freezing it. Thus the physical remains of Oradour would provide a permanent commemoration.

The display of objects saved from the ruins was also to play a role in Dr. Masfrand's effort to instruct the public. He announced a plan for the creation of a Museum of Memory, "where objects gathered from the ruins of the town will be piously conserved and exhibited, objects that will evoke for the visitor the most striking vicissitudes of this monstrous affair." Dr. Masfrand had already gathered many objects which, in his judgment, were "particularly interesting from this point of view," such as baby carriages perforated by bullet holes, and the remains of the church bell, which had melted from the heat of the fire.[32] Displaying items taken from the church as museum pieces did not just transform them into artifacts; the attitude brought to bear on these remains would endow them with the aura of religious relics.

In a subsequent meeting, the Comité du Souvenir continued to place importance on preserving the details of violence and death. Dr. Masfrand requested that the bullet holes in the wall of the church be protected by a layer of straw. As for the bloodstains in the same part of the church, he told the meeting that he had written to the conservator of the Louvre for information about a fixing procedure to ensure their conservation.

The last feature in Dr. Masfrand's plan for Oradour entailed expanding the cemetery and building a chapel and ossuary, topped or accompanied by a monument. The remains of the victims of the massacre had been buried in three mass graves in the cemetery. Dr. Masfrand had received numerous complaints from mourning mothers, distraught at not knowing at which grave to pray. Erecting an ossuary would unite the ashes of all those who died.

The Comité proposal to inscribe Oradour on the roll of historic monuments was nothing less than an effort to demonstrate in cultural terms that France had been martyred at the hands of the Nazis. In France, fewer than one hundred buildings have been deemed worthy of designation as *monuments historiques;* normally this classification has been reserved for such revered edifices as the great cathedrals of Mont-St-Michel and Chartres. From the point of view of architects and experts on national heritage, steeped in the tradition of France, it was quite absurd to think that the ruins of a country town should be counted as a national treasure.

The Comité's plan was radical from the point of view of city planners as well. According to Gabor Mester de Parajd, the government architect responsible for Oradour in the late 1980s, in the past "one always rebuilt from the old foundation [*tissu ancien*], or at least followed the trace of a road. There are few cases where one conceived of a new village starting from scratch. . . . That came thirty years later."[33] After the war, for example, ruined towns such as St-Mâlo and La Chapelle-en-Vercors were rebuilt on their original locations.

Technical experts within the Fine Arts Administration immediately characterized the proposal as unfeasible. The architect Creuzot voiced his concerns in a long report to the general director of the Fine Arts Administration three days after attending the meeting in Oradour:

FIGURE 5

Mourner at the entrance to the church at Oradour-sur-
Glane, November 1944.

It has been decided to put in a request with the purpose of creating a perimeter that would encircle the ruins of the burned town. This classification will immediately present a particularly difficult task: the conservation of the ruins. In the spirit of the Comité Provisoire, the conservation of the village in the state it was found after the departure of the Germans is the theme that must take precedence over carrying out architectural projects or plans for a monument, which would be done only to complement the presentation of the ruins. . . . But is it possible to maintain this state of affairs? The growth of invasive vegetation is considerable in the Limousin; storms during one winter could cause considerable damage to the ruins that still remain. . . .

In the course of his visit, Creuzot reported, he had observed ruins crumble before his eyes:

. . . the vestiges make a line of high ruins whose silhouette and color are truly impressive. While standing for a few minutes in the rain, we saw sizeable portions of these ruins crumble. After the winter none of it will remain.[34]

Creuzot had identified the central problem that has dogged Oradour to this day: the enormous difficulty and expense of trying to maintain a ruin in a ruined state. A memo dated 24 November from the office of the Minister of National Education came to the same conclusion:

The Comité Provisoire for conservation has expressed the wish that the ruins of the village be "crystallized" in their current state as much as possible. . . . Indeed, it is relatively easy to maintain the church in the state in which it appeared after the fire. . . . It is unfortunately not the same for the ensemble of the village because of the materials used in its construction. The houses of Oradour are largely made of puddled clay [a mixture of sand and clay] or mud wall, materials that readily crumble and cannot be conserved in a ruined state.[35]

Yet after just one meeting of the Comité Provisoire, it was clear to Creuzot that the political momentum in favor of the project would be difficult to resist. "In any case, the classification of the site is inevitable. . . ."[36]

Indeed, the technical difficulties of preserving Oradour did little to dampen the overwhelming political appeal of the gesture. Creuzot's superior, Inspector General Georges Lestel, reported that he had asked that a *dossier de classement* for Oradour be opened immediately. Yet he went even further, inviting regional inspectors throughout France to gather the necessary documentation for similar propositions. "The measures prescribed," wrote Lestel, "constitute, in my opinion, the minimum . . . that the *Historic Monuments Service* can do to assure the necessary perpetuation [of the memory] of these ignominious tragedies."[37]

Two days later, on 28 October, the Commissioner of the Republic in Limoges received a telegram from the Minister of National Education announcing the "institution of an action to classify the entire ruins of Oradour-sur-Glane as a historic site and the ruins of the church as a historic monument."[38] Though clearly supportive of the spirit of the project, these officials would not designate the entire town as a historic monument, as Masfrand and the Comité du Souvenir had asked. A historic *site* would require less protection, and was a more appropriate category, in the Ministry's opinion, for such an extensive area. The head of the Historic Monuments Service suggested designating a "red zone" around the church within which the houses would be preserved as much as possible in their current state. The implicit conclusion was that the rest of the town would be torn down or allowed to crumble away. The government was clearly trying to avoid taking on the burden of maintaining the vestiges in their entirety. But that solution was rejected out of hand in a meeting of Oradour's Comité du Souvenir on 14 November 1944: "Mr. Masfrand declared that it is fitting, in his opinion, to classify all the houses of the bourg and their outbuildings as a site. In classifying only a part, one risks reducing the value of the intended goal."[39]

The provisional government (Gouvernement Provisoire de la République Française, or GPRF) adopted the grand outlines of the Comité du Souvenir's demands despite foot-dragging by experts in the Fine Arts Administration who judged these matters from an architectural and aesthetic point of view. Only a few of Masfrand's more extravagant suggestions went unexecuted—the most sensational being the proposal that on Saturday and Sunday (the days of the week on which the town was destroyed, and on which the ruins received the greatest number of visitors) a flame and plume of smoke be maintained on the tower of the ruined church.[40] In a meeting on 28 November 1944, President de Gaulle's cabinet decided to make Oradour "the object of particular protection by the government"[41] and adopted four proposals presented by René Capitant, the Minister of National Education: classification of the church as a historic monument, classification of the ruins as a historic site, construction of a new town on a different site, and official recognition of the Comité du Souvenir.[42]

From now on, Oradour would be invoked in the name of the Nation.

Though the highest members of government had concerned themselves with commemoration of the massacre at Oradour, in 1944 it was not yet clear what they intended the ruins to symbolize. What was Oradour to stand for? Transforming Oradour into a national symbol meant assigning it some particular commemorative meaning, but that meaning had not yet been identified, beyond general statements about the need to preserve this particular testimony to Nazi barbarism. Lestel, the Inspector General of Sites, had alluded to the malleable nature of what Oradour could represent in his report of 26 October, in which he applauded the notion of preserving the ruins: "Hereafter it will be advisable to examine in what form national piety should finally be expressed regarding these martyred towns and martyred populations."[43] In other words, Oradour should first be saved to become a symbol that would be useful to France. Its exact utility could be determined later.

Lestel's reference to "national piety" and "martyred populations" gave a strong hint of what was to come. The moves to commemorate Oradour occurred within a general trend at the end of the war to take stock of the suffering inflicted by the Germans. For a short while, after the Allied invasion in June, dramatic military events had dominated the pages of most newspapers. But once Paris was freed and the GPRF established, atrocities reemerged as a major theme in the press. In its editorial of 5 September, the leftist newspaper *Ce Soir* exhorted the French to remember their martyrs:

It is essential that the list of victims be drawn up now, that the martyrology of our unfortunate country be brought up to date. 75,000 men were put to death in the Paris region in the course of four years. How many others perished under torture, those of Châteaubriant, Ascq, Oradour, of so many cities where "terrorists" were executed for the only crime of having loved their country too much. These documents must be published, and distributed all over, so that they engrave into our memory and the memory of that people who permitted themselves to be dishonored by so much barbarism. As for the sinister torture chambers, the bloodied walls, the torture instruments, they should be left intact as witnesses in front of which our descendants will come to exalt the memory of our dead and fortify legitimate hate of their murderers.[44]

In its litany of martyrs, *Ce Soir* did not distinguish between resisters and random civilians who died in reprisals. Over time, Oradour would be removed from the context of the Resistance to stand as "pure" martyrdom.

The more politically moderate *L'Aurore* called for German crimes to be anchored in the public consciousness to prevent the falsification of history:

These atrocities of the past months, don't they fill everyone's memory? . . . These memories need to be fixed because man's attention is, by nature, short. They need to be authenticated in order to avoid later dispute, or I don't know what kind of facile accusation of exaggeration and romanticizing. History is not legend: it is based on documents. . . . Yesterday we knew helmeted Germany of the battlefield and military occupation.

> Tomorrow we will find Germany in top form or in the soft
> felt hat of international conferences and political
> congresses. . . . She will explain that Hitlerian domination
> . . . was nothing but a bad dream, that nothing of it remains
> beyond the Rhine and that it is preferable to forget what we
> learned about it.

But bearing witness to Nazi barbarism was not just a *mise-en-garde* against Germany. The message of France's suffering was meant for an international audience—in particular the western Allies. *L'Aurore* elaborated:

> Our English and American friends just got here. Most of
> these incidents happened before they arrived. Certain [inci-
> dents] are so outside the laws of nature that even their verity
> isn't credible. To the Anglo-Saxons we sometimes pass for an
> imaginative people. It is said without cause that we exagger-
> ate. . . . This is why an official collection needs to be estab-
> lished, bringing together unimpeachable evidence and con-
> clusive photographs. . . . It's not a question of increasing
> hate. It's a question of proclaiming the truth and satisfying
> justice.[45]

It is perhaps with this in mind that, in July 1945, the Commissioner of the Republic requested that the departmental railway increase service to Oradour during the fifteen-week period that American troops would be stationed in Limoges. He specifically asked that every Friday during this time, service from Limoges to Oradour be sufficient to transport four hundred soldiers.[46]

At its third meeting, the Comité du Souvenir received the visit of a government official who also had these concerns in mind. M. Billet, attaché at the Ministry of Information, contacted the Comité and attended the session of 12 December 1944. Billet informed the group about an exhibit being prepared, in which Oradour would figure, about "Fascist Crimes and Prisons." Dr. Masfrand loaned some of Oradour's most striking relics, including a child's toy car and a baby carriage, both riddled with bullets, as well as various objects gathered from the ruins of the church (corset stays, nails from clogs, and so forth). Billet explained that "an enormous national propaganda campaign needs to be carried out, directed especially toward the Allies."[47] The government's involvement in establishing the *village martyr* as a national symbol had more specific political objectives than simply bearing witness to Nazi brutality; it was part of an effort, led by General de Gaulle, to claim legitimacy for France as a country that had suffered under the Nazis and deserved to reclaim her rank as a great nation.

In autumn 1944, the Allies had not yet decided to recognize France's sovereignty. President Roosevelt considered de Gaulle an unknown entity at best, a potential demagogue at worst, and in any case a leader with no political mandate. Roosevelt believed that France, like any other liberated nation, should be administered by the Allied Military Government of Occupied Territories (AMGOT) until elections could be held. It was not until 23 October 1944 that the Allies formally recognized the GPRF.

In this atmosphere of uncertainty, President de Gaulle decided that his physical presence, as the head of state, would promote the cause of order around the country and, by eliciting massive popular support, would convince the Allies of the provisional government's claims to legitimacy.[48] During his period as president of the Provisional French Republic, from September 1944 until he resigned on 20 January 1946, de Gaulle undertook fifteen presidential trips to the provinces. During all of these trips, de Gaulle constantly stressed themes of national unity; much in the way that he had sought to rally the different elements of the Resistance, he now sought to unify a fragmented nation.

On 4 March 1945, at the ruins of Oradour, de Gaulle elaborated the message of national unity in suffering. His visit to Oradour came as part of a triumphal two-day tour of the Limousin and the Dordogne that included all the hallmarks of de Gaulle's official visits. The presidential delegation arrived in Limoges by train at nine o'clock in the morning and was met by the Commissioner of the Republic and five prefects from departments of central France. The president proceeded to the square de la Poste, where he laid a wreath at the World War I memorial. From here he went on foot to the prefecture. All along the way, cheering crowds lined his route. "By the thousands Limousins acclaimed General de Gaulle" heralded *Le Libérateur*, one of the single-page, regional, weekly papers that had sprung up since the Liberation.[49] Another, *La Marseillaise*, described the city as "trembling with patriotic faith" and rejoicing in the "intimate contact between the government and the Nation."[50] In the main hall of the prefecture, before the gathering of administration officials, the regional military commander, various local notables, and delegations, de Gaulle enumerated the conditions necessary to attain the goals of renovation and reform.[51] Later, he addressed an enormous crowd from the balcony of the Hôtel de Ville.

The emotional tenor of de Gaulle's visit shifted from celebration to somber pilgrimage when he set off for Oradour in the afternoon. No public announcements had been made that the

president would be touring the ruins.[52] When official arrange-
ments were being planned, Subprefect Pauchou, displaying a
fine instinct for staging, had proposed that the visit take place
"without a milling crowd," so as not to reduce the impact of the
ruins or detract from the horror of the massacre.[53] Only a small
group was permitted in the ruins to receive the president. A reporter accompanying the president and his entourage described
the drama of the scene:

> Finally, suddenly, through the trees, we perceived, even more
> tragic in the sunshine, the ruins of Oradour. Oradour, a
> name that sounds like a tolling bell to the ears of an entire
> people: Oradour, which in one day saw its population annihi-
> lated and its houses ruined. By way of the sloping street bor-
> dered by gutted and blackened façades, where the wind
> blows a sinister moan through the gaping windows, the gen-
> eral and his retinue ascended to the little square.[54]

Assembled on the marketplace were Subprefect Pauchou; the
mayor of Oradour, Louis Moreau; the five survivors of the Laudy
barn (Yvon Roby, Clément Broussaudier, Mathieu Borie, Marcel
Darthout, and Robert Hébras); the sole woman to survive the
slaughter in the church, Marguerite Rouffanche; the two little
boys who had escaped, Roger Godfrin and André Pinède; members of the Comité du Souvenir; and a number of bereaved families. De Gaulle then addressed a few sentences to the gathering:
"Oradour is the symbol of what happened to the country itself.
In order to mend, and to maintain the memory, it is necessary to
remain together, as we are in this moment. A place like this remains something shared by all. Never again; a similar thing must
never happen anywhere in France."[55] With these few sentences,

FIGURE 6

Some of the survivors on the occasion of de Gaulle's
visit to Oradour, March 1945. From left to right: Armand
Senon, Mathieu Borie, Daniel Senon, Yvon Roby, Clément
Broussaudier (front), Marcel Darthout (behind), Maurice
Beaubreuil, Roger Godfrin, Joseph Beaubreuil,
Hubert Desourteaux, Robert Besson, Aimé Renaud,
Paul Doutre, and Martial Machefer.

President de Gaulle made Oradour an exemplar of the national experience; Oradour was to be a symbol that would bring the French together in commemoration of the horrors of Nazi barbarism and the suffering of the nation. The local view was expressed in Pauchou's short speech. He called for "exemplary punishment of the guilty" and revenge. He finished by crying: "You are our saviour; today we are asking you to avenge us." Only *La Nouvelle République du Centre-Ouest* bothered to quote that.

From the marketplace the president was led on a tour of the ruins, following the itinerary taken by the victims. Pauchou directed the presidential group to the barns and sheds where the men had been shot and then down the main street to the ruined church. Only a small party entered the church, which was shown to them by the Bishop of Limoges. The "pilgrimage" ended with a "pious visit" to the cemetery, where President de Gaulle placed a bronze plaque that read, "To Oradour, witness to Nazi barbarism, the government of the Republic."[56] After signing and dating the first page of the memorial book of the martyred village, the president departed for Limoges. The final image conveyed by the newspapers was one of the president comforting the mourning nation: "At the exit to the village and on the road to Limoges, the inhabitants of the region crowded along the route of the head of government. He ... had his car stopped and bowed before numerous groups of people in mourning, all of whom wept for the victims of the tragic day of 10 June."[57]

At the ruins of Oradour, de Gaulle had extended the message given at Grenoble a few months earlier. There he had celebrated the sacrifices of the Resistance as a national endeavor; at Oradour he broadened the sufferings of the ruined town to stand for the trials of the nation as a whole. This time France's martyrs

FIGURE 7

President Charles de Gaulle at the cemetery of Oradour,
March 1945.

and heroes were not Resistance fighters but the ordinary citizens of a peaceful village destroyed by marauding SS soldiers. De Gaulle's visit established Oradour's reputation as the outstanding example of an ideal French village that, through no fault of its own, became the hapless victim of Nazi barbarism. The commemorative effort at Oradour, begun by the Comité du Souvenir and legitimated and enlarged by de Gaulle, reduced the tension between the image of the French as active resisters and the fact that the great majority of the population had survived the war by getting by. The implicit message was that every French person, regardless of political choice or wartime activity, had been at risk.

The concept of martyrdom went beyond the physical suffering of the French to the heart of the moral dilemmas posed by the Occupation and collaboration. In the newspaper commentaries written in the fall of 1944, one hears strains of anxiety and dismay that France had somehow faltered morally. In *L'Aurore* of 14 October, the paper's editor depicted France as a "victim state" in the postwar international arena:

> One often says that the united nations divide up into great
> and small states. Instead of small states it would be better to
> speak of victim states, because that would better define their
> position. . . . There were a large number of states that were
> occupied and ravaged by the Hitlerian armies, and due to
> this fact, their moral situation and their political situation are
> very particular. . . . France, for example, finds herself to be
> one of them.[58]

Honoring the French civilian victims as "martyrs" ennobled an experience that had been, in many respects, humiliating, and in some cases dishonorable.

Martyrdom, which suggests physical weakness but moral superiority, implies a sacred cause—in this case, the cause of the nation. The national cause had long been represented as sacred, but the use of the term "martyr" reflected the overwhelming belief that France had been powerless in the face of the Nazis. The willingness on the part of the French to accept this assessment may also have been reflected in French attitudes regarding postwar justice. Historian Jean-Pierre Rioux has questioned the good faith of the French on this count:

> Indeed, one can ask if the population as a whole was quite as innocent in its attitude to the victims of the *épuration* as it cared to believe. In 1943, General de Gaulle had promised that France would need to know vengeance. Yet after 1944 the desire for vengeance foundered amidst the reticence of the Nation. Was this not, in part, because too severe a judgement on those involved in the Occupation implied a judgement on everyone?[59]

The decision to make Oradour a commemorative site of national importance was part of the leniency, on the part of de Gaulle and the larger political community, toward the recent past.

By his visit, de Gaulle not only assigned meaning to the ruins but also provided help of a practical nature. Until the legal character of the site was settled, no major work could be done to consolidate the ruins. The administration planned to make the ruins a historic site, while the Comité du Souvenir and the mayor of Oradour continued to insist on the status of historic monument. Subprefect Pauchou used the occasion of de Gaulle's visit to press his case with the Minister of the Interior, André Tixier, who was part of the presidential delegation. On 22 March, Tixier sent a testy memo to the Minister of National Education, René Capitant, requesting that a compromise decision (classification of the village as a historic site and the church as a historic monument) be published in the *Journal officiel:* "It would be opportune that it be published without delay, soon after General de Gaulle's trip." He also urged his colleague to get work underway immediately to save the ruins: "At the present hour the ruins in their entirety threaten to disappear."[60]

In early April, Capitant took the first legal steps to classify the "entire agglomeration of the ruins" as a historic monument. This decision gave the ruins the provisional status of historic monument for one year and permitted the technical services of the Office of Historic Monuments to begin conservation of the ruins. In announcing his decision, which was only a step short of full classification as a historic monument, Capitant noted that he had taken this measure in deference to local demands.[61] With the help of de Gaulle, the Comité du Souvenir had succeeded in securing Oradour's place on the official commemorative landscape of the Second World War.

Classification of the ruins of Oradour as a historic monument was complicated by the very facts of the massacre. The law governing such classifications requires the agreement of the owners, which was obviously not possible in this case. Under these circumstances, the Fine Arts Administration and the Ministry of Reconstruction decided to simplify matters: they arranged for the state to expropriate the ruins and land of the old town.[62] Once the government decided to make itself owner of the ruins, it became permanently involved in the commemoration of the massacre.

Dr. Masfrand had spoken of piety—the "pious conservation" of objects from the ruins, and the cemetery as a place of "pious

FIGURE 8

Postage stamp issued in 1945.

pilgrimage." Now the French government adopted these terms. A press release issued on 5 January 1945 announced the government's desire to make the "martyred village" a site of "national pilgrimage" and, by conserving the ruins, transform the site into a "Temple of Memory" (Temple du Souvenir).[63] Another communiqué referred to the ruins as a "Museum of National Piety" (Musée de la Piété Nationale).[64] The language of this discussion was reminiscent of the language of episcopal investigations into the authenticity of miracles in order to decide whether to sanction the founding of an official cult.[65]

Franck Delage, the author of *Oradour, ville martyre*, a small book published in March 1945, called most explicitly for a blending of nationalism and religious faith as part of the cult of national memory:

> After this war, whose ravages ceaselessly increased, ruining provinces that had been spared by other wars, after victory, after the crushing of an inhuman enemy, France will want to have her national pilgrimages. Oradour-sur-Glane, the innocent martyr, will rank highly in these ceremonies where the French people will partake of the sacrament. One will not come only to pray for the dead while mourning unutterable suffering. These will be ceremonies of French faith and, at the same time, of Christian faith.[66]

The "Martyr of the Innocents" at Oradour would serve as a "national lesson." Pilgrimage to this site would strengthen the will to restore the nation's greatness; just as Christian pilgrims renew their faith by visiting holy relics of martyrs, so at Oradour would French citizens restore the national zeal: "The pilgrimage to the ruins of Oradour will strengthen the will of all Frenchmen to restore France to her fine place in the world. . . . In this modest village of the Limousin, from the contact of death and ruin, will surge forth the vitality of a great nation, which does itself honor by detesting iniquity and cruelty, which loves justice, law, and peace."[67]

These notions of "national pilgrimage" were not new. In fact, they harkened back to the religious revival of the Third Republic, which came in response to the French defeat in the Franco-Prussian War of 1871 and the violence of the Paris Commune that followed. As historian Thomas Kselman has shown, the early 1870s saw an intense religious revival among believers and an upsurge in pilgrimages to miracle sites that had been established in the nineteenth century—the most famous of these being at Lourdes in the Hautes-Pyrénées.[68] The pilgrimage movement reached a high point in 1872, when a national commission of laymen and clergy organized the first National Pilgrimage to Lourdes.[69] By the last third of the century Lourdes "served as an unofficial but widely acknowledged national shrine."[70]

From 1871 to 1873, the French reported an increased number of apparitions and experienced a major revival of the French prophetic tradition. The most famous apparitions occurred at Pontmarin, in the department of the Mayenne in western France—an area under threat by Prussian troops. On 17 January 1871, the Virgin appeared to two children, saying: "But pray, my children, God will answer your prayers in a while." Indeed, a few days later Pontmarin was spared. An episcopal investigation concluded that a miracle had indeed occurred.[71] In this period of political and social crisis following the French defeat at Sedan, prophecies served an important social and psychological function: "to explain and justify political and social disorder as a result of moral decadence and religious indifference. After describing the expiatory chastisements, prophecies assured their readers that France would recover her position as the wealthiest and most powerful state in the world."[72]

The same combination of Catholicism and nationalism inspired the construction of the Basilica of the Sacred Heart on Montmartre in Paris.[73] In the aftermath of the Franco-Prussian War, the religious revival of the Third Republic represented the culmination of a common religious and political theme in nineteenth-century French Catholicism: "The belief that France was being punished for the unexpiated sins of the Revolution, and a hope that public prayer and ritual could serve as reparation."[74]

In 1944 there was no comparable outpouring by Catholics of a sense of guilt for failures of the Vichy period (the Catholic Church, after all, had been a bastion of support for Vichy and Pétainism). Yet in their quasireligious rhetoric, the proponents of Oradour as a national monument drew on a tradition of mixing religion and nationalism; with this blending of Christian belief and patriotic faith they designated the dead of Oradour as martyrs who died not for their faith but for their country. This tone in memorialization contributed to a peculiar tension between the vision of France as a victim of the Nazis versus France as a proud country of resisters among the victor nations.

In France, the decision to classify an edifice as a historic monument or site is usually made within the channels of the bureaucracy with little publicity. But in the case of Oradour, four cabinet ministers took the extraordinary measure of introducing special legislation in the National Assembly to enshrine the ruins of Oradour as a historic monument and to provide for the construction of a new town. Without debate, the Assembly voted unanimously for the bill. It was signed by President Félix Gouin and promulgated on 10 May 1946.

In the preamble to the law, the government echoed de Gaulle's statement made at Oradour in March 1945: "It is necessary to leave to future generations the testimony to Nazi barbarism and the suffering of the French people during four years of occupation. The ruins of Oradour-sur-Glane are one of these testimonies." The law formally provided for the protection of the ruins, their classification as a historic monument, and the building, by the state, of a new town. "Thus French and foreign pilgrims will have, next to the image of France ravaged [*la France meurtrie*], that of France renascent."[75]

A report that had been submitted with the bill, drafted by the Commission on National Education and the Fine Arts, Youth, Sport, and Leisure, used stirring language to expand on these two founding points. It stated that the commemoration of Oradour would be the vigilant call against "a policy of forgetting and moral weakness." The vestiges of Oradour, "implacable in their silence," would stand as "the indictment drawn up by history against every regime of oppression and violence." Then, in an enormous leap in logic, the report further broadened the victimization the ruins were meant to evoke to include those who had been deported and died in the camps: "Thus one will make the ruins of Oradour into a national necropolis, where decency, austerity, respect, and silence will reign. One will make these remains into witnesses of one of the greatest tragedies of history, the symbol of those who disappeared in the camps of extermination and suffering."[76] This claim was certainly freighting the symbol of Oradour with more than was reasonable. Equating the death inflicted at Oradour with the killing that took place in the camps indicated a need for France to see itself as a victim. The suggestion that Oradour would serve in this way worked to efface France's own role in persecution and deportations. In the end, these claims were not included in the law.

Creating a memorial site required enclosing, redefining, and sorting out space. For the first six months after the massacre, what remained of Oradour was a mass of charred ruins. The main street was still a thoroughfare for automotive traffic and the departmental tram. Visitors wandered about freely in the ruins. In order to create a memorial/pilgrimage site, Oradour had to be marked off as sacred ground. Once the government assumed ownership of the site, visitors as well as surviving members of the community were gradually shut out of places where once they could go as they pleased.

The principles for preserving the ruins were developed by Pierre Paquet, the architect put in charge of the "special mission" to conserve the ruins and build a new town. Already seventy years old at the time, Paquet was nearing the end of a distinguished career in the service of the Fine Arts Administration, where he had held the rank of Inspector General of Historic Monuments since 1920. He brought a high degree of expertise to the Oradour project. After the First World War he had held a post on the National Committee for Reconstruction, and he had also overseen work on such architectural treasures as the Hôtel de Cluny and the Ste-Chapelle in Paris. In 1923 he had been entrusted with the care of one of the jewels of historic monuments,

Mont St-Michel. Although Paquet officially retired in 1947, he remained the chief architect for Oradour, both the ruins and the new town, until his death in 1959.

Having accepted the Oradour assignment in January 1945, Paquet made numerous trips to Oradour to survey the ruins and to choose a site for the new town. On March 27, he submitted his general program for conservation and reconstruction to the ministers of National Education and Reconstruction and Urban Planning.[77] This report was no less than the government's blueprint for shaping the meaning and commemorative purpose of the blackened wreck of the former town.

Paquet outlined two specific goals. The first was to transform the ruins of Oradour into an "evocative cemetery," a witness to "one of the greatest tragedies of the war." This "sacred place" would impose respect and silence. The second goal was to make the ruins a national monument that "in the eyes of the whole world would perpetuate [the memory of] the savagery of the German race."[78] To accomplish this task, Paquet proposed to reroute the main road so that traffic would no longer pass through the ruins, enclose the site with a low wall, shore up portions of the ruins that were in danger of falling down, protect the church from damage by weather, and build an underground chapel in which to house the ashes of unidentified victims. A year later he added the task of keeping up the gardens of the former inhabitants.[79]

Work to protect the ruins began in earnest in the late spring of 1945. A private company from the nearby town of Confolens was hired for the most urgent job: tearing down walls that threatened to collapse onto the main street. By midsummer, a special tram from Limoges was bringing one hundred workers a day to clear and consolidate the ruins. They repaired the crests of the burned walls with new stone and cement and buttressed the weakened structures. Wooden lintels were replaced with reinforced concrete. As Paquet was careful to note, "All of this work was done with the greatest care to keep the look of the ruins without adding anything."[80] As the work progressed, Pierre Masfrand supervised the positioning of furniture and other objects gathered from the ruins.

It was not just the physical remains that had to be organized. The public and what remained of the community had to be induced to behave appropriately. Pierre Paquet expressed concern about visitors taking objects from the ruins. "In order to avoid this looting," he decided to place iron bars across the doorways of the ruined houses to prohibit intruders. "But," he noted, "this is just a reminder; it is necessary that the guardians make it effective."[81]

The local inhabitants presented a different problem; they still considered the old town to be their home, and they continued to make use of land inside the enclosing wall. If Oradour-sur-Glane was to become a national monument, the former proprietors had to be shut out. In 1947, Dr. Desourteaux's surviving son requested the right to cultivate his parents' garden: "Since I have not yet been given any land to replace the garden in question, I have the honor of asking you for authorization to cultivate again this year, and until All Saints' Day 1947, my parents' garden, which is situated in the ruins. . . ."[82] Though he expressed regret, the Director General of Architecture, R. Danis, gave an unfavorable reply.

Though the enclosing wall was almost completed by 1949, it had not successfully stopped foot traffic through the ruins. In 1949 the Director General of Architecture reported four cases of local people going through the ruins to gain access to their fields. One of them was getting to his garden by walking through the streets of the old town and then climbing a ladder he had placed against the enclosing wall behind the church. In another case, the inheritors of a barn that had not burned were making use of it. "I call your attention," the Director General wrote to the Minister of Reconstruction and Urban Planning, "to this situation, which is particularly detrimental to the mood of contemplation and composure which this national necropolis must have."[83] The Chief Architect, Creuzot, foresaw that completion of the entrance gates to the ruins would completely close off such access to the old town.[84]

By the 1950s the government had achieved its aim. All local claims of the living to the old town of Oradour-sur-Glane had been removed. Oradour was now a sacred place that belonged to the nation.

Chapter Four

THE MEMORIAL LANDSCAPE

I n the design of the monument and in its use, government architects and planners, working in conjunction with the ANFM,
shaped the ruins of Oradour into an instructive narrative. The
staging of the ruins as well as their decay over time influenced
how the place worked as a *lieu de mémoire* and as a commemorative site. A variety of people have made use of the memorial space:
survivors, families of the victims (in both a private capacity and
as part of the ANFM), the general public, and representatives of
the state. Their differing relationships to the site shed light on
the interplay of space and place with memory, history, commemoration, and mourning.[1]

Though national commemoration included elements of
mourning (witness, for example, de Gaulle's visit to Oradour), the
survivors and the families of the victims also mourned their losses
personally and individually. The physical remains in Oradour
contribute to and are enhanced by the nostalgic memories of the

survivors. For those who once lived in the old town, the landscape of Oradour is imbued with memories and emotional associations related to personal and family history. For them, the ruins are not just a scene of destruction but the scene of their youth; this landscape has deep meanings quite apart from the political or historical significance developed by the official commemoration.[2]

In Oradour, verbal testimony—the recollections of the survivors, books about the massacre, and the speech of the tour guide—has taken second place to the site itself; spoken and written renditions of the story are told in reference to the vestiges of the dead town. When survivors relate the story of their escape, they set it in the physical context of the ruined town—where they lived, where they were when the SS soldiers arrived, the route they took in getting away. During the spring and summer months, when many visitors come to Oradour, an official guide to the ruins, Jean-Jacques Hyvernaud, recounts the story of the massacre to tourists in the church. As they gather around to listen, Hyvernaud describes the events of the afternoon of 10 June. His performance, with all its gravity and dramatic intonations, attempts to give life to the physical frame presented by the ruined buildings and preserved artifacts.

Although the commemorative site of Oradour is technically limited to the ruins (they alone constitute the historic monument), the memorial landscape is broader, including the vestiges of the old town, the cemetery (belonging to the commune of Oradour) lying along the eastern edge of the ruins, and the new town, a few hundred meters to the north of the ruins. Official commemoration, community memory, family memory, and the memories of individuals are tied to these places. Going to these places to remember—to take part in official commemoration, mourn as a group, or visit as an individual—shapes and reinforces memory. Those who drafted the legislation for preserving the site intended the ruins to gather power and meaning from their contrast to the new town and their relationship to ideas of homeland and nation.

In his elaboration of a sociology of memory, Maurice Halbwachs proposed that "Every collective memory unfolds within a spatial framework. . . . We can understand how we recapture the past only by understanding how it is, in effect, preserved by our physical surroundings."[3] For Halbwachs, locale was essential for the maintenance and recovery of memories: "Each group cuts up space in order to compose, either definitively or in accordance with a set method, a fixed framework within which to enclose and retrieve its remembrances."[4] In his effort to articulate universal laws about the nature of memory, he insisted upon a correspondence between physical locale and memory for all social groups.[5] Halbwachs's analysis of space and collective memory works best for small, cohesive communities like Oradour, where members lived together over time. These societies bear out most clearly his assertion that "place and group have each received the imprint of the other."[6] In his view, this collective memory is threatened by the advent of modern, fragmented society. He believed that it is precisely a change or breakdown in the structures that form the "social frameworks of memory" (family, religious group, and social class) that causes a society to forget or deforms its collective memory.[7]

Noting that spatial frameworks are a source of community stability, Halbwachs offered an insight that illuminates the workings of memory among the survivors at Oradour: "Extraordinary events are also fitted within this spatial framework; because they occasion in the group a more intense awareness of its past and present, the bonds attaching it to physical locale gain greater clarity in the very moment of their destruction."[8]

Owned by the state and maintained by the Ministry of Culture for public viewing from dawn to dusk, the forty acres of ruins are the centerpiece of a permanent commemoration by the state of the massacre. Government officials estimate that approximately three hundred thousand people a year come to Oradour. On summer afternoons a constant stream of visitors floods the main avenue. On certain days during the height of summer travel, ten thousand people visit the ruins.[9] Even on the bleakest days in winter, one happens across the occasional tourist.

The typical summer visitor is French, between the ages of 35 and 49, coming with family or friends. A quarter of the visitors come from the western regions of France. For 71 percent of visitors, this is their first visit to Oradour. Half heard about Oradour from a family member. Visitors to Oradour give, as their most common explanation for the trip, a desire to see "a town that testifies to barbarity"—barbarity which many consider "to still exist."[10]

The ruins of Oradour were originally figured as a site of national pilgrimage, and all those who come—whether referred to as pilgrims, visitors, or tourists—are heirs to the Catholic tradition of making a pilgrimage. It is no accident that the ruins are considered a "martyred" village, or that the eight who escaped the hands of the SS (The survivors of the Laudy barn, Roger Godfrin, and Madame Rouffanche) have been designated as *miraculés*—a term used to denote those ailing pilgrims cured at the shrine of a miracle cult. Oradour can, without exaggeration, be considered a shrine in a secular cult of memory, which expresses much of its meaning in Catholic imagery. Even among nonbelievers, the *miraculés* of Oradour are venerated not unlike the *miraculé* who, after the miraculous cure, was "regarded . . . as a cultic object, a living symbol of the omnipotence and mercy of God."[11] This is not to say that the survival of certain individuals is seen in an unambiguously positive religious light. If anything, the fact that God permitted women and children to die in a church caused a crisis and even loss of faith among many believers who lived in Oradour.[12]

At Oradour one can map out a memorial landscape that makes visible various forms of memory associated with the massacre. The ruins are the site of national commemoration by the state and the general public. The cemetery is where families come to grieve the death of their loved ones and the death of the community. The new town combines aspects both of commemoration and mourning in the way it was designed and built, and in its residents; the survivors of the massacre and the families of the victims formed the kernel of the new town and established a sense of community within the ANFM. There is, of course, overlap. The ruins, the focus of national commemoration, also figure in the efforts of individual survivors to remember their personal history. Yet each of these places is characterized by distinct approaches to the past.

The visitor to Oradour usually enters the ruins at one of two iron gates situated at either end of the old main street. Approaching on the road from Limoges, one can park in a small lot at the lower entrance, cross the bridge over the Glane, and walk in below the church. However, most cars and tour buses continue along the highway. The view opens out. To the right is a broad view of the ruins, while straight ahead the tower of the new church perches on the crest of a small hill. As the main road curves sharply west, bypassing the new town, one turns off into an unpaved lot between the new town and the ruins, only a few steps from the upper entrance. Just inside the gate, a young woman employed by the Historic Monuments Service sells postcards, slides, and books.[13]

Proceeding down the road, one passes under a stand of dark pine trees before stepping out into the sun. The atmosphere is at once ghostly and peaceful. One hears the sounds of birds and, from a distance, the cars passing on the highway. Tracks of the regional tram, now rusted, still run down the center of the road. To the right a narrow lane joins the main road. A small sign at the intersection raises a sense of horror and anticipation: "tragic well." Following the arrow, one comes to the spot where Nazi soldiers dumped cadavers into the well of a small farm. Here, as at the sites where groups of people were shot, a sign bids the viewer "Recueillez-vous." The verb *se recueillir*, a word full of religious resonance, means to collect one's thoughts for an inner meditation.

Back on the main road, continuing toward the church, one passes a high wall. A stone plaque marks the impressive stone house set off from the road as the former residence of the two local doctors, Paul and Jacques Desourteaux. Until recently this was one of only a handful of plaques that named particular people, but in 1990 the Departmental Architecture Service installed plaques on all the buildings of the marketplace and the main street, indicating the profession and name of the person who once lived or worked there. This new attention to individuals has shifted the emphasis in the ruins away from an evocation of anonymous, collective death. Reading the names of professions that for all practical purposes no longer exist (clogmaker, cooper, welldigger) gives the sense not only of a lost town but of a lost epoch as well.

By now one has arrived in the former town center. Most of the houses stand flush with the street. Low wooden fences prevent entry, but tourists lean over and peer into the broken-down interiors of houses where rubble and rusted pieces of metal strew the ground. In one an old sewing machine has been left on the window sill. These humble buildings have deteriorated more rapidly than the public buildings and rare houses built of massive stone. Efforts to fend off decay are visible; along the façades of the main street the white of new cement contrasts with the grey and molded mortar of the original walls.

Crossing toward the central marketplace, one is brought up short by another stone plaque: "Place of torture. Here a group of men were massacred and burned to death by the Nazis. *Recueillez-vous.*" With the aid of the map provided in the official book on Oradour published by the ANFM,[14] and also in a newer brochure sold at the kiosk, one can locate all five barns and sheds around the marketplace where the men of Oradour were machine-gunned.

The marketplace is a now a green expanse of lawn ringed by the façades of houses. Sky shows through their gaping windows and open roofs. In places, only door frames and fragments of wall remain. The only object in this open space is the body of an old car. A postcard purchased at the kiosk indicates that this is the car of Dr. Jacques Desourteaux. Reading the official account of the massacre, one learns that the doctor had been paying a house call in an outlying village when the German soldiers entered

Oradour. The soldiers stopped his car as he came back into town. One climbed in and ordered Dr. Desourteaux to drive on and join the rest of the townspeople, including his family, who had been rounded up on the marketplace.

Continuing down the rue Emile Desourteaux, one arrives at the steps leading to the church. Though the tiles on the roof of the church and the bell tower burned during the fire, the nave and transepts, built from granite in the fifteenth and seventeenth centuries, survived with only some discoloration caused by smoke. On the outside wall an iron crucifix still remains. During the summer months, tourists gather round to hear M. Hyvernaud's account of the events of 10 June 1944. Dressed in the dark blue blazer of the Historic Monuments Service, Hyvernaud combines the authority of an official spokesman with the pathos of local feeling; he was four years old in 1944 and lost many cousins and extended family members in the massacre.[15] The government has always permitted the ANFM to appoint those who serve as guides to the ruins from among their membership. Hyvernaud's role as both insider and guide is in keeping with the basic tenet that at Oradour those most affected by the massacre are the ones to bear witness and present the event to the public.

In his speech, Hyvernaud weaves an actor's dramatic account of the massacre with an exposition of the material evidence of the atrocity. He tells his listeners how the population was rounded up, the men shot and the barns set on fire, the women and children machine-gunned and then smothered to death by smoke and burnt to ashes. A bullet-ridden baby carriage in front of the altar evokes the 205 children massacred in the church: "You can also see a baby carriage. An eight-day-old baby was burned here, a twelve-day-old baby, month-old babies, two months, two years,

FIGURE 9

Children at the altar of the old church, 10 June 1994.
The only survivor from the church escaped through
the center window.

FIGURE 10

Visitors to the church in the old town.

all ages." The escape from death by the eight *miraculés* and the fate of the church is imbued with religious drama and mystery; near the end of his rendition Hyvernaud directs the visitors' gaze to evidence of other "curious" events. Twisted fragments of the church bell still lie where it fell, by the church door, beneath the bell tower. He notes that this bell, cast out of bronze, melted in the heat of the conflagration, while the wooden altar survived unscathed, as did the wooden confessional booth. "You see," he remarks, "there are things that are difficult to explain."

He gestures to the right side of the church. Here, opposite the door where the Nazis stood when they shot the women and children, he points out the blood stains on the floor and the bullet holes that mar the walls and pock the white marble tablet listing Oradour's "glorious dead" from the Great War. "You can read about it in books and hear Oradour talked about," Hyvernaud concludes, "but you have to see it to believe it." He then invites the visitors to look around the church and recommends that afterward they visit the cemetery, where the bones and ashes of the 642 martyrs have been deposited in an ossuary. Across from the cemetery gate, he adds, is a crypt where visitors can view the victims' possessions, gathered from the ruins.[16]

Leaving the church for the cemetery, one walks a few yards up the rue Emile Desourteaux and takes the second lane on the right. One passes the ruins of a stone barn filled with the rusted bodies of old cars. A few yards farther on, a plaque marks the spot where the body of Pierre-Henri Poutaraud, the local mechanic, was found. Poutaraud, as the guide in the church has told, managed to escape from the Laudy barn with the five other survivors—only to be shot by a German sentinel as he tried to make it to the woods beyond the town.

FIGURE 11

Ossuary for the ashes of massacre victims.

The path from the main entrance of the cemetery bisects the graveyard, drawing the visitor past gravestones toward the huge ossuary and bank of memorial plaques that dominate the west end of the cemetery. The effect is not unlike that of approaching the altar of a cathedral. The column of the ossuary rises from a large, slightly raised concrete platform on which stand two miniature coffins, encased in glass to display relics: the bones of Oradour's "martyrs," gathered from the ruins. Ashes of the unidentified dead have been placed in the column, which is framed by eight black marble plaques mounted on a low wall behind the ossuary. These plaques bear the names and ages of all 642 victims. Over the years a myriad of veterans' groups, political parties, trade unions, widows' associations, municipalities, and districts have made the pilgrimage to Oradour to deposit their own plaques, in many shapes and sizes, to pay tribute to the victims of Oradour. These have been mounted on a grille that stands in front of the wall, between the lists of names. On the ground, at the base of the wall, families of unidentified victims have put individual funerary plaques to the memory of their loved ones.

Retracing one's footsteps, one comes out of the cemetery through a wrought iron gate across from a broad, smooth gravel path leading to the heavy stone portal of a windowless low-lying building. A narrow stone staircase descends into a dark vestibule. The wrecks of two children's bicycles lean against the wall. The inner chamber of the crypt is cool, quiet, and dim, like a chapel. A stone plaque on the wall is carved with the number who died and a quotation from Balzac: "Of all the seeds entrusted to the earth, the blood shed by martyrs is that which renders the most rapid harvest." Objects have been artfully laid out in museum-quality display cases. The mood is hushed and respectful; one is

FIGURE 12

Plaques listing names and ages of those
who died in the massacre.

FIGURE 13

Commemorative plaques at Oradour cemetery.

in the presence of the relics of martyrs. Indeed, these objects were described as such by the ANFM when, in 1948, they first requested the right to set up their Maison du Souvenir:

> Ever since the day after the Liberation, the National Association of the Families of the Martyrs of Oradour-sur-Glane intended to further the memory of this horrible massacre and piously gathered in every gutted house, in the schools, in the church, a rather important quantity of objects, which, having belonged to the victims, are valued like relics by us. . . . In our minds, these objects should be exhibited in a barn, which was miraculously spared, near the church. . . . We could thus carry out what we consider to be an imperative task and a testimony of our loyalty to the memory of our martyrs as well as a permanent reminder of their sacrifice to the pilgrims who have been called to visit Oradour.[17]

In the center of the room, four glass cases, the shelves lit from within, have been set in a circle. Handwritten labels, slips of yellowing paper, indicate that these relics were gathered in the barns where the men were shot. The relics have been sorted and set out according to the gender of the owner, reflecting the fact that the men died separately from the women and children. The central cases display the contents of the men's pockets at the moment of death. Two contain an assortment of broken pocket watches. Another exhibits jackknives, identity papers, a ration card for tobacco, and a snapshot of the local soccer team. The fourth case holds coins and franc notes, some of which bear the traces of fire.

Against the back and right wall of the crypt, tiers of glass shelves exhibit articles once owned by women and children: a sewing thimble, an iron, tapestry scissors, keys, spoons, a cup, a china shoe, a toy donkey, a statue of a dog, a figurine of a fisherman, buttons, keys, and a toy sewing machine. These artifacts, mostly undamaged, evoke a tender image of domestic life in which women worked at home while small children played. The bottoms of these cases are filled with sand, lending a mood of archeological discovery. Looking down through the top is like peering into a deep pool or wishing well. On the sandy bottom one can see coins visitors have dropped between the cracks of the glass top. This gesture is reminiscent of the Catholic practice of dropping coins into a collection box at the entrance to a church, as well as the folk custom of going to the *bonne fontaine* (good fountain or wishing well) which still persists in parts of the Limousin.[18] Whereas the men's artifacts portray sudden, violent death, among the intimate objects of the women and children there is little to remind the viewer of the particular historical conditions of the war and Occupation; they conjure up instead an innocent vision of a golden past.

Oradour was first conceived of and described as a pilgrimage site. Yet those who have spent time in the ruins over the years have noted a change in attitude that denotes a shift toward tourism. In 1988 Dr. Robert Lapuelle, mayor of Oradour for thirty years, walked among the crowds during the summer season. With some dismay, he remarked on the change: "In the years after the war, people who came had experienced the war and were very bound up with what had happened. And little by little things evolved to a sort of tourism. . . . I've established that it's no longer a place where one reflects, but a stopping point on a longer trip, or a sort of outing. And that pains us a little."[19]

Dr. Lapuelle had remarked one of the fundamental differences between tourism and pilgrimage. For Alphonse Dupront, a contemporary scholar of religion, an essential difference between the two activities is that the pilgrim, by definition, seeks a fixed, sacral goal, a spiritual summit. The tourist, on the other hand, does not necessarily designate any one point of the journey as the high point before departure. As Dupront goes on to demonstrate, however, though at first glance tourism and pilgrimage may appear as divergent activities, they nonetheless show many affinities and cannot always be clearly distinguished. The primary link between these two forms of "collective migration" is the participation of crowds. The crowd imposes an element of sacredness: "The onrush, even when it becomes tyrannical, is never without some confession of faith. It tells us what the insular or literary egoism of the pioneer tourists of the first decades of the last century jealously tried to hide: the vital quest for something else."[20] Thus pilgrimage and tourism share an element of spirituality, even if the tourist is moved by a sense of history rather than the presence of the miraculous or marvellous.

Visitors to Oradour are also heirs to a shift in sensibilities by which cultural activities have become increasingly focused on the visual. Scholars of fin-de-siècle France have written much about the influence of "realism" as a new way of seeing the world that equated "reality" with truth. Historian Vanessa Schwartz has shown how this fascination with the real extended beyond the high arts of painting and literature to more popular forms of entertainment in which the distinction between the real and its representation was often collapsed. In such popular nineteenth-century activities as going to the morgue to view dead bodies, or to wax museums to look at dioramas of actual events and real people, Parisian crowds expressed intense interest in "reality." In the case of Oradour, visitors come to see the actual site of the atrocity, the traces of the violent act, and real objects that belonged to the martyrs.[21] While this desire for the authentic has roots in the Catholic practice of visiting the sites of miracles and viewing relics, a newer, late-nineteenth-century sensibility contributed to the *frisson* of being in the presence of "the real thing."[22]

Two extremes in the spectrum of remembrance are represented in the ruins of Oradour-sur-Glane: highly formal commemoration by the state, and individual recollection by survivors. The key to commemoration and pilgrimage, as opposed to reminiscence or recollection, is that one does not have to have a personal memory of the event in order to participate in the remembrance. The site of the old community has become the most public place in the landscape. But for the handful of people who grew up in the old town and are still alive today, it is also the most private. Whereas the tourist is shocked by the traces of violent death, for the old timers of Oradour these traces are the site of their intimate childhood memories. Of course these survivors go to the ruins to participate in the ceremony commemorating 10 June 1944 as well as the other days recognized by the ANFM.[23] Their presence at these events is of great importance, as they are considered by the community as the vessels of memory. But in recent years they have also come to the ruins in search of their own, individual pasts.

For André Desourteaux and Robert Hébras, the emotional power of the ruins lies in the fact that this landscape was the scene of their youth. They grew up together as schoolmates and friends in Oradour. At the time of the massacre, Desourteaux was nineteen and Hébras was twenty. Except for one uncle who hid when

FIGURE 14

Cortege at a "tragic well" where some
victims were found, 10 June 1994.

the Germans arrived, Desourteaux lost all of his immediate family: both parents, his two sisters, all four grandparents, and numerous aunts and uncles. Hébras is a *miraculé:* one of the five men who survived the massacre in the Laudy barn. He lost his mother and two sisters. For Robert Hébras, being a *miraculé* is not what marks him most:

> Oh, but that, no, that doesn't have anything to do with it. It's a piece of luck I had, that's it. For me what's important—we lost our families, we lost everything one could have. We lost our youth at Oradour. We lost everything. . . . From one day to the next you have nothing. Just think about it. One no longer had a family life where one sits down together in the evening, at midday, where everyone was there, with the advantages and the inconveniences of family. One found oneself alone like . . . like a stray dog.[24]

Desourteaux was a well-known name in Oradour. Forebears on both sides of André's family had been mayors of the town. The main street was named after his great-grandfather, Emile Desourteaux, who was a Radical mayor from 1892 to 1906. Emile was succeeded by his son Paul, who remained mayor until he was defeated in 1919 by André's maternal grandfather, a Socialist named Joseph Beau. Beau stayed in office until 1941, when the Vichy government reinstated Paul Desourteaux, who as a Radical Republican was more congenial to the Vichy authorities. Paul Desourteaux was shot in a barn along with the other men from Oradour, after having offered himself and his family to the Nazis as hostages.

André Desourteaux is a small, fit, lively man who lives in a modest neighborhood near the train station in Limoges. He spends his summers in Oradour, in his house in the new town. Since he retired from the postal service in 1985, Desourteaux has devoted his winters to researching the history of Oradour. He began the project ten years earlier, in the municipal library in Limoges, by reading the issues of a regional newspaper from 1900 to 1939. He painstakingly copied, word for word, all articles concerning Oradour. At home he would carefully recopy his notes and store them in looseleaf binders. For Desourteaux, what counts is the town he knew before the massacre: "For me, Oradour stopped on 10 June 1944. That's it. Everything that came afterwards is something else. . . . For me, who has done a fair amount of research on Oradour's past, for me, Oradour has always existed in the olden days. . . ."[25]

This project is his way of recapturing the past—his own as well as that of his parents and grandparents. In copying the certificates of births, marriages and deaths in Oradour at the turn of the century, Desourteaux has learned not just the names of the residents and where they lived: "I managed to get to know people from my hometown whom I actually didn't really know. I know people now that I didn't know well before."[26] He becomes particularly animated when he describes the rich social life in the region before the war. With pride he lists the fairs, the *fêtes*, the *bals*, and the singing societies: "It gives proof of the vitality of the place. There was a dance almost every Sunday."

Although he participated actively in the ANFM, until recently Desourteaux did not talk directly about the massacre to his family, even to his wife: "One never talked about it, one never really went deeply into the question. One eluded . . . one avoided, one evaded." In 1983, at the age of fifty-nine, he began visiting the ruins with his family and close friends. The Desourteauxs' visits are private. "We don't like to go when there are a lot of people," his wife says. For Desourteaux the mood is not one of sadness or mourning but of recovery. "He remembers stories, jokes, we laugh, we never cry," his wife adds. These visits have a ritual quality. "We always stop in the same place and relate the same things."[27]

Desourteaux offers a psychological explanation for his interest in Oradour's past: "Maybe it's the shock, this brutal cutting off that one never accepted. . . . It's difficult to accept that, you know, it's very difficult." Is this search for the past a means of denying or assimilating the trauma of the massacre? Desourteaux began his methodical research on Oradour with the old days. "I've managed to go back to 1700. One manages to find out a lot of things. . . ." Slowly he is working his way up to the more immediate past. "That's coming. That'll come."[28] His hope is that assembling the history of Oradour will help bridge the rupture of the massacre:

> One puts back together the general history of the locality a little bit . . . before the massacre. There were people who disappeared on the tenth of June, 1944. Life in the *bourg* picked up again, but without those people. There's not really a continuity. It'll certainly be recreated over the course of generations, I hope. My dearest wish is that it will be recreated here—the history of the whole locality. . . . People lived and then they disappeared. Other people came. I hope that those people . . . will remember that Oradour existed before their families came—well, then maybe there would be some continuity after all.[29]

To walk through the ruins of Oradour with André Desourteaux on a late summer afternoon is to be taken on a tour of his boyhood memories. As with many survivors, aging plays a part in his interest in visiting the past and his childhood memories. Desourteaux's observations are filled with historical detail, his memories suffused in the glow of nostalgia.

Arriving from the new town at the upper entrance to the ruins, we found a tour bus parked at the gate. To avoid the tourists, we took the narrow road that skirts the western edge of the ruins and curves around the cemetery. Here one is on higher ground and can look down onto the abandoned gardens and the backs of the ruined houses that face the old rue Emile Desourteaux. On our left we passed three new houses. Moments later we entered the ruins by a small gate next to the cemetery. This is a "back door" used by local people who come to visit the graveyard without going through the ruins.

On the way down to the church, Desourteaux pointed out what were once the fine residences of Oradour. Peering into the interiors, one can see wide steps, indicating that there were once large interior stairways. Desourteaux noted a carved lintel dating from the fifteenth century at the back of the church. Just around the side of the building is the window from which Madame Rouffanche escaped—the architectural feature for which the church is known today. But the Oradour that interests Desourteaux is not the Oradour the tourists come to see.

Proceeding up the main street, Desourteaux stopped to point out a well that had been in the courtyard of a small farm. A little farther along we passed by the front of the grocery store run by his parents before arriving at the stone wall in front of the house where the families of his uncle and his grandfather, the two local doctors, had lived. We had reached our destination. Desourteaux clambered over the crumbling garden wall and invited his guest

to join him. Signs posted throughout the ruins and wooden bar-
riers erected in the doorways by the Historic Monuments Service prohibit visitors from going inside, but the unspoken understanding in Oradour is that those rules apply only to tourists.
People from the old town can still go home.

The remains of the office where the doctors Desourteaux received their patients were still there, just on the other side of the
wall. Stepping into the broken-down structure, one could see
patches of a black-and-white tiled floor. Beyond this small building, the body of an old car lay against the inside of the garden
wall. Set back from the road and surrounded by a large lawn
stood the impressive stone structure of the Desourteaux house.
The front garden was peaceful and green but not completely
abandoned. The grass had been recently mown by a gardener.

For the old-timers of Oradour, the family house, rather than
the ruins in their entirety, is the pole of memory. As Robert
Hébras explained, "My strongest feelings are when I pass in
front of my house . . . well, what *was* my house." Not in front of
the barn where he was shot and survived? "No, the barn . . . no,
I repeat myself, but the fact of being a survivor, that's a big word.
It's been talked about too much. Okay, I had the luck to survive
this massacre, but really, well, for me, it's just a question of
chance."[30]

For Marcel Darthout, also a survivor of the barn, the experience is similar. He goes to the ruins for the annual commemorative ceremony on the tenth of June, on the first of November for
All Saints' Day, and when out-of-town friends or relatives ask him
to accompany them. Otherwise, he goes to the cemetery: "I go to
the cemetery, but not to the ruins, not much, not much, not much.
For me personally, no. But I consider them to be absolutely

necessary—but not for me. No, the ruins, they're ruins, and I, in my memory I see my house just as it was. In my memory I find images just as I saw them. So the ruins don't add a lot."[31]

In his classic work *The Poetics of Space*, the French phenomenologist Gaston Bachelard explores this powerful link between personal memory and what he called the "poetics of the house": "The questions abound: how can secret rooms, rooms that have disappeared, become abodes for an unforgettable past?"[32] Like Halbwachs, Bachelard discerns a link between space and memory. But whereas Halbwachs rejects the psychologists' emphasis on individual memory, Bachelard suggests a new avenue of psychological investigation into memory, which he dubs "topoanalysis":

> Of course, thanks to the house, a great many of our memories are housed. . . . All our lives we come back to them in our daydreams. A psychoanalyst should, therefore, turn his attention to this simple localization of our memories. I should like to give the name of topoanalysis to this auxiliary of psychoanalysis. Topoanalysis, then, would be the systematic psychological study of the sites of our intimate lives. In the theater of the past that is constituted by memory, the stage setting maintains the characters in their dominant roles.[33]

Indeed, for many old-timers of Oradour, the ruins provide a physical and psychic frame for their intimate memories. Desourteaux experiences personally a concept stated abstractly by Bachelard: "For me, when I go into the ruins, everything is not dead and gone. As I get older . . . my youth and all the pranks I pulled in this town come back to me. Well, . . . and I'm at home. Even if it might be a void in reality . . . in my mind it's not empty.

They're there. At every door, at every window, there's a face. It's not necessarily sad."[34] For his childhood friend Jeanette Montazeaud, the ruins function in a similar way—although for her the experience is painful: "Before the ruins didn't bother me. Now that I'm getting older I'm getting more sensitive. I see everyone. It's quite painful."[35] For both, the existence of the ruins makes their past more present and accessible. Desourteaux explained: "When I go to the town, I don't see what you see. . . . For me, life in Oradour was stopped, yet it's still alive. If Oradour had been rebuilt on the same spot, we would have seen the same thing. If the ruins weren't there I would remember less."[36] This sentiment was echoed by Montazeaud, who now lives in the new town across from the church: "The ruins have a moral influence on memory. It's much more present."[37]

Clearly, the ruins are not necessary for remembrance. The kind of remembering described by Bachelard, for example, is inspired by the mental image of a childhood home, not the physical object itself. Jeanette Montazeaud, among others, said she would feel the same with or without the ruins. Her childhood friend Lucette Bichaud concurred; she does not need the ruins to evoke the past and only goes there on the ceremonial days of 10 June, Palm Sunday, and All Saints' Day. For some survivors it is the receding of the event in time that makes the past more accessible: "As time passes it gets easier to evoke the 'old bourg,' " Bichaud said. "Before, all I saw was destruction."[38]

The slow decay of the ruins may also play a role in this emotional evolution. As their shape softens under the impact of erosion, the traces of violent destruction become more benign; for Lucette Bichaud, this may permit recollections of life before the massacre to emerge. So although the ruins may not be necessary for memory, they impinge on memory nonetheless. The survivors of Oradour cannot be indifferent to their presence. Some, like Jeanette Montazeaud, find it increasingly burdensome to live within sight of the visible traces of their trauma. In a wistful tone, she remarked, "The only thing I don't like is that the new town is so close. I'd like to be able to open my window and not see the ruins."[39] The reverse is true for Lucette Bichaud, for whom, only recently, the image of destruction has started to fade. In the case of André Desourteaux, the ruins enable him to better grasp his past; but they also underscore the rupture between past and present, and reinforce the immobile quality of his memories.

The tourist comes to Oradour to see the ruins of the old town. Even though the cemetery lies on the itinerary proposed by the guide, the most intent visitor might well pass it by without realizing its central role in the themes of memory and commemoration played out at Oradour. Apart from the Glane river, the cemetery is the only part of the old village that survived the events of 10 June 1944; it is the only link to the past that still serves its function today and continues to grow. In this small, cramped space one discovers a dense layering of private mourning by families and formal commemoration organized by the ANFM. History, sentiment, and interpretation are piled on top of each other to create a collage that is more complex than the ruins' image of an arrested moment. A study of Oradour continually leads back to this plot of land.

On a first visit to the graveyard, one is likely to be overwhelmed by markers of the massacre. But those who spend time in the cemetery become aware of distinct zones, like geological strata, by which one can chart the history of the community. The oldest graves lie by the main entrance. Here one finds grave-stones, decorated with hand-painted enamel plaques, of people who lived out their lives in the previous century. Walking toward the back of the cemetery one moves forward in time, and evidence of the massacre begins to appear. On top of family tombs relatives have placed funerary plaques, often in the shape of an open book with a portrait of the deceased. The epitaphs ring of bitterness and anger: "Madeleine Bois, 1935–1944. To our dear little Mimi, burned to death by the Nazi barbarians, 10 June 1944." Another speaks of a local schoolteacher: "To the memory of Poor Little Martyr, Denise Bardet, Schoolteacher. Born 10 June 1920. Burned to death with her Dear Students by the Germans, 10 June 1944." An eighteen-year-old boy who hoped to join that profession is also remembered: "To our son Lucien Raymond Clavaud, Student Teacher at the Lycée Gay Lussac. Martyr of 10 June at the age of 18. *Regrets éternels.*" Each plaque represents a fragment in the mosaic of the community's trauma.[40] Here in the cemetery the memory of the massacre is joined to the community's earlier history.

In attempting to read the cemetery of Oradour one should never lose sight of a key fact: the cemetery belongs to the commune of Oradour. This is the one place still connected to the old town over which the people of Oradour have complete control. This is their turf. In 1953, the ANFM began building its own ossuary; this ossuary and the lists of the victims make a statement to the outside world. The front of the cemetery is a stage for associational commemoration, but the space among the tombstones is for private grief and remembrance.

For the survivors of the massacre, the cemetery—not the ruins—is the emotional focus of mourning. Many people from

Oradour rarely visit the ruins except for the ceremony of 10 June but will go to the cemetery on their own or with their families. In the ruins the state has commemorated anonymous, collective death. In the cemetery people come to remember in the context of the family and community.

Immediately after the massacre the cemetery became the center of community mourning. Mass graves were dug for the unidentified corpses cleared from the ruins. (Bodies that were identified were placed in family tombs.) Photographs from the first anniversary of the massacre show women weeping in front of these graves, which are heaped with flowers, wreaths, and crosses. Just on the other side of the cemetery wall, the government built a makeshift wooden chapel to house coffins filled with human ashes.

The cemetery took on particular importance for the women who came to visit the graves of their children and husbands. It became their meeting place to share their sorrow. The men met in the course of work. The re-creation of the soccer team—an event often cited as marking the rebirth of community life—also provided a milieu for male companionship. But women, especially those from the outlying villages, had no organized forms of sociability. They were isolated except for trips to the cemetery.

Marguerite Hyvernaud was a member of a generation of women marked by mourning. She wore traditional black after 1918, when her brother was killed in the last days of World War I. After the massacre, Madame Hyvernaud never attended any festivities: no marriages, baptisms, or first communions. Until she entered a nursing home in 1992, she would walk down the little road from town to the cemetery every day in the early afternoon, accompanied by her daughter Amélie. They visited the mass graves and the tombstones of her husband and two sons. Occasionally the two women would return home by way of the ruins.

The survivors and their families, represented by the ANFM, decided to observe "a generation of mourning," a period that lasted twenty years. Yet even when the mood in Oradour began to shift in the early 1960s, the effort to build a normal daily life for the community faced many obstacles. A few old women, such as Madame Hyvernaud, never abandoned their mourning.

Preserving the vestiges of a village was an endeavor radically different from erecting a monument, which is a more or less abstract representation. The ruins of Oradour were not meant to represent or symbolize the destruction of 10 June 1944. They would be presented to the visitor free of interpretation or mediation—the bare facts, hard evidence of the event itself.

Though Oradour was one of the more striking examples, it was by no means the first or only place where the French sought to perpetuate the memory of war through such literal representation of destruction. In 1919, the city of Verdun considered plans to rebuild after four years of war—the most extensive damage having been inflicted by intense artillery fire during the ten months of the Battle of Verdun in 1916. A group of citizens led by a former mayor of Verdun proposed preserving "in a ruined state" a portion of the town center and building modern neighborhoods nearby, on empty property ceded by the state. Proponents of the plan claimed that it would permit rapid construction and economic revival of the city, while the ruins, a testimony to the sacrifice of Verdun, would become a tourist attraction. Others foresaw insoluble problems with this plan, referred to in the local press as "Verdun-Pompeii"; they predicted that the ruins would deteriorate quickly and, in the process, lose any emotional appeal or aesthetic interest. Strong opposition also came from citizens who wanted to rebuild their town where it had always been.

Although the merits of this plan were vigorously debated in the local press, the elected officials never seriously considered the proposal, and this possible predecessor to Oradour as *village martyr* never made it past the drawing board.[41] In the face of colossal military losses (1,139,800 French soldiers died in World War I, 270,000 of them at Verdun), the destruction of civilian property was not the most compelling story for the French after World War I. It was the building of an ossuary at the battlefield of Douaumont, a key site in the defense of Verdun, that attracted the public interest and financial support necessary to make Verdun the *haut lieu* in the national commemoration of the First World War. The French state contributed one million francs to the construction of the ossuary. The rest, fourteen million, was raised by the private committee that oversaw the construction.[42] The common soldiers of the trenches, the *poilus*, were the primary subject of commemoration in the First World War, and the sites that fostered a national response were the battlefields where they died.

The idea of creating a memorial to Jewish life that would have worked like a martyred village occurred to the exiled Jewish poet Julian Tuwin when, in late 1943, he learned of the uprising in the Warsaw ghetto. In a lament entitled "We, Polish Jews," Tuwin called for a monument that would consist of vestiges of the old ghetto: "And there shall be in Warsaw and in every other Polish city some fragment of the ghetto itself left standing and pre-

served in its present form in all its horror of ruin and destruction
... so that the memory of the massacred people shall remain forever fresh in the minds of generations to come, and also as a sign
of our undying sorrow for them. Thus a new monument will be
added to the national shrine."[43] By the time Tuwin first publicly
read these words, at a ceremony in 1948 to dedicate Nathan
Rapoport's monument to the ghetto uprising, the Germans had
systematically destroyed the ghetto, and the city of Warsaw,
leaving the earth covered by a pile of rubble sixteen feet deep.
The kind of monument Tuwin imagined was no longer possible.

Memorial sites such as the concentration camp of Auschwitz
in Poland operate on a principle similar to that at work in
Oradour, seeking to edify the viewer by showing the scene of the
crime. But the source of the emotional effect of these sites is different from that of a martyred village. The martyred village is tied
less specifically to the discrete historical period of the Second
World War. Its particular power comes from the echoes of life
during peacetime, before its destruction. The memorial site of
Auschwitz, by comparison, harkens back to no other history than
that of the camp itself. This is true of both the camp at Auschwitz
(Auschwitz I), which has been carefully preserved, and the one at
Birkenau (Auschwitz II) two miles away, which has been left to
decay. The ruins of Oradour, on the other hand, elicit for the
first-time visitor as well as for local people the destruction of a
community that existed long before the war. The element of
horror remains in the foreground, but as the event of the massacre recedes and the ruins crumble and soften, other layers of
meaning come forth. The monument gathers more of its power
from the image it presents of a mythic, idealized, rural French
village of the past.

The differences between the martyred village and other war sites become more apparent when one compares the effect of the material objects displayed at Auschwitz and Oradour. At both places, common objects gathered from the site are displayed in glass cases; but they call forth the past in very different ways. At Auschwitz the barracks that housed inmates have been preserved, and some now serve as a museum. Here the visitor is confronted with huge piles of baggage taken from the deportees. These suitcases evoke the lives of individuals—the owner's name and address are painted on the side—from their forced departure from their homes to their arrival in the camp, when they were deprived of these last possessions. In another glassed-in window, an enormous stack of shoes summons up the moment when victims stripped before entering the gas chambers. The presentation of these objects evokes the staggering number of people killed and the extent to which the methodical efforts of Nazi extermination reached into communities all over Europe to single out particular inhabitants. In Oradour, the emphasis is on portraying the destruction of one particular community. The debris collected from the ruins is exhibited in the more intimate setting of an underground crypt. The objects are small, and one has to peer into the lit glass cases to see the assembled material.

David Lowenthal has noted that relics promote an unchanging view of the past: "Relics are . . . static. Whereas the recorded and remembered past can convey the sense of a sweep through time, most tangible survivals yield only arrested moments."[44] At both Auschwitz and Oradour, relics yield such arrested moments. The moments remembered at Auschwitz have to do exclusively with the Holocaust. At first glance, the memorial of Oradour seems even more particular; it is a conscious attempt to freeze time at the moment after the massacre. But the sense of time conveyed in Oradour extends back from the catastrophe of 10 June 1944 to evoke a nostalgic vision of life in this place.

Europe's other martyred village, the town of Lidice in the Czech Republic, offers a counterpoint. The circumstances of its demise have elements in common with Oradour's. The Nazis destroyed this village twelve miles east of Prague in reprisal for the assassination of Reinhard Heydrich, the Deputy Reichprotektor for Bohemia and Moravia and a high-ranking Nazi official. In the early morning of 27 May 1942, Heydrich took his accustomed route to downtown Prague from his residence in the northern outskirts of the city. At a point where a sharp turn required his driver to slow down almost to a stop, two men ambushed the car and mortally wounded the Nazi leader. The Nazi response was massive, swift, and brutal. Heinrich Himmler came to Prague to personally direct search parties. In prisons and concentration camps Nazis took reprisals against Czech partisans; the three thousand Czech inmates of the Mauthausen were exterminated.

Six days after Heydrich's assassination, circumstantial evidence linked the assassins to the town of Lidice. On the night of 9 June, SS soldiers surrounded the village. Of Lidice's 503 inhabitants, 476 were present. The women and children were taken off in trucks to the nearby town of Kladno. The next day, 173 men were herded into the courtyard of a farm and shot on the spot. In Kladno a few days later, the Nazis separated the 203 women from their children and deported them to concentration camps. Of the Lidice women, 143 survived. Most of their children did not. Eighty-one children from Lidice were sent to the Chelmno concentration camp, where they died. Others, deemed suitable for Germanization, were interned and then sent to SS families in the Reich. Seventeen of these children were found after the war.[45]

Only the barest traces of Lidice remain today. In the month following the massacre, the Reich Labor Service razed Lidice to the ground, uprooted its trees, and spread two feet of dirt over the area where buildings once stood. Today the visitor to Lidice finds a martyred village reminiscent of Oradour that is, at the same time, its inverse. Whereas in Oradour ruined walls meet the eye, at Lidice one walks through a wide, open valley. New stones have been laid down to trace the old main road. A low wall, not more than a foot high, has been built to recreate a corner of the barn where the men of Lidice were shot. The foundations of the school and the town church have been uncovered. And that is all. The rest is for the visitor to fill in and imagine.

In Lidice too, a new town has been built close by the original. On 10 June 1945, three years after the massacre of Lidice and a month after the end of the war, the government announced a plan for commemoration similar to the one being worked out for Oradour. The memorial plans called for the entire area of the original town to be set aside as "a natural preserve . . . a sacred orchard with as few buildings as possible."[46] Three hundred meters away from the original village, overlooking the valley, a modern town was built to house the women who returned to Lidice. As in Oradour, the main street of the new town was named after the date of the massacre.

A small museum has been built on a plateau above the ruins. The exhibit consists of photographs of the people of Lidice and a short history of the German occupation and the massacre. Yet whereas the ruined buildings in Oradour provide the atmosphere of a French village, and thus a specifically national tone, nothing is left in Lidice to evoke Czech village life or culture. Furthermore, the Czech government, in keeping with the universalist tenets of Marxist ideology, chose to give an international message to the commemoration of the massacre. In 1955, a "Rose Garden of Friendship and Peace" was built on a strip of land between the new town and the museum. A low, semicircular stone wall facing out toward the old village of Lidice bears the emblem of cities and towns considered to have suffered the same fate as Lidice.[47]

In the absence of tangible remains of the town, at Lidice the land itself—its color and shape and climate—have become the dominant features of the memorial. The overall effect is one of emptiness. The visitor notices what is not there rather than focusing, as in Oradour, on what remains. Though the events that transpired in these two places are so similar (down to the uncanny coincidence that both massacres occurred on 10 June), their memorials produce different effects. The ruins of Oradour give this martyred village the sense of a particular and specific place. In contrast, the openness of the memorial landscape of Lidice gives it a more serene and abstract quality. One has a sense of space in Lidice, a sense of place in Oradour.

Chapter Five

THE BORDEAUX TRIAL

In January 1953, the long-awaited trial of twenty-one soldiers who had participated in the massacre at Oradour-sur-Glane took place in a military court in Bordeaux. For eight years the families of the victims had been demanding that the killers be tracked down and punished for their crimes. The survivors wanted vengeance: justice should be done swiftly, efficiently, and with appropriate severity.

Yet as the case came to trial, it became clear to the French public that the task of dispensing justice would be difficult, divisive, and perhaps impossible to achieve. Many of the officers responsible, including Major Otto Dickmann, who had planned and led the attack, had been killed on the Normandy front. Others had gone into hiding in Germany or were otherwise unavailable to be tried. The commander of the SS Division Das Reich, General Heinz Lammerding, was known to be living in Düsseldorf, in the British-occupied zone, but the British proved unresponsive to French demands for his extradition.[1] And most troublesome of all, investigations after the war revealed that among the sixty-six soldiers and officers still alive who could be identified as having belonged to the SS company, fourteen were French, from Alsace. These were the men brought to trial in Bordeaux, along with seven German soldiers who had been in prison since the end of the war.[2]

In 1953, the people of Oradour were about to move into the new town that had been built for them by the government. Understandably, they were still preoccupied with the events of June 1944. The rest of the country, however, was ready to leave the past behind. The trial took place during the last stage of a long national debate about how severely collaboration during the Occupation should be punished. While the people of Oradour wanted never to forget what had happened to them and who had done it, the French parliament was more interested in promoting reconciliation among the French by wiping out the wartime records of many of its citizens.

The debate about punishments for crimes of collaboration began before the war ended. As the purge trials began in October 1944, Albert Camus and François Mauriac argued in the pages of *Combat* and *Le Figaro*, respectively.[3] Mauriac, expressing de Gaulle's concern for moderation and conciliation, desired that sentences not be harsh. Camus argued that forgiving collaborators meant sacrificing the ideals for which resisters had died, as well as betraying the dead by allowing their executioners to go free. In parliament, the same moral arguments were raised in the debates on amnesty legislation that took place in 1950 and 1952. All political parties in the French parliament were caught up in the controversy. The stakes were enormous, as Henry Rousso has remarked, because the debate took place "at the crossroads where the law, ethics, and memory meet. '*Oubli juridique*' [juridical forgetting], by the very terms of the law, could singularly modify the perception of the Occupation; notably by the shroud of silence it imposes on verdicts that have been handed down."[4]

Christian democratic members of the Rassemblement du Peuple Français (RPF) and the Mouvement Républicain Populaire (MRP) led the movement in parliament to pass amnesty legislation. The debate on the first law opened on 24 October 1950. In the name of national unity and reconciliation, they argued that clemency was necessary to correct the injustices of the purge. They pointed to the examples of Germany and Italy, which had already begun to move in this direction. Anti-Communists insisted that national unity was all the more necessary in face of the Soviet threat. The Communist Party, on the other hand, saw in amnesty the threat of neofascism, as well as an attempt to rehabilitate the discredited Right. The Communists also sounded an alarm at the coincidence of efforts to absolve collaborators with the beginning of international consideration of German rearmament. The Socialists, for their part, supported clemency (also in the interest of national unity) but opposed any rehabilitation of former collaborators.[5]

The debate about creating new laws and modifying sentences had been overtaken to some extent by events. French prisons were being emptied of convicted collaborators. The postwar presidents (de Gaulle, Gouin, Bidault, and Auriol) had all used their presidential power to shorten or suspend prison sentences and to release prisoners. Of the 40,000 people who had been arrested for collaboration at the Liberation, only 13,800 were still in jail in December 1948. In October 1949, 8,000 remained. In

1951, on the eve of the first amnesty, only half that number were still in custody.[6]

After two months' consideration, with a vote of 327 to 263, the National Assembly enacted the first amnesty law, promulgated on 5 January 1951. It benefited those who had been punished for *l'indignité nationale* (civic unworthiness), which encompassed violations of moral, patriotic values and was punished by "national degradation." The amnesty law granted clemency to those who had received national degradation as a chief penalty, reduced the list of punishments included in national degradation, and provided for the early release of some prisoners. Clemency was not, however, extended to those who had been judged by the High Court (Pétain, cabinet officers, and colonial governors), nor those who had informed, tortured, or worked for the German police.[7]

Eighteen months later a second, broader amnesty bill was introduced. After a year of maneuvering and debate, the final bill passed on 24 July 1953. This time, national degradation was abolished altogether. Those who had been stripped of voting rights had them restored, and objects of the administrative purge were given back their pension rights. All but the most flagrant collaborators were released from prison. The first amnesty law had reduced the number of collaborators jailed from 4,000 to 1,570. When the second had taken full effect in 1956, only sixty-two of those jailed in 1945 remained in custody.[8]

Until the Bordeaux trial, the treatment of French citizens accused of wartime crimes had been debated in terms of individual crimes and punishments. But the conflict about the culpability of soldiers at Oradour became a conflict between regions; the trial pitted against each other two French provinces with very different experiences of the war and Occupation. The images of the Limousin and Alsace were freighted with symbolic meaning for the French nation. Looking back at the highly publicized postwar trials, the court reporter for *Le Monde* from 1945 to 1985, Jean-Marc Théolleyre, recalled the passions of that time: "Oradour had become a symbol. The name of this village in the Limousin wiped out in a single afternoon in June 1944 had acquired such resonance that it alone echoed in France of the Liberation with an emotional charge equal to that of Verdun...."[9] The older myth of Alsace as the French hostage to the rapacious Germans also came into play. But now the Bordeaux trial put it in question:

> And suddenly surged back to mind the whole legend of the lost province, all the stories, all the songs, all the sentimentality bound up with this part of the national history.... This shattered the myth of the good guys and the bad guys, the good Alsatians and the bad Germans. The old nationalist clichés [*la vieille imagerie d'Epinal*] engraved in our memories since 1870 could not hold up. This trauma tore apart the whole country. Still today, in the Limousin and in Alsace, these times are not to be mentioned.[10]

At the opening session the judge who presided over the trial declared, "This trial is, and will remain, a trial of Nazism."[11] Instead Oradour, a symbol intended to unify the French in the contemplation of Nazi barbarism, turned the French against the French.

Only one of the Alsatians on trial had volunteered for the SS. The rest—known by their sympathizers as the *malgré-nous* (against our will)—had been drafted into the German forces in late 1943 and early 1944. As their defenders were quick to point out, eight of them had been under eighteen years of age at the time they were drafted into the German Army, only to be transferred to the SS a few weeks later.

In the days preceding the trial, Alsatian politicians and veterans' associations rallied to defend the *malgré-nous* and to plead for understanding of Alsace's special situation during the war. Despite the 1940 armistice in which Germany had agreed to respect France's sovereignty, the Germans had annexed, de facto, the departments of Alsace and Lorraine. In August 1940, they had appointed a *Gauleiter* (Nazi Party regional commander) for each province.[12] The institution of German civil, racial, and penal codes soon followed. In January 1942, membership in the Nazi youth organizations became obligatory for everyone between the ages of ten and eighteen. Both men and women were compelled to work in Germany as part of the Reich Labor Service. And on 25 August 1942, the *Gauleiter* decreed that military service in the German armed forces was now obligatory for all men born between 1920 and 1924. Those who refused were often sent to the security camp (*Sicherungslager*) at Schirmeck in the eastern foothills of the Vosges. Others saw their families forcibly resettled in the Reich.[13] By the end of the war, though an estimated 40,000 young men deserted or escaped to other parts of France, 160,000 men from Alsace and Lorraine had been mobilized. At the end of the hostilities, 25,000 were officially counted as dead, 22,000 were missing, and approximately 12,000 still remained in Russian prisoner of war camps.[14]

Whatever compromises they had made while serving in the army of the enemy, the *malgré-nous* were not caught up in the coils of postwar justice. At the Liberation, the provisional French government had passed a war crimes law, but it applied only to "nationals of enemy countries or non-French agents in the service of enemy interests."[15] It made no provision for the legal pursuit by the military tribunal of French citizens for war crimes.[16] Thus, though a number of the Alsatians who took part in the killing at Oradour had been interviewed in English prisoner of war camps and, at the end of the war, made depositions to French authorities, only two Alsatians had been jailed along with the German soldiers who had been caught.[17] The others were considered to be only witnesses and were allowed to return home. It seemed likely that these men would never be held accountable for their actions at Oradour.

All this changed in 1947, when President Vincent Auriol addressed the crowd at the commemorative ceremony of 10 June in Oradour. Auriol and his entourage (including François Mitterrand, then Minister of the Veterans and War Victims Administration) were met by an enormous crowd and an array of local politicians and dignitaries: the prefect and subprefect of the Haute-Vienne, the well-known Communist Resistance leader Georges Guingouin, now mayor of Limoges, and the five parliamentary deputies of the Haute-Vienne. After visiting the ruins and laying wreaths on the mass grave at the cemetery and at the wooden chapel housing the ashes of the victims, the procession assembled at the marketplace. Standing in for the president of the ANFM, the secretary of the association, Madame Laurence, made an impassioned plea to the Minister of Justice: "We insistently demand that your administration . . . do everything possible and neglect nothing to arrest the culprits, and the moment they are captured that they be judged right here. In the name of our martyrs, let justice be done!"[18] The president promised satisfaction. He evoked the image of Oradour as an ideal French village wiped off the map by the SS. Then he revealed that the French government had designed special legislation "aimed specifically at the authors of this odious crime that we commemorate today." The proposed legislation would consider any member of a criminal unit (and the SS had been deemed such in the Nuremberg trials) as a coauthor or an accomplice in any crimes the group had committed.[19]

This announcement of the government's commitment to Oradour's cause brought an overwhelming response. According to an official observer, "M. Vincent Auriol's promise to rapidly punish those guilty of the massacre at Oradour was the only thing to receive unanimous approval."[20] Auriol ended his speech with a call for "the solidarity of all the French" in the tasks that lay ahead. Eventually, however, it would become clear that the effort to remember and punish particular crimes would undermine the parallel attempt to further French national unity.

Fifteen months later, the parliament unanimously passed the law of 15 September 1948, which introduced a new notion into French penal law—the collective responsibility of groups that committed war crimes.[21] The legislators' intent was clear: since individual participation would be difficult to establish in most cases, the presumption of collective guilt of criminal organizations would allow all members to be charged with a crime committed by a unit to which they had belonged. In other words, anyone who, on 10 June 1944, had been a member of the third company of the regiment Der Führer of the division Das Reich could be presumed guilty. It should be noted that the presumption of collective guilt was still left to the judge's discretion and was not considered automatic. Nonetheless, "the law of collective responsibility," as it became known, went against the principles of established law; now, in the case of war crimes, the burden of proof shifted from the prosecution to the accused, who would have to prove his innocence.

The third article of this law specifically addressed those not included in the war crimes law of 28 August 1944—French citizens. They could now be included in prosecution by the French military court: "Notwithstanding all provisions to the contrary, individuals not included in article one of the law of 28 August 1944 who are coauthors or accomplices to a war crime or a crime associated therewith can be included in the prosecution in military court in case of legal action against at least one of the coindicted." Under this article, French citizens would not be prosecuted by virtue of collective guilt but rather as "personally coauthors or accomplices."[22] This fact did little to appease the Alsatian public or their representatives in parliament. They considered it an outrage that the Alsatian *malgré-nous* had been charged under a retroactive law, and that they would sit in the dock side by side with the accused Germans.

With the trial impending, the veterans' association of *malgré-nous*, l'Association des Evadés et Incorporés de Force (ADEIF), raised the alarm. On 10 December 1952, all the regional newspapers in Alsace published a letter from Georges Bourgeois, the ADEIF president in the Haut-Rhin (as well as a deputy in parliament and president of the Conseil Général of the Haut-Rhin), calling for the Alsatians and the Germans to be prosecuted separately.[23] By the end of the month, nine other veterans' associations in Alsace had joined the ADEIF in its demand.[24] The Alsatian public followed their lead. Though there was continued support for the prosecution of the Alsatians based on their personal conduct, demands for the motion to sever continued to grow: "This painful affair . . . is agitating public opinion more and more. The vast majority back the opinion expressed by the duly constituted bodies and the patriotic associations, that is: severance of the Alsatian defendants in the prosecution of this case."[25]

In a remarkable show of solidarity, the regional press and politicians from all parties rallied to defend Alsace from what they considered an accusation against the entire province: "The papers expressed the fear that the conditions in which the trial will take place (the absence of higher-ups and real culprits; Alsatians side by side with the German defendants) will turn this into a trial of the Alsatians who were forcibly drafted and will cast a moral slur on Alsace and, as a consequence, will lead to a judgment of the Alsatian population's attitude toward the nation."[26]

The intensity of local feeling took outside observers by surprise. One journalist from Paris reported: "I was in Alsace a few days ago. One is stupefied by the importance that the Oradour affair has taken on. One Alsatian clearly told me: 'Watch out! Don't take this lightly; the Oradour affair, for us, is a new Dreyfus affair. . . .' "[27]

The Communist Party in Alsace was the notable exception to the general sympathy for the *malgré-nous*. Since the end of the war, the PCF had been calling loudly for the punishment of soldiers who had taken part in the massacre. Furthermore, the Limousin region (though not Oradour itself) had been a center of Communist resistance. With the affair of the *malgré-nous*, Alsatian Communist leadership was caught between regional loyalties and the Party policy. But, reported an agent of the Renseignements Généraux, they soon fell into line: "Now they call for exemplary punishment for all the accused without making distinctions between nationalities."[28] Throughout the trial, the Alsatian Communists defended the interests of the Limousin victims. As a result, the Communist Party in Alsace would see its regional following drop precipitously.

Alsatian politicians warned that the special law threatened to alienate Alsace from France. Paul Kalb, senator from the Haut-Rhin and vice president of the upper chamber of the legislature, cried out at the unfairness: "We insist on protesting against such proceedings, which plainly risk provoking a new Alsatian drama. The trial of Oradour-sur-Glane will call into question all the *incorporés de force* . . . and will raise painful feelings in our province, land of loyalty, which was within its rights to expect something other than intolerable humiliation."[29] In an intelligence report filed in Colmar, an agent of the Renseignements Généraux made explicit reference to a concern that, from the beginning, loomed in the background of the Bordeaux trial: "A trial under these conditions could revive political difficulties in Alsace that might summon up those of the prewar period."[30]

The "political difficulties" he referred to had a complex history. When the Prussians defeated the French in the Franco-Prussian War of 1870, they annexed Alsace and part of Lorraine, which they kept until the 1918 defeat of Germany in World War I.

Once the French recovered Alsace, politicians and government administrators immediately turned their attention to bringing the border province back into the national fold. French nationalists in Paris had been acutely concerned that after forty-eight years as part of Germany, Alsace might have succumbed to German habits and ways of thought. This was hardly surprising, considering that in 1918 rural folk in Alsace spoke only a dialect of German, and that regional culture resembled that of Baden, across the Rhine, more than that of the Ile-de-France. In most areas of the province, French remained a language spoken only by the educated middle class and nobility[31]—and many members of this group had migrated to France after the annexation of 1871. In 1919, the French government found it necessary to launch a campaign to foster Alsatian allegiance to France through the expansion of civil administration and promotion of French culture.

The integration of Alsace into France did not prove easy; during precisely the years that historian Eugen Weber has deemed the watershed of a transition in France from regionalism to nationalism, Alsatians had been subjected to the government and modernizing influences of the German Empire.[32] And while the separation of 1871–1918 had strengthened the French patriotism of some Alsatians, many others who resisted the Germanizing influence had grown more attached to their regional, Rhenish culture, not to the French nation. In any case, Alsace's experience as part of Germany had not been purely negative. Although forced to join Germany against her will and subjected to an unpleasant Germanization program, Alsace was swept along in the powerful economic growth that made Germany Europe's strongest industrialized nation on the eve of the First World War. After the war, though most Alsatians were pleased to be French citizens again, many nonetheless resented the government's efforts to "Frenchify" them. Soon the French were speaking of the "Alsatian malaise."[33]

In 1924, a proposal to extend to Alsace all French legislation passed during the annexation radicalized the politics of assimilation. During the annexation, Alsace had missed the introduction of the Ferry education laws and the abrogation in 1905 of Napoleon's Concordat of 1801. The Alsatian clergy violently protested the government's intention of abolishing religious education in schools and declaring that members of the clergy would no longer be considered civil servants.[34] From 1924 through the early 1930s, an Alsatian autonomist movement gained momentum. The German annexation in 1940 effectively put down Alsatian autonomism, and suffering under German fascism turned Alsace toward France again. But with the Bordeaux trial, questions about Alsace once again threatened to damage France's national unity—a unity that the experience of the Vichy regime had already undermined severely.

These considerations were of little interest to the people of the Limousin, who remained unmoved by the Alsatian pleas for special understanding. In an editorial published at the end of December, the *Nouveau Rhin français* cited a letter from Jean Brouillaud in which the president of the ANFM had asserted the validity of the provisions of 15 September 1948. Brouillaud added: "If they participated in the crime, then they must be punished. . . . It is too convenient to claim years later that they acted under duress." For Marcel Jacob, the newspaper's editor-in-chief, this attitude was ominous: "We are terrified—despite all the bitter experiences—of such an unheard-of and total lack of understanding vis-à-vis the Alsatian tragedy. Just as we bow deeply in front of the victims of Oradour and their families, we will just as resolutely continue to stand up against attitudes like the kind revealed in this letter."[35]

As the trial approached, the opposing parties became more deeply entrenched. In the Limousin, politicians continued to oppose any attempts to shield the Alsatians. As one parliamentary deputy commented on the front page of the regional Socialist paper:

> The problem is clear. If the Alsatians detained in Bordeaux are not guilty, if they did not participate in the crime, if on 10 June 1944 they desperately tried, as was their duty, to save human lives, if they don't have French blood on their hands, their innocence will shine forth on its own. . . . But if they are guilty, if they killed and burned, the fact they are Alsatians should not shield them from punishment. . . . I'll go even further. In this case they are more guilty than the German soldiers. . . . An Alsatian had less right than a German to fire on civilians. . . . For us, at the Trial of Bordeaux, there are no Alsatians and Germans. There are the accused. Let justice be done and the ultimate punishment be brought down on the guilty![36]

In an atmosphere heavy with tension and acrimony, the trial at Bordeaux began.

In the early morning of 12 January 1953, a train pulled into the station at Bordeaux carrying eleven of the accused Alsatians, who had come to turn themselves in to the clerk of the military prison. Jean-Marc Théolleyre described the scene for the readers of *Le Monde:*

> It was truly a pretty curious sight, this arrival in the middle of the night. . . . They found themselves on the platform, suitcases in hand, left to themselves, vainly looking for the lawyers who, they said, should have come to meet them. Instead they found only a handful of journalists and a few photographers, who lit up the night with magnesium. Thus one caught sight of these men, passive, at sea, distrustful and worried, all modestly dressed. . . . They rented taxis and de-

cided to drag one of their lawyers out of his hotel bed. It was a strange vision, these sleepy boys with rustic faces, out of their element, gathered in the entrance hall of a sumptuous hotel waiting for a resting place (hotel or prison) where they could finally finish out the night. . . . Shortly afterward another train would bring the representatives of the Association of the Families of the Victims of Oradour, who were received at the town hall in the morning.[37]

In the afternoon, in a small, cramped courtroom in a suburb of Bordeaux, the accused and their lawyers appeared for the first time in front of the military tribunal composed of six active officers and a presiding civil magistrate, M. Nussy Saint-Saëns. From their bench, these judges looked down on the row of the accused. The absence of any high-ranking officers made the Alsatians appear all the more like ordinary individuals: "They are above all common folk," wrote Théolleyre. "All—their names matter little under the circumstances—practice manual professions: machinist, postman, worker, mason, driver, farmer, cowherd, etc."[38] The lawyers were seated behind the accused. Behind them, three rows of metal chairs had been set up for the families of the victims. Approximately fifty members of the public fit into the standing room provided in the back, "on the condition," as Théolleyre wrote, "that they are willing to stand like metro passengers during rush hour." The press received no special treatment either: "Farther back, the press is going to suffer from a stiff neck from trying to peer over all these backs."[39] Over the next few days, the court heard arguments in which lawyers for the Alsatians gave long exposés about the situation of Alsace during the war. They protested against the provisions of the law of collective responsibility that placed their clients side by side with the German defendants. On the second day of the trial, Nussy Saint-Saëns became exasperated with requests to rule on the application of the law of collective responsibility. To do so would have the effect of declaring the court incompetent to try the case: "There we have it! That's the whole problem: they pass laws in the parliament and then it is to us, the military court, that they come to suggest ways to avoid applying them."[40]

The court would have none of it, and the trial finally proceeded to an interrogation of the accused. Their pasts were scrutinized. The Germans had gone through the habitual indoctrination in the Hitler Youth. Among the Alsatians one could find some evidence of French patriotism. One had received the *croix de guerre* in May 1940. Others had skirmished with the German authorities before being drafted into the Wehrmacht. A handful had deserted to the Canadians in Normandy. But efforts to establish their guilt in the massacre produced only evasive answers, as all but one of the accused denied any participation in specific acts of killing. Here too the trial seemed to bog down:

> "This trial is and will remain a trial of Nazism," M. Nussy Saint-Saëns had declared at the opening of the proceedings. But for the moment it seems to still be that of a [military company]. One discusses maps, laid out on a table or hand-held, like in a military headquarters. Everything is dissected, analyzed, bit by bit. Minutes and gestures are put under the microscope. In the end one loses sight of the drama as a whole, its heinousness and its outrageousness.[41]

While Nussy Saint-Saëns tried to move the trial forward, the parliamentary deputies from Alsace managed to have the law of collective responsibility brought up for debate before the National Assembly. The representatives from Alsace used this forum to argue passionately for reestablishing the principle of individual responsibility and for returning the burden of proof to the prosecution in the case of the *malgré-nous*. Once again, they asserted that the *malgré-nous* had little in common with the accused Germans, and even claimed that they shared the victimization of Oradour: "How much we would have liked to mix our tears with theirs, in common suffering from an evil that, in truth, far from dividing us, unites us in blood, humiliation, and infinite sadness."[42] Others argued that to try the Germans and French together was, in effect, a ratification of the Nazi annexation of Alsace. And always they invoked the political imperative of integrating Alsace into the national union: "The law that, dear colleagues, I hope with all my heart you will pass, will provide Alsace the certainty that nothing remains of the de facto annexation of which she was a victim—that with no reservations or second thoughts, she has regained her place in the bosom of the motherland."[43]

For his part, a representative of the Limousin called on the Assembly to contemplate the ruins of Oradour, which cried out for justice:

> Dear colleagues, the ruins of Oradour . . . remain as incriminating evidence, bearing, more than any other, the signature of Hitlerism. . . . Whoever contemplates our ruins, our cemeteries, will refuse to accept that such deeds not first be expiated . . . and then rendered impossible. Let the tortures of Oradour be avenged without any further delay, as required by justice. Then the ruins can teach the world that from now on what is at stake, among people of good will, is to save civilization.[44]

Jean Le Bail, a Socialist deputy from the Haute-Vienne, stated his concerns less grandiosely: "Is it enough for a province, which is dear to all our hearts, to have a fit of touchiness, believe its honor wounded (its honor which no one here doubts), that another province, which has been waiting for justice for eight years, can say today that justice may never be done?"[45]

The answer was yes. On 27 January, while witnesses from Oradour were testifying in Bordeaux, the National Assembly voted 365 to 238 to exempt the Frenchmen from "the law of collective responsibility."[46] The next day, the first article of the law of 15 September 1948—the article that established the notion of collective responsibility itself—was quietly abrogated.[47]

The Alsatians were gratified. The Renseignements Généraux in Colmar reported "relief . . . in all quarters."[48] In Strasbourg, the vote "brought some satisfaction to the self-esteem of the Alsatians, whose patriotic feelings had been hurt."[49]

Elsewhere, there was indignation. President Auriol was disgusted with what he considered the pusillanimous conduct of the Assembly: "It is the most saddening thing to have occurred while I have been in office."[50] In the courtroom in Bordeaux, Jean Brouillaud of the ANFM threatened to boycott the trial, crying out: "We victims, we don't want, in a couple of days, to have to watch the assassins, on their way home, leaving this city free. There's nothing more for us to do here!"[51] But Nussy Saint-Saëns expressed once again his determination to let nothing impede the trial: "For us, nothing has changed. The court will continue to hear this case in this session and if severance were to be granted it cannot enter into question until sentence is imposed."[52] In a final comment, he brandished a little red law book and remarked that, if necessary, "the good old penal code" would suffice to prosecute: "Since this was written, no one has come up with anything better."[53]

As the trial continued, the defense presented witnesses from the Alsatian Resistance to testify about the overwhelming difficulties of defying the German occupying power. Another spoke of the near impossibility of desertion: "If someone from the SS had come to me in the unoccupied zone to desert, I would never have wanted to do something to help him, out of fear of dealing with some kind of informer." Joseph Rey, the mayor of Colmar, questioned how much heroism one can expect of teenagers. What would he have done if he had found himself at Oradour? "I don't know," he responded. "I would have maybe chosen death. But the streets aren't full of heroes, not here, not elsewhere. And then one thinks of one's family."[54] While this testimony increased awareness in the interior about the infernal situation of Alsace, the witnesses from Oradour, when they finally took the stand, presented the inconsolable anguish of those who suffered as individuals.

The starkness and simplicity of the survivors' testimony made a striking and dramatic contrast to the legal arguments and tactics that had so far characterized the proceedings. As Le Monde remarked:

> What a strange trial! One could even call it a trial with two faces. On one side the law, the interpretation of texts, scheming in the corridors, and on the other, a deep horror, a sum of indelible suffering, deeply upsetting accounts of a simple and aching humanity that make one weep. As events unfold, one shifts from one to the other. One observes the courtroom performance of erudite variations on legal topics. After which one returns to the witnesses. . . . It is truly their drama, and their drama only, that interests the tribunal.[55]

FIGURE 15

Marguerite Rouffanche, sole survivor of the burning
of the church, with President Vincent Auriol (on the right),
10 June 1947.

First men and women from outlying hamlets described seeing the Germans arrive, and the horror and carnage they found in the ruins after the massacre. By all accounts, however, the dignity with which Marguerite Rouffanche told her story made the greatest impact on the court.

> What great writers achieve by the power of art—a stripping away, concision, the power of sober lines and density like marble—Mme. Rouffanche, a peasant of the Limousin, achieves effortlessly. . . . A perfectly sober account, and, in that, overwhelming, reduced to the essential facts. . . . Since the ordeal has left her very weak, the magistrates, instead of asking her to come forward, draw themselves completely around her chair. She holds herself dignified and austere, dressed in clothes of deepest mourning. . . . Her face under her black hat is white as chalk. She leans her head a little to the right. Her voice, without the least trace of easy sentiment, reaches us clear and implacable. She is Nemesis, calm and inexorable.[56]

In her final words to the court, she spoke with "an intense illumination of a visionary":[57] "I ask that justice be done with God's help. I came out alive from the crematory oven, I am the sacred witness from the church. I am a mother who has lost everything."[58]

Though the presiding judge expressed his hope that the suffering on both sides might become "an element unifying French people who suffered under the same doctrines and the same men," the days shared in the courtroom did little to increase mutual understanding. Alsatians continued to view the trial at Bordeaux as a trial of the entire province. The Limousins resented the testimony on behalf of Alsace, which cast the *malgré-nous* as victims.[59]

The Limousin's legacy of Resistance contributed to the alienation of the two regions. The Renseignements Généraux in the neighboring department of the Creuse warned, "It is certain that acquittal of the twelve Alsatians would provoke a pained and disillusioned reaction in the heart of the population, which still has recent memories of its own Resistance dead."[60] The Limousin's Resistance tradition also contributed to the Communist Party's position on the Bordeaux trial. Besides being a center of Communist-led Resistance during the war, the Limousin had been a center of rural communism since the founding of the Party in 1920. The Communists had taken a dominant and often polemical role in commemorating the Oradour massacre. In choosing sides in the Bordeaux trial, political acumen and the Communist sympathies of the Limousins led the Central Committee to defend the Limousin at the expense of their Alsatian supporters, who had never been very large in number.

The Limousin as a region rejected the arguments in defense of the Alsatians, but the families of the victims perceived them as a personal affront. The president of the ANFM refused to shake the hand of an Alsatian resister who testified for the defense.[61] The entire ANFM walked out of the courtroom when Georges Bourgeois, president of the ADEIF of the Haut-Rhin, rose to testify.[62] Back home, the people of Limoges rallied in support of Oradour. On the evening of 3 February, forty-thousand Limogeauds filed past a catafalque in an expression of sympathy and solidarity for the families of the martyrs of Oradour. While church bells tolled and sirens rang, all business as well as public transportation in the city came to a standstill. After listening to declarations demanding the punishment of the perpetrators of the massacre and the extradition of General Lammerding, an enormous cortège marched to the city's *monument aux morts* before silently dispersing.[63] The German-language edition of the *Nouveau Rhin français* took note: "This demonstration took place after fourteen days in which the most gifted orators of our province sought to waken understanding for the drama of Alsace. Their skills and effort seem to have been for naught in Limoges. . . ."[64]

On 12 February, the court heard the last of the closing arguments. The courtroom emptied and the judges went into conference to conduct the sentencing. The next evening, while the judges' conference was still going on, thousands of citizens of Bordeaux filed slowly passed a cenotaph draped with the tricolor flag of France while bells of a neighboring church tolled for an hour.[65] The members of the ANFM returned home to the Limousin without waiting for the verdict. Finally, after thirty-two hours of deliberations, the judges pronounced their sentences at 2:10 A.M. on Friday, 13 February. The highest-ranking German, Sergeant Lenz, received the death penalty. One German soldier who had proved his absence from Oradour on 10 June 1944 was freed. The court condemned the four other Germans to sentences ranging from ten to twelve years of hard labor. The Alsatians received somewhat lighter penalties. Georges-René Boos, the one volunteer in the group, was sentenced to death. (Boos's case had been separate from the *malgré-nous* from the very beginning of the trial. As a volunteer in the SS, he was tried not for war crimes but for treason.) Nine Alsatians were given sentences ranging from five to twelve years of hard labor. The remaining four were sentenced to between five and eight years in jail. All except Paul Graff, who had already served most of his sentence, immediately requested an appeal.

The morning editions of newspapers announced the verdict throughout France. Most of the Alsatian papers had delayed printing in order to include lengthy reports and comments, and by 8:30 in the morning the newsstands were sold out. The *Nouveau Rhin français*, which had fiercely defended "the thirteen," covered much of the front page with a defiant headline: "Alsace does not accept this shameful verdict."[66] In the streets of Strasbourg, the verdict was the subject of intense discussion.[67] The *Nouveau Rhin français* reported similar consternation in Mulhouse: "In the streetcar, in the trolley, at the street corners, wherever acquaintances and friends met, there was the same astonishment, the same incomprehension, the same rancor in the breast."[68]

Throughout the province, Alsatians vehemently objected. In Colmar, the Association of Mayors of the Haut-Rhin called a meeting at which they passed a motion protesting "against the lack of understanding of which the *incorporés de force* are the unhappy victims" and demanding that the government immediately suspend the sentences against the *malgré-nous*.[69] Pierre Pflimlin, deputy from Alsace, made the same demand in a telegram to the Minister of Defense, René Pleven; since the trial had taken place in a military court, Pleven was the highest responsible authority in the cabinet. And in Paris an Alsatian deputy in parliament, Michel Kauffman, entered a request at the National Assembly for an inquiry into the "condition and atmosphere in which the trial of Oradour took place," the verdict itself, and the "moral repercussions for the youth of Alsace" and "the future of the province."[70]

Within hours of the news, twenty buildings along the main street of the Alsatian town of Guebwiller, including the town hall, were hung with the French tricolor flown at half mast or furled and draped with black crepe.[71] In Strasbourg, flags hung in mourning could be seen along a main thoroughfare near the cathedral. A shopkeeper in Mulhouse made an autonomist statement by raising the flag of Europe on his storefront.[72] Later in the day, posters went up in every commune in the Haut-Rhin emblazoned with a message from the department's Association of Mayors: "We don't accept it." The text went on to assert, "All of Alsace declares solidarity with her thirteen sons wrongly condemned in Bordeaux and with the 130,000 *incorporés de force*. . . . Alsace will stand by them in their suffering."[73] At six o'clock in the evening, church bells tolled for fifteen minutes throughout the Haut-Rhin.[74]

The ADEIF of the Bas-Rhin made the most inflammatory gesture. It plastered kiosks in Strasbourg with yellow signs listing the names and sentences of the *malgré-nous*. These posters were identical in color, format, and lettering to those that had been put up by the Nazis to announce death sentences against Alsatian resisters.[75] As night fell, silent men and women with drawn faces stood grouped around these signs.[76]

The next morning, while the Alsatian members of parliament were meeting in Strasbourg to draw up strategies of protest, Deputy Pierre Pflimlin received a response to his telegram requesting the suspension of the Alsatians' sentences. Though the request was denied on technical grounds, the Minister of Defense made clear that the government would facilitate parliamentary efforts to grant amnesty to the Alsatians: "I have been informed that you have the intention to introduce a bill providing measures of amnesty that would favor the *incorporés de force*. In agreement with the Président du Conseil, I am advising you

FIGURE 16

Street demonstration in Strasbourg, protesting the verdict
of the Bordeaux trial, February 1953.

FIGURE 17

Strasbourg World War I monument veiled in protest,
February 1953.

that the government will accept the urgent debate of this bill if it is introduced."[77] Thus the possibility arose that, in *l'affaire d'Oradour*, the legislature would once again intervene in a judicial matter in order to ease the political crisis.

Pleven's telegram immediately brought some calm to Alsace. In order not to impede parliamentary action, the mayors of the two Alsatian departments canceled the administrative strike they had been planning. But they kept up the pressure with dramatic ceremonial gestures. On Sunday, the mayor of Strasbourg led six thousand people on a march from the town hall to the Place de la République, where the city's monument to the dead of First World War loomed under a black shroud.[78] In Haguenau, Schirmeck, Sélesat, Molscheim, and Schiltigheim, demonstrators gathered at their own *monuments aux morts*, which were similarly veiled in protest.[79] The design of the Strasbourg monument made it a particularly powerful site for the expression of distress over the latest eruption of the *drame d'Alsace*. It is a pietà in which a female figure supports two dying soldiers on her lap—sons of Alsace who fought in the opposing armies of France and Germany. Two nude male figures, sculpted in the style of Rodin, clasp each other's hands in the last moments before death. This group of figures faces in the direction of the old town, where the spires of the cathedral of Strasbourg pierce the skyline. In keeping with the sober mood of the statue, there are no heroic inscriptions or names of individuals on the monument. The base is carved with the simple inscription "A NOS MORTS 1914–1918."[80]

The unrest in Alsace caused such concern that the government gave its support to yet another *loi d'exception*. This bill proposed full and complete amnesty for those who had been "forcibly incorporated into the German armies." So that the amnesty would be interpreted as gesture from the entire nation toward Alsace, the draft legislation was proposed by eight deputies from "provinces of the interior," representing all political parties except the Communists. On the morning of 17 February the president of the cabinet, René Mayer, went to the Palais-Bourbon to prepare the way for the debate and vote that would take place the next day. "The government is uttering a solemn appeal to the unity of the nation," he told the Chamber of Deputies. "The mourning and the trials of our diverse provinces should bring us to understand each other, not to tear each other apart."[81]

In the Limousin, those who had attended the trial had not been surprised by the verdict, but they had taken the news bitterly. The families of the victims found the sentences scandalously lenient. The only sentence they would have accepted was the death penalty for all who participated in the crime. The proposed amnesty four days later completed the outrage. In the regional Socialist Party paper, *Le Populaire du centre*, Deputy Jean Le Bail railed against the bad faith of his Alsatian colleagues in the Assembly. He pointed out that only weeks before, during the debate over the abrogation of the law of collective guilt, they had insisted that they were not trying to subvert justice but wanted only to do away with an unjust law. That had been achieved. Now they were proposing yet another exceptional measure to skirt the judgment of the court.[82]

In a tone more restrained than the vociferous complaints of the Limousin and the Communist Party, the newspapers born of the clandestine press of the Resistance expressed discomfort with the arguments made by the defense and the subsequent protests in Alsace: "It is not Alsace that is on trial. Other French people, alas! in other provinces were shot for having gone over to the enemy. Their home provinces felt solidarity on their behalf. Do not let it be said that in convicting those guilty of the massacre at Oradour, one has condemned Alsace." *Libération* expressed sympathy for the Limousins: "The people of the Limousin felt this verdict like a hot iron applied to their wound. And if that did not do it, it is enough to hear Chancellor Adenauer in Bonn proclaiming himself, on top of it all, very pleased.[83] Though one could certainly make a case that Alsace had suffered exceptionally during *les années noires,* the proposition that French citizens could have been forced to act "in spite of themselves" raised troubling questions about how the French were to judge any act of collaboration. Resisters in particular were offended by the logic of the Alsatian defense, which might contribute to apologetic attitudes toward other French citizens, who had accommodated or collaborated with the occupation.

President Auriol was apparently troubled by such thoughts when, on 18 February, five days after the verdict had been handed down, he received a delegation of Alsatian deputies. This meeting took place only hours before the National Assembly was to vote on the legislation to grant amnesty to the Alsatians. First, Auriol commented on the conditions that had permitted the passage of the original war crimes law of 1948, which had proved untenable: "Everyone was like me, under the impression of those little white coffins; doubtless the horror of the drama got the better of them." But he went on to remind them that none of them had opposed the law at the time: "You made the law of 1948, you accepted the judgment in advance." Auriol indicated that he was willing to provide some sort of clemency for the Alsatians: "A [presidential] pardon is possible. . . . Of course, pardon [*la grâce*] does not efface the conviction, but it dispenses with the application of the sentence. I am not opposed to an act of clemency. But I am calling on you for a return to calm. I beg you not to welcome these men with triumphal arches and to think of the victims."[84] These remarks indicate that Auriol was ready to grant clemency for the sake of appeasing Alsace and resolving the painful situation. He did not approve, however, of the proposed amnesty, which would have the effect of expunging the court's conviction. Nine years after the end of the war, Vincent Auriol, who had been a *grand résistant*, remained committed to the ideal of Resistance and uneasy with a gesture that appeared to absolve the *malgré-nous*.[85] Notes in his diary make plain that Auriol would have been happier with a presidential pardon (granted on an ad hoc, case-by-case basis) rather than amnesty voted by parliament, which is a sweeping decision by society to wipe the slate clean.

In the parliamentary session of 18 February, deputies from the Limousin passionately warned their colleagues of the serious threat the bill posed to the principle of the separation of powers: "If the lawmaker now takes it upon himself to annul the judgment before the ink has dried, where are we going, in what sort of state are we?" asked Socialist deputy André Bardon. He went on to question whether the proposed bill, coming so quickly after the court's judgment, could claim the moral legitimacy of a true amnesty: "They are saying to us: 'amnesty.' Amnesty, according to the Greek etymology, is forgetting, it is the law of forgetting. Amnesty is a gesture that one makes only with a cool head. What forgetting is there in our hearts? . . . Not exhibiting the character of a true amnesty, it shreds the pronouncement of conviction."[86]

The proponents of the amnesty did not engage in discussion of its legal ramifications but rather sought to frame the debate by what they considered the overriding consideration at hand: the exigencies of national unity. "The country is a mother," cried the President of the Assembly, Edouard Herriot. "She cannot let her children tear each other apart on her breast." The Minister of Defense asked the deputies to consider the problem apart from the juridical issues: "The decision by politicians should be taken on a totally different level than that of the judges, a level which is not that of judicial reasoning but of the national interest and of the unity of the French community."[87] Even General de Gaulle, despite his essential role in establishing Oradour as a national symbol, had also appealed for understanding of the Alsatians in the interest of national unity: "What French person will not understand the inflamed suffering of Alsace? In this serious affair what we have to avoid, above all, is that after having lost so many of her children assassinated by the enemy in the tragedy of Oradour, in addition France lets a bitter wound be inflicted on national unity."[88]

The deputies from the Limousin could see that if political considerations prevailed, the interests of Alsace would take priority. As Jean Le Bail, the Socialist deputy from the Haute-Vienne, remarked in bitter protest:

> One doesn't work . . . for national unity by sacrificing one province for another province, whose bruises and uncertain lot . . . do not give it the right, whatever may have been its misfortunes, to a special law. Ladies and gentlemen, there's the rub, and when one speaks of national unity, one does not have the right to sacrifice a province that presents no autonomist threat, because that is what is dominating everything in

this debate: the fear that imprudent people will drive French Alsace to commit regrettable errors.[89]

In the eyes of the Limousins, the national unity invoked for reasons of state could only come at their expense.

The people of Oradour would not be reconciled. In revolt against the verdict in Bordeaux, the ANFM had already decided to return the *croix de guerre* presented to Oradour in 1947. When Deputy Jean Tricart took the podium, he read a letter in which the ANFM listed the drastic symbolic measures the group would take against this "new insult to the memory of our martyrs": they would return the *croix de la Légion d'honneur* bestowed on the organization in 1949; they would refuse to transfer the ashes of their "martyrs" into the crypt built by the state; they would refuse to accept any government representatives at ceremonies in Oradour. And to identify those who, in their view, had interfered with justice, they would display at the entrances to the ruins the names of the deputies who voted for the amnesty.[90]

In the end, it seemed that the Assembly deemed the alienation of a poor, rural, leftist region to be less of a threat to national unity than continuing unrest in populous, prosperous Alsace. Three hundred nineteen deputies—the great majority from the MRP and RPF—approved the amnesty. All of the Communists, three-quarters of the Socialists, a third of the Radicals, and a dozen isolated members from other parties—211 in all—voted against the bill. Eighty-three deputies abstained.[91]

Three days after the vote of the Assembly, in the wee hours of 21 February, the thirteen Alsatians walked through the gates of the military prison in Bordeaux. They quickly climbed into four waiting vans that drove northeast, through the dark and fog. By the early afternoon they had arrived home in Alsace, where they were received by their families with relief and joy.[92]

While the newspapers in Alsace published pictures of the *malgré-nous* reunited with their wives and children, in Oradour those who had lost their families in the massacre reeled with shock, anger, and despair. For the people of Oradour, this amounted to a second martyrdom—this time at the hands of their own countrymen. In the face of this blow, they responded as promised. On 20 February a delegation of the ANFM, led by André Desourteaux, returned to the prefect the *croix de la Légion d'honneur.* It also gave back the bronze plaque presented in the name of the Republic by President de Gaulle.[93] The next day, the mayor of Oradour, and a delegation that included five other Communist mayors from the canton of St-Junien, returned the *croix de guerre* that the community had received in 1948.

The Communist Party called for protest against the amnesty in the Limousin and throughout France. In Paris, on Sunday, 22 February, groups of Resistance veterans joined with the Parti Socialiste Unitaire and the PCF in a procession of approximately four hundred people to lay wreaths on the Tomb of the Unknown Soldier under the Arc de Triomphe.[94] The Communist Party organized a demonstration in Limoges that drew one thousand people and urged all the communes of the department to join them in an administrative strike. In the Communist-led protests that took place in departments throughout France over the next two weekends, the Party explicitly linked the amnesty of the Alsatians to its criticism of Franco-German rapprochement and the European Defense Community (CED).[95] Rivalries within the French Left, however, as well as the sense that the Communist Party was exploiting the massacre at Oradour, hindered the success of these protests. In the Limousin, for example, the bitter and vindictive battles between the Communists and the Socialists surely played a part in the decision of the Socialist mayor of Limoges, Léon Betoulle, not to support the strike.[96]

Although the Communists dominated the active protest, the Renseignements Généraux noted sharp disapproval of the amnesty among *anciens résistants* in general—particularly in regions of France where there had been widespread Resistance. In the Haute-Savoie, an area which had been known as the "citadel of the Resistance," a broad range of Resistance veterans disapproved of the parliament's decision.[97] On the other end of the spectrum, unapologetic supporters of Vichy demanded a sweeping amnesty, "one and indivisible," for "victims of the purges."[98] The German government, which had approved of the sentencing that did not distinguish by nationality, was dismayed that only the Alsatians had been absolved.

In the end, the president of the Republic pardoned the two men condemned to death (the German, Lenz, and the Alsatian, Boos). By 1958, five years after the trial, all prisoners had been freed. This fit into the larger pattern of leniency for collaborators. In all of France, only nineteen people accused of collaboration remained in jail in 1958. In 1964, twenty years after the Liberation, there were none.[99]

Calm returned to Alsace immediately after the amnesty and ferment died down in the rest of the country. The Bordeaux trial had produced an intense but brief national crisis. In Oradour, the shock and bitter disappointment endure. For many old timers of Oradour, recollections of 1953 are as gloomy as those of 1944. Robert Lapuelle, who took up a medical practice in the new town of Oradour in 1949, remembers: "So, to this feeling of very great pain and of having survived there was added a sentiment of injustice, abandonment, and, at times, revolt.[100] Alienation and anger had an enormous impact on both the commemoration of the massacre and the evolution of the new town. To this day, many of those who lived through the shock of the amnesty divide the postwar history of Oradour into two periods: before and after Bordeaux.

Chapter Six

THE NEW TOWN

The backlash from the Bordeaux trial also produced consequences for elections for local office; it ended the dominance
of the French Communist Party, which had come to power
in Oradour in the aftermath of the massacre. By 1953, although
the PCF had defended the Limousins throughout the Bordeaux
trial, many in Oradour felt that the Party had exploited their
cause for its own political purposes. Indeed, beginning in 1947,
as the Cold War flared up, the national strength of the PCF had
ensured that ideological struggles reverberated at every level of
French domestic politics.

The Communists' immediate postwar success in Oradour had
been in keeping with their political fortunes throughout the
Haute-Vienne. Their important role in wartime Resistance had
benefited the Party everywhere, and the effect had been particularly marked in the Limousin. In 1945, Communists were elected
to local office in 155 out of the Haute-Vienne's 206 communes,

as compared to only 31 in 1939.[1] In the legislative elections of 1946, the PCF became the majority party in the region, gathering 38 percent of the vote.[2] The municipal elections of May 1945 brought Communists into Oradour's town hall for the first time; the entire Communist list was voted into office, headed by Aimé Faugeras, leader of the local Communist cell.

Although the Left had dominated Limousin politics since the First World War, in the Haute-Vienne the Communist Party had never before extended its power beyond a few key communes. Between 1919 and 1936, Oradour regularly voted Socialist in legislative and municipal elections.[3] There was a Socialist mayor from 1915 to 1939. At the local level the PCF never came close to challenging the traditional rivals for the office of mayor, Socialist Joseph Beau and Radical Republican Paul Desourteaux. Both these men died in the 1944 massacre, creating a vacuum of political power in Oradour. The Communist Party seized the opportunity. From 1948 until 1953, Mayor Faugeras, inspired by the regional Party leadership, used Oradour as a platform from which to address an array of domestic and national political issues. In 1948, at the offical presentation of the *croix de guerre* by the Secretary of State for the Armed Forces, Faugeras criticized the national government for its efforts toward rapprochement with Germany.[4]

The following year, the Communists' continued politicization of the symbol of Oradour led to an acrimonious split between the ANFM and the city council. The Minister of National Defense planned to present the ANFM with the *croix de la Légion d'honneur* at the annual ceremony of 10 June. But in mid-May, an article in *L'Humanité* announced that the municipality would decline to accept it.[5] Indeed, a week later the municipal council of

Oradour voted unanimously to turn it down. At this point the affair escalated into a political brawl. The prefect of the Haute-Vienne advised Paris to take a strong stand: "It is, in my opinion, of capital importance that the government not cede in the face of blackmail by the Communist municipality, probably inspired by Paris."[6] In the forum of the regional Socialist paper, the ANFM rebuffed the mayor: "You have refused, Mr. Mayor and municipal councilors, to accept the *Légion d'honneur* as long as the executioners are not punished. It is a point of view that would have all our sympathy if it had been bestowed on you. But the *Légion d'honneur* has been bestowed on THE DEAD of Oradour-s/Glane. They deserve it. . . ." At the official ceremony of 10 June, the ANFM went ahead and accepted the medal.[7]

Meanwhile, the PCF had refused to participate in the annual ceremony on 10 June, announcing throughout the region its own event for 12 June. A crowd estimated at ten thousand assembled in the ruins of Oradour for a ceremony attended by members of the PCF-affiliated "Peace Movement" who had come on a special train from Paris. Speakers included Frédéric Joliot-Curie, the High Commissioner for Atomic Energy, and the leading Communist intellectual/activist, poet Louis Aragon. On the marketplace, Joliot-Curie called for the punishment of the perpetrators of the massacre and added a pointed political message: "Meanwhile, one speaks of clemency, one condemns resisters, one imprisons them and rehabilitates traitors. All of this is part of a plan of psychological preparation for war against the Soviet Union."[8] The next day, the local Socialist press decried such polemics: "Five years after a first martyrdom, why is it necessary for Oradour to undergo another by being the scene of discordant demonstrations? . . . Suffering and pity are one thing

. . . exploitation of these sentiments is another and is particularly intolerable. Oradour and her children belong to the whole nation; and it is inadmissible that the Communist Party use them for the purposes of its cause."[9] But no consensus emerged. From 1949 to 1952 the city council continued to organize its own separate ceremonies to commemorate the massacre.

In 1950, the Communists organized under the banner "Pilgrimage for Peace," and the annual commemoration of the massacre became, in essence, a political rally. In the regional press, the PCF called on its members and sympathizers to demonstrate against the rearmament of West Germany and the proliferation of the atomic bomb: "SIX YEARS AFTER [the massacre of Oradour]: France risks being turned into a gigantic Oradour by atomic bombs. COME ALL, resisters, republicans, patriots, show . . . your deep disapproval of this abdication and your will to oppose it. To save PEACE, for the outlawing of the atomic bomb, BIG RALLY."[10] On the afternoon of 11 June, a crowd estimated at 2,500–3,000 converged in the new town to hear speeches by Charles Tillon, former national leader of the Francs-Tireurs et Partisans Français, the Communist paramilitary Resistance group, as well as by poet Paul Eluard, who had been active in the Resistance.

The success of the event was marred, however, by a fistfight that broke out next to the ruins. An agent of the Renseignements Généraux filed this report:

> Numerous people coming and going from visiting the church . . . were parked nearby on the square. Among them, a completely disabled veteran from the department of the Dordogne was calmly saying to his comrades that, during the war, he had seen completely destroyed towns and villages in

Germany. At that moment he was called a provocateur and received a violent punch in the chest. . . . A violent discussion followed, blows continued to accompany invective, a mob of 500–700 people formed immediately. The intervention of the guardian of the ruins . . . who himself was punched, was necessary to restore calm.[11]

Appalled by this turn of events, the ANFM enjoined visitors to conduct themselves with respect: "We beg you, all of you who come to Oradour, leave your hatred and rancor, your partisan passions, at the door. Tell yourself that you are entering a sanctuary!"[12]

Nonetheless, Oradour continued to be the site of political demonstrations. In 1951, the Communist-led ceremony in the afternoon, attended by 1,500 participants from all over France, overshadowed the ANFM's smaller gathering held that morning.[13] In 1952, Faugeras launched his by now familiar criticisms before a crowd of three thousand gathered for a separate commemoration on 8 June:

> The rulers have consecrated the rearming of militaristic and vengeful Germany, in which the assassins of Oradour will doubtlessly be promoted to the rank of instructing officers. This betrayal of French interests is done under the cover of anti-Communism and anti-Sovietism. They want to drag us onto the same path that, in 1938, went by way of Munich and led, after the arrests of the Communists, to the death camps, to Oradour.[14]

One year later, in the wake of the Bordeaux trial, the politics in Oradour shifted abruptly. Tired of seeing the anniversary of the massacre used for purposes other than commemorating their dead, the survivors turned against what they considered to be political exploitation of their emotional suffering. Furthermore, at Bordeaux, Mayor Faugeras had proven inadequate in representing Oradour to a greater public. At this point, Socialists and Gaullists pulled together to eliminate the influence of the PCF. As the municipal elections of 1953 approached, the lawyer who had represented the ANFM at Bordeaux (who was also deputy mayor of Limoges and a Socialist) proposed that the ANFM and like-minded citizens create a *liste d'union* of Socialists and Gaullist moderates to run against the PCF. That year Oradour-sur-Glane voted Faugeras out of office and replaced him with the *liste d'union* headed by Jean Brouillaud, president of the ANFM, who had better defended their interests at Bordeaux.

It was agreed that members of the *liste d'union* would not engage in national party politics in Oradour. The new municipal council banned speeches in the ruins or from the balcony of the town hall. It imposed a moratorium on political discussions within the town council and the ANFM. No member of the municipal council was allowed to hold office in a political party or attend party meetings.[15]

In the spring of 1953, a few months after the Bordeaux trial, a group of surviving families moved into twenty of the two hundred new houses that had been built a few hundred meters from the ruins of the old town. The rest of the houses remained closed, waiting for new inhabitants. During the construction of the new town, these families had been living in wooden barracks erected by the Ministry of Reconstruction.[16] In 1949 they had been joined by Dr. Robert Lapuelle, who became the physician for the community.

Oradour Sur Glane

HᵀᴱVIENNE

FIGURE 18

Postcard of Oradour, showing the old and new towns.
Pictures in center and upper right are of Oradour before
the massacre. In the lower left, aerial view of the ruins.
Lower right shows the town in the 1950s. The church
in the new town is at upper left.

For the next ten years, the families in the new town maintained continual mourning. From 1953 until the early 1960s, there were no public activities or gatherings: no first communions or baptisms, no weddings, no dances. No associational life took place in Oradour other than that of the ANFM. Community life revolved around visits to the graveyard and observance of commemorative ceremonies. Dr. Lapuelle remembered those early days of the new town: "At the time, this was an extremely sad town. Deserted streets. One saw few people. And above all what was striking, one didn't see children. . . . Sure, a few children had been born in the barracks. But since the school was at the edge of town, one didn't see children in the center. And this sadness was something indescribable."[17]

The emotional trauma caused by the massacre was further complicated by the bitter experience of the trial at Bordeaux. The sense of injustice occasioned by the Assembly's amnesty vote led the community to turn in on its sorrow and reject relations with the French state. Not only did the municipal council and the ANFM return the government's medals, they announced that government officials would no longer be invited to participate in the yearly ceremony on 10 June.[18]

The ANFM took its strongest stand at the ruins by reclaiming the commemorative site. To the dismay of the Historic Monuments Service, the association scrapped plans for putting the bones and ashes of the "martyrs" in the costly underground crypt built by the state for this purpose.[19] On a routine visit to Oradour in November 1953, a departmental architect noted construction work going on in the cemetery, which belonged to the commune of Oradour-sur-Glane:

In the course of a recent inspection at the Ruins of Oradour s/Glane, I learned that the National Association of the Families . . . was proceeding to build a relatively large monument in the cemetery to receive the remains of the victims of the tragedy of 10 June 1944. Following discreet investigation, I established that, in fact, earthworks were in progress. I believe that it is my duty to report this state of affairs, when the state, wishing to honor the victims, has built a monument at its own expense worthy of receiving them.[20]

The ANFM was indeed erecting its own ossuary—which still contains the remains of Oradour's martyrs. Since 1974 the crypt has housed objects gathered in the ruins (formerly kept in the Maison du Souvenir), but it has never served its original purpose.

The antigovernment gesture that caused the greatest embarrassment to the national government and elected officials was the posting of large placards at all entrances to the ruins, listing the members of parliament who had voted for the amnesty. If visitors to Oradour found their deputy's name on these signs, they often wrote him outraged letters. Disconcerted deputies wrote the Minister of the Interior to demand removal of the signs. The minister, in turn, would pass on the request to the prefect of the Haute-Vienne. In some cases, the prefect would then order the mayor of Oradour to have the signs taken down. Each time, the mayor refused, in a show of solidarity with the ANFM.[21] But in most instances, the prefect let the matter lie, not wishing to provoke a showdown. In 1955, the beleaguered prefect of the Haute-Vienne wrote to the office of the President of the Republic to explain his predicament:

I have the honor of informing you that my predecessors and I have, repeatedly, received the same suggestion. . . . the climate surrounding this delicate affair has not improved . . . and I can say that a lot of the population is still bitter. . . . The malaise is real and, whether it's latent or sharp, according to the circumstances, it is not any less deep. That is why it is still impossible to imagine removing the signs, which would provoke incidents out of proportion with the desired goal. Such a measure would outrage the population and its representatives, would serve Communist propaganda, and would needlessly set opinion against the government and certainly the President of the Republic. Besides, such measures would require the presence of a large police force in Oradour and would lead to serious trouble. Moreover, identical signs would be put up . . . every night, in the same place, as soon as they were not permanently guarded. . . . That is why it appears to me useless, as it is inopportune to revive the passions that I had a lot of difficulty pacifying, and to provoke incidents the extent, duration and violence of which are unpredictable. . . .[22]

The prefect's reasoning carried the day; the placards were on view for ten more years, until the presidential elections of 1965 created a temporary division within the ANFM.

In the first round of these elections, Charles de Gaulle (Union pour une Nouvelle République), François Mitterrand (Fédération de la Gauche Démocratique et Socialiste), and Jean Lecanuet (Mouvement Républicain Populaire) opposed each other. With another poster, the ANFM informed the public that Mitterrand and Lecanuet had voted for the amnesty. During the campaign, embarrassed supporters of Mitterrand within the ANFM took away the signs in the middle of the night. Though other members wanted to replace them, Mayor Lapuelle declared that the signs should remain down—which they did. In the end, then, this important step toward a modus vivendi came about as the result of a local political squabble, rather than in response to pressure from the government.

At the ruins of the *vieux bourg*, the ambition was to stop time. In the new town, however, there was an ongoing struggle to balance the survivors' need to mourn and the community's need to be viable. Over the years, the nature of memory and mourning shifted as new people moved into the community, as the survivors grew older, and as the ruins of the old town continued to deteriorate.

New buildings could not free the settlers from the weight of the past. The second Oradour could not be a truly new town, without history, like a new suburb or satellite city. Townspeople did not think it appropriate to come out of mourning just because the physical setting had changed. When, in 1952, the owner of the Hôtel de la Glane marked its opening with a ball, a group of families came, rifles in hand, to prevent the party.[23]

The extensive mourning desired by the ANFM gained strength from the close proximity of the ruins. Janique de Catheu was told by her mother what it was like to walk to school from one of the outlying hamlets:

> All the kids who lived at Les Bordes had to go through the [ruined] bourg. In winter . . . they were all scared to go through this town—and there wasn't any other way through. They had to go . . . by the main street. Mom said that when one went through, if there was a strange sound, everyone started to run. And she says, "to run in wooden clogs," because

that's what they wore then, "well, it wasn't easy." This nightmare stayed with them for years.[24]

Dr. Lapuelle's recollections indicate that in the early years the presence of the ruins weighed heavily on adults as well: "When I made calls at night I still went through the ruins. One still smelled this burnt odor and one had the impression that the fire had just happened. And the people who had . . . suffered from the war, who were coming out of that [experience], couldn't accept seeing normal life next door [to the ruins]. . . . I think that the proximity of the ruins enormously complicated, and complicates, life in the new town of Oradour."[25]

The rules of mourning were particularly hard on children and teenagers—especially the girls, who had greater restrictions imposed on them than boys. Amélie Lebraud was fifteen in 1944. For two and a half years, she and her sister wore only black. They were forbidden by their mother to go to parties in the months of June and November (which were considered *les mois des morts*) or to wear lipstick or jewelry: "How to tell you? For me, mourning was something that marked me terribly. Horribly marked me, I should say. It's not that I wanted to forget what happened, but to walk in procession every Sunday, in black, in the old bourg, became almost torture. Because, well, one always met people there who had suffered, one spoke about people who had suffered, one talked about the dead, and one never talked about life." Although they were later allowed to wear navy blue and white, Amélie Lebraud wore bright colors only after she married. The effects of the years of mourning were long-lasting: "Besides clothing, we didn't laugh anymore, we didn't sing at home anymore. . . . It was really sad. . . . You feel less like having fun, you feel less like

FIGURE 19

Amélie Lebraud with her mother
at their home in the new town.

laughing. . . . It took my children growing up for me to understand life better . . . that they wanted to go out and have fun."[26]

Christiane Jude, born in the new town, has painful memories of her childhood there:

> I felt this mourning very deeply. . . . I was born in the new town right at the beginning. Of course, at the time the school hadn't been built yet, and there were very few children. I don't remember having little friends to play with, little girls to play with me. Well, when the school was built, it was marvellous. The children played in the courtyard and I took my toys, my little teddy bear, and then I crossed the street and I went to watch those children play—I was missing something.[27]

People like Christiane Jude are part of the first generation that did not know the old Oradour or the people who died there. During childhood they suffered from the sorrow and pain of their parents and from the sadness of their families.

As the provider of medical care for the community, Dr. Lapuelle was well-placed to judge the emotional impact of the massacre on the families of Oradour. He recalled the suffering of the women from outlying hamlets who lost their school-aged children in the massacre:

> What struck me most in my life as a doctor when I set myself up in practice—you know that in medicine one makes charts. You ask women about their previous history, if they have been sick, how many children they've had. I saw women who said, "I had six children, eight children." And to uncover a little more, one often asks what has become of these children, what they do. And in the first years there were women who answered, "I had six children, they were burned alive at

Oradour." I think this trauma, however long one lives, doesn't change. . . . The women never went into it, we spoke a little about it, like that, and then they cried.[28]

In the early 1960s, people in Oradour began to make an effort to revive the social life of the town. The municipal council focused on activities for young people. They built a recreation hall and initiated a campaign called "Le Droit de vivre" (the right to live).[29] A group of men put their energy into reestablishing Oradour's soccer team. Though young men who survived the massacre had started playing with a group from towns nearby, it was not until 1964 that there were eleven teenage boys from Oradour to make a full team. The Union Sportive d'Oradour became the symbol of the rebirth of Oradour. By 1970 the team made it to the departmental championships—which is still a great source of pride for the team's boosters.[30]

Rebuilding a social life for Oradour was the most important aspect of *la reconstruction morale* of the community, but creating an economic base was necessary for survival. In this regard, Oradour faced a particularly difficult set of circumstances. Its estrangement from the central government left the town in no position to solicit special financial subsidies. Local commerce was not enough to support the town economy. (The sale of postcards or books benefitted only the ANFM.) Nor did the leaders of Oradour want to build the town around tourism or become a bedroom community for people who worked in Limoges. With the decline of agriculture that followed the Second World War, new industry was particularly important to the regional economy. Starting in 1960, the community sought to attract small entrepreneurs by offering tax incentives and inexpensive housing for their employees. Four small factories were built, creating two hundred jobs and bringing new people into the community. Though all of these new enterprises went bankrupt during the oil crisis and economic recession of the mid-1970s, the municipality bought the buildings and later managed to establish new factories and workshops. From a commune that had been predominantly agricultural before the war, Oradour developed an economic base of small industry, artisanal production, and commerce.

The economic development of Oradour in the 1960s also changed the make-up of the community. The influx of outsiders created two distinct groups within Oradour: the survivors and their descendents, and newcomers who were not affected by the massacre. According to Dr. Lapuelle, relations between these two communities have not always been easy: "Often the new inhabitants tell me that they have difficulties fitting in."[31] Amélie Lebraud regretted that, in the past, the solidarity among the oldtimers of Oradour worked to exclude newcomers: "We were a little turned in on ourselves. That is, the massacre tightened the bonds of friendship almost into ties of family. . . . There is a time for that, but it is also necessary to extend oneself . . . and I think that we didn't always know that at the requisite time. . . . I'd even say that there was a little too much sectarianism vis-à-vis others. It's a little late to be saying it. . . ."[32] Others, like André Desourteaux, feel dismayed by the increasing influence of the newer residents: "This town was made without us," he remarked with a trace of bitterness.

Among younger people, the demographic shift created tensions between the newcomers and the old residents of peasant stock. One twenty-six-year-old was quite outspoken: "Their attitude is really bad, and we don't get along . . . [with] the new people, the young ones. Because they play papa's boy. 'My dad is so-and-so,' but really, they want to be better than us. . . . At home we say, they play the know-it-all. For them, when you get down to it, a peasant is a nobody!"[33] As time passed and new people moved into Oradour, the community became less focused on the past. How could it be otherwise? The newcomers do not share in sustaining the memory of the massacre, and the children of survivors are now grown and have their own children, who are less concerned with the past.

As the massacre recedes in time, the intensity of mourning has diminished. In 1988, the ANFM cut back its prohibition on weddings and public events from the entire month of June to the five days before and the five days after the tenth of June.[34] There were other signs that Oradour would present a more cheerful face. The pharmacist on the town square had his stucco redone in yellow, and the municipal council decided to do the same.[35] Until then all buildings in town had been left their original grey. In 1991, the town planted trees along the avenue du 10 juin, renovated the fountain on the town square, and set up flowers boxes at the main intersection.

For some of the children of survivors who have stayed in Oradour, getting on with life has sometimes required getting some physical distance from the ruins. Christiane Jude and Jean-François Beaulieu both grew up in the new town when mourning pervaded all aspects of community life. As an adult, Madame Jude freed herself by moving to Les Bordes—out of sight of the ruins:

FIGURE 20

The town hall in the new Oradour.

FIGURE 21

The avenue du 10 Juin in the new town.

I wanted to get out of this context of Oradour. This context of mourning, all of that. I wanted to live a little on the edge [of the community] because it marked me so much—this memory. . . . I wanted to leave it behind a little bit, distance myself a little bit from all that. . . . It's not far away, but I don't see the ruins anymore, there are so many trees that separate me. It's not very far away. But I don't see them anymore, so [the memory] fades a little bit.[36]

Beaulieu also seeks to strike a balance between the past and present. Across the street from his house are the crumbling ruins of the house and garden that once belonged to his grandparents. Beaulieu planted a dense screen of trees in front of his house, blocking his view of the ruins. When pressed about the reason, he responded much like Madame Jude: "One has to admit that aesthetically it is not particularly agreeable to look at. . . . It's not a barrier, [but] one wants to put oneself in a setting for living; one tries to protect oneself, after all."[37]

Though the children of the survivors are determined to lead normal lives, they are still committed to protecting the memory of what happened at Oradour. They consider themselves caretakers of a familial and communal memory that they have inherited. With the passage of time, the call to remember is no longer tied explicitly to the desire for vengeance or the need to mourn; the chief task, as they see it, is to prevent exploitation of the story of Oradour and to preserve an accurate record of what happened.

In the 1980s, the massacre at Oradour-sur-Glane became the subject of a number of films, novels, and "historical" accounts that romanticized or fictionalized the events of 10 June 1944. Most nefarious, in the eyes of the ANFM, are books and films that give untenable motives for the massacre. These explanations attack the notion of Oradour as a massacre of innocents and the raison d'être of the monument itself as a testimony to the gratuitous savagery of the SS.

In the summer of 1987, a British film director, Geoffrey Reeve, came to the region to make a movie called *Souvenir*.[38] In this story a former German soldier, Ernst Kestner, returns to the Limoges region, where he was stationed during the war. He goes to a small town looking for a young French woman with whom he had a passionate affair. He knows that German soldiers massacred the townspeople and suspects that she was one of their victims. During the filming, an interview with actor Michaël Lonsdale appeared in the mass circulation television guide, *Télé 7 jours*. Lonsdale described his role in the film as the mayor of the town, Oradour-sur-Glane, who confesses to Kestner that he provoked the massacre by killing two German soldiers.[39]

The ANFM alerted the prefect and called in their lawyer. After meeting with a representative of the ANFM at the mayor's house in Oradour, the producers of the film sent out a press release declaring that "all people and all places portrayed in 'Souvenir' are fictitious and have no relation to the historical reality of Oradour."[40] The Ministry of Culture contacted the producers of the film to ensure that the final version would "conform with the historical truth" and warned that if they found it unsatisfactory, they would not hesitate to prohibit its distribution in France.[41]

In March 1988, an English writer claimed to have discovered the key to the mystery of why the SS chose Oradour as its target. In *Oradour: Massacre and Aftermath*, the most fanciful retelling of the massacre to date, Robin Mackness told how in 1982 he met a former *maquisard*, whom he called by the pseudonym "Raoul

Denis," who wanted help in smuggling six hundred kilos of gold to Switzerland. Raoul revealed that his *maquis* had ambushed a convoy of the SS division Das Reich in the early morning of 10 June, not far from Oradour. Everyone except Raoul had been killed in the attack. While searching a German truck, Raoul discovered a cache of gold bars, which he buried and returned to dig up after the Liberation.

This book received a favorable response in England. The *Sunday Times Magazine* (London) published a long excerpt.[42] M. R. D. Foot, the leading scholar on English wartime operations in France, judged that until a better explanation could be given, Mackness's account deserved serious consideration. The ANFM, the regional press, local politicians, and French historians took affront. The ANFM declared its intent to block any attempt to publish the book in France. The historian Jacques Delarue, a specialist on Nazi crimes in France, debated Mackness on French radio and effectively demonstrated the incredible nature of his story.

If the need to defend Oradour from exploitation by outsiders is a subject on which everyone in Oradour can agree, it has not been so easy to arrive at a position toward local commercialism related to the ruins. In the early years, the first inhabitants of the new town discouraged efforts to capitalize on the flow of tourists to the ruins. The Historic Monuments Service also kept a vigilant eye on efforts to advertise anywhere near the ruins.[43] A survey taken in 1991 showed that only one-quarter of the visitors to the ruins stop to eat a meal in the new town.[44] People in Oradour today bridle at the accusation that they seek profit from the ruins: "There are a lot of people who say that it's not right because we are living off the dead," remarked the young woman who works in the kiosk at the entrance to the ruins.[45] But as the massacre of Oradour recedes in time, it has become more difficult to deny the wish of Oradour's merchants to attract those who visit the ruins. In recent years, the municipal council has sought to integrate Oradour into regional tourism. The local chamber of commerce established a tourism office in 1993 that is open from June through September. The mayor presented this development as part of the perpetual challenge to balance the demands of the past and the present: "Our old point of view can no longer be defended, and I think we have to accept the fact of tourism in the region. . . . But with a fair amount of decency nonetheless. As long as we are here, we will maintain a certain decency."[46]

For many years, the moratorium on partisan politics in Oradour left a strange mark in the new town. In the center of town, only the street leading from the main square to the ruins had a name: l'avenue du 10 Juin. The six others were designated by number, according to the architect's blueprint. Due to the sharp political feelings in Oradour, when construction was completed, agreement could not be reached on street names. Dr. Lapuelle remembers:

> There was one who said "No, that won't do, we have to call the town square General de Gaulle Square." "Oh, if that's called General de Gaulle Square, the main street, street number three, has to be called Vincent Auriol Street." And then there was, "Michelet was a great resister from the region, we have to call it Michelet Street." But Michelet was very politically engaged. And then another said, "We have to put the names of the former mayors." And then we stopped completely. We left it like that.[47]

Thirty years later, in the mid-1980s, when the municipal council addressed the issue again, it faced the same problem. One suggestion was to name the streets after the plots of land on which they were built. André Desourteaux, a municipal councilor at the time, drew up a list of appropriate Limousin names, but it came to nothing. Most towns in France give at least passing homage to history in the naming of streets.[48] For Oradour, itself a relic of a historical event, any incidental commemoration may have seemed trivial.

In 1992, the town council was finally able to pick names for the numbered streets. Three hark back to an idealized pastoral Oradour: rue des Hortilliers, rue de la Glane, rue des Carderies. Two allude to the character of the town as a martyred village: rue de Charly and rue de Distoman honor two other towns, in the Lorraine and in Greece, whose populations were massacred by the Nazis. The names of one street looks forward: rue de l'Europe. None of these names could be considered controversial. This choice of names reflects Oradour's evolution from a provisional settlement preoccupied with its bitter past to a place that aspires to normality.

By presenting a moment captured in time, the proponents of conservation intended the ruins to be a bulwark against forgetting. But people have not been the only force to act upon the ruins and shape their meaning and history. Over the years the ruins are inexorably shrinking, melting away under the impact of time and weather. As the ruins are eroded by rain and cold they become less a commentary on "Nazi barbarism" and more a general metaphor for broader notions of time, catastrophe, destruction and decay. Though preserved to freeze a specific moment, the ruins also contain the story of their own ephemeral nature and the fragility of human memory.

Jean-François Beaulieu remembered that during his boyhood, the blackened ruins dominated the nascent new town—not only emotionally, but also in terms of the physical area they covered. But now the new town, which has continued to grow, exerts a stronger presence for the people of Oradour. Similarly, as the old-timers of Oradour become fewer, the old town is slowly ceding its place in the community's memory. Yet the relationship of old and new within the landscape of Oradour-sur-Glane is not only a metaphor for change in collective memory; the ruins also influence how people think about the past. The physical deterioration of the ruins has raised a whole set of dilemmas— technical, aesthetic, emotional, and political—for the survivors and their descendents, as well as the architects of the Historic Monuments Service.

Within a decade of the massacre, progressive erosion of the ruins brought to light the technical impossibility of preserving the entire ruins of Oradour forever. In 1958, Pierre Paquet, the Inspector General of Historic Monuments in charge of Oradour, first broached the need for an overall policy regarding conservation of the ruins.[49] In the meantime, the Historic Monuments Service continued to repair the most dilapidated parts of the ruins on a case-by-case basis, with an eye to ensuring the safety of the visitors. Every spring, architects would survey the damage wrought by winter freezing and restore or tear down weakened structures. From their professional point of view, the limited aesthetic and cultural value of the ruins justified this method.[50]

Even without a detailed, long-term plan for the ruins, by 1966 the government architects had decided that the emotional impact of the ruins, rather than the physical integrity of the site, was the most precious quality of the ruins. Yet, as the regional conservator noted in 1966, the appearance of devastation proved most difficult to preserve. The removal of fallen masonry made room for vegetation and created "expanses of lawn" that detracted from the mood of desolation. The rain washed the jagged walls of the smoke and soot of the fire that had consumed the town. As the old town crumbled, the outline of the ruins became softer, smoothed like a seashell washed by the tides.

Extensive restoration created its own problems: "One risks ending up intervening in too visible a way, which would give an artificial character and in the end would alter the character of the site." The conservator judged that the best he could do was to stave off deterioration as unobtrusively as possible: "The only reasonable solution appears to be being content with slowing down the inevitable deterioration of the ruins, and to get to the point where the equilibrium that will be reached some day represents a state still sufficiently evocative of the historic event that it is all about."[51]

The care and maintenance of the ruins proceeded, bit by bit, without much comment or complaint until the early 1980s. Then a widespread public interest in the history of the Vichy years increased the attention given to Oradour. In the 1970s, after years of uneasy quiet on the subject, France's Vichy past had first emerged as a pressing historical issue on the national agenda. Les années noires became the object of intense investigation and open contention in the wake of May 1968 and the departure of General de Gaulle from office. Vigorous probing by filmmakers, writers, and historians broke down any consensus about French behavior during the Occupation. Marcel Ophuls's documentary Le Chagrin et la pitié (The Sorrow and the Pity) marked this turning point in 1971, launching an attack on the cherished myths that had exaggerated the extent of French Resistance and minimized the significance of the Vichy regime. Young French historians soon followed the direction provided by two foreign colleagues, Eberhard Jaeckel and Robert Paxton, in their path-breaking works on the relations between the Vichy government and the Nazi regime.[52] The effects of the new discussion were far-reaching, for, as historian Henry Rousso observed, "Contrary to other periods of reactivation [of the memory of Vichy], in which agitation was localized in a few places (Parliament, court-rooms, the press, or the intelligentsia), the new representations offered at the beginning of the 1970s met a real demand in [public] opinion."[53] French society responded with a fascination and curiosity that Rousso has characterized as a national "obsession."

If the breakdown of taboos surrounding the Occupation permitted an attack on myths about the Resistance, reexamination of the past emboldened the extreme right to make its traditional arguments in public. In 1978 Robert Faurisson, a scholar, and Louis Darquier de Pellepoix, one of the major architects of Vichy's war on the Jews, independently denied the existence of the gas chambers. In 1987 Jean-Marie Le Pen, the leader of the National Front, referred to the extermination in the camps as "a detail of history." In the light of these efforts at revisionism, Oradour took on renewed importance as physical proof of Nazi crimes.

In the early 1980s, with public sensibility heightened by the approach of the fortieth anniversary of the Liberation, the French courts once again became the forum for excavating the crimes of the Occupation. The amnesties of 1951 and 1953 had submerged the strife of the purges. But in the early 1980s, the application of the law on crimes against humanity permitted the courts to bring charges not only against Germans but against Vichy officials as well. The names Touvier, Leguay, Bousquet, Papon, names heretofore bathed in obscurity, became well known to readers of the French press.

The Limousin also lived through another episode in the postwar search for justice. In 1983 Heinz Barth, a junior officer who had participated in the massacre at Oradour, was brought to trial in East Berlin. Once again, a delegation from the ANFM went to face the accused in court. Barth, who had nothing to offer in the way of new information about the massacre, was sentenced to life imprisonment in East Germany. Outside the Limousin, the trial of Heinz Barth was hardly noticed, overshadowed by the extradition of Klaus Barbie, the former Gestapo chief of Lyons, from Bolivia and his arrival on 5 February in France, where he was indicted for crimes against humanity. There was an enormous expectation that the Barbie trial would reopen old wounds that many of the French had tried to forget. The race against time to bring these war criminals to justice increased awareness that members of the generation that had lived through the war were getting old and dying. The survival of memory itself suddenly seemed at stake.

These concerns revitalized the political and moral message of the memorial of Oradour. Yet renewed appraisals of Oradour also showed the failure of the physical site to withstand the test of time. By 1983, government funding for maintaining the site had dwindled to the point that brambles and nettles had encroached on the town gardens and open spaces in the ruins had turned into grassy lawns. The prefect urged that something be done to allay the impression of desertion:

For our country it is a matter of a showcase of an international dimension which it is unthinkable to leave in its current state—all the more since a record crowd seems to be expected in the course of the next months; taking into
consideration the public's increasing sensitivity to the events
of the last war after the arrest of Klaus Barbie; and most of
all, the trial of one of the principal men accountable for the
massacre at Oradour-sur-Glane, Heinz Barth, which just
took place in East Berlin.[54]

Those responsible for conserving the site declared an urgent
need for a long-term plan for the ruins.

In August 1983, Gabor Mester de Parajd, the principal architect responsible for Oradour, submitted a general study of
Oradour to the regional representative of the Ministry of Culture. Mester de Parajd laid out the problem: "A ruined state is, by
definition, a furtive state, a moment in an evolution, more or less
rapid but irreversible, toward complete disappearance. To conserve ruins in a ruined state thus demands artificial intervention."[55] Considering the size of the site and the condition of the
ruins, Mester deemed it "hardly realistic," if only from a financial
point of view, to attempt to preserve the entire site in a state that
would ensure public safety. He proposed to mark out for attention a route that would include the main road and key sites.
Mester made clear that his only objective was to stabilize and restore a limited portion of the ruins and to preserve the poignant
character of the site: "It is not being considered in this case 'to
improve' the current presentation of the vestiges by seeking to
return the ruins to their state of 1944. Too much erosion has
taken place in 39 years for the result of such intervention, which
moreover would be too expensive, not to be purely contrived."

Greenery would also have to be held in check if the ruins were not to completely lose their impact: "The encroaching vegetation lessens the moving character of the site and softens the testimony [of the ruins]. Can one permit the site to become a place for 'romantic walks'. . . ?"[56] A romantic element would certainly contradict the desired effect, for romantic ruins convey a mood of not-unpleasant melancholy rather than one of horror.

In February 1984, the Minister of Culture, Jack Lang, committed one million francs for the first stage of the project to create a defined circuit through the martyred village, repair ruins along this path, and close off public access to the rest of the town. The ANFM and the town council of Oradour approved the plan in time to prepare the site for the fortieth anniversary of the massacre. A billboard posted by the Ministry of Culture at the northern entrance to the ruins let the public know that Oradour had not been forgotten.

While the government architects saw the dilemma of conservation from a technical and aesthetic point of view, the problem presented itself more painfully to those with an emotional investment in the site. For the generation that knew the old town, contemplating the deterioration and eventual disappearance of the ruins is like witnessing the disappearance of their own past. The old-timers of Oradour worry about the future of the ruins, which are indeed changing before their eyes, as Marcel Darthout admits:

> I think that the ruins have to be kept. . . . It's necessary. But they are going to evolve. I'm afraid of that. I'm afraid they're changing. On the one hand they're going to fall down, they're going to collapse—or it will be necessary to put in a lot of money to protect them. What they're going to become,

I don't know. Will they become in a few years like what one
sees at the ruins of a chateau or for that matter a fortress? . . .
Are they going to become like that? I wouldn't want that.
That's the goal of our Association, not to forget. That the
ruins don't become lifeless. One would like to make them—
to make them live again. It's awful.[57]

It is almost as if the ruins mock the very effort of this particular
commemoration, as their progressive erosion reveals the impossibility of fixing both time and memory.

Continued restoration raises a dilemma that has dogged the
ruins of Oradour from the start; if the ruins are taken as historical truth in and of themselves, any attempt at preservation that
introduces artificial elements also risks falsifying history. The extent to which the issue of authenticity inheres in the very origins
of the commemoration at Oradour was dramatically illustrated
in 1988, when restoration experts came to study how to halt the
decay of the car of Dr. Desourteaux. The rusted body of the
sedan, which stands on the edge of the marketplace, has enormous symbolic value in the portrayal of Oradour's destruction. It
evokes the moment when the town doctor, Dr. Jacques Desourteaux, returned from attending a patient in the countryside to
find his town in the hands of the Nazis. Like the ruins, the car of
Dr. Desourteaux had been continuously exposed to the weather,
and the corroded orange shell seemed to be sinking into the
ground. The technical experts discussed a number of options to
prolong its life without producing an artificial effect. But the car
over which they leaned, like surgeons over a body on an operating table, was not the car of Dr. Desourteaux at all.

The facts are common knowledge among the old-timers of
Oradour. When Dr. Desourteaux arrived at the entrance to town,

soldiers forced him to drive up the main street and stop across from the marketplace, where he joined the assembled townspeople. He died with the others that afternoon. A few weeks later, the doctor's brother and his nephew moved the Desourteaux car to the family property, where it still lies inside the garden wall. The car on the marketplace actually belonged to the wine merchant. When the rescue teams came to clear the ruins, they found this car blocking the road and moved it out of the way, onto the marketplace. Over time, it became referred to as the car of Dr. Desourteaux.[58] The Historic Monuments Service invested considerable time and resources to preserve "the car of Dr. Desourteaux." In 1992, after completing a detailed study, restoration experts dismantled the wreck, sanded the body, painted the interior with tar to prevent further decay, and waxed the outside to repel moisture.[59]

The story of Dr. Desourteaux's car is emblematic of the contradictions facing Oradour as a monument. As time goes by, the artificial will continue to encroach upon the real as long as conservation remains a priority. Conservation thus risks undermining the basic premise for preserving the ruins—for it was their authentic character that was supposed to give them meaning.

If the ruins change, become unrecognizable, or disappear, according to the logic of the monument, so too can memory. The old-timers who knew the site as it appeared in the first years after the massacre are faced with the irrefutable evidence that time erodes and alters even the most carefully guarded memories. With the passing of the generation of survivors, it is the fading of memory itself that worries the people who care about Oradour.

In March 1988, Marguerite Rouffanche, the sole survivor of the massacre in the church and the only female *miraculé*, died at

FIGURE 22

The "car of Dr. Desourteaux" on the marketplace.

FIGURE 23

The real car of Dr. Desourteaux, next to the garden wall
of his former house.

FIGURE 24

The ruins of Oradour, preserved as a historic monument.

the age of ninety-two. In the driving rain of a spring thunderstorm, members of the ANFM accompanied the funeral procession as it passed through the southern entrance to the ruins. The hearse carried her body past the church and the window from which she had jumped to save her life forty-four years earlier. It continued on through the ruins to the cemetery, where the coffin was placed in front of the ossuary holding the ashes of those who died in the massacre. The members of the funeral party passed in front of the coffin and sprinkled it in turn with holy water. In a quiet discussion at the end of the ceremony, Amélie Lebraud expressed her sense of loss in an anxious voice: "After us, who will remember?" Indeed, every commemorative effort faces a severe test when it is no longer sustained by the memories of the people who experienced the event. All monuments face what the art historian Kurt Forster has called "a kind of historical double jeopardy: memory is all that sustains its meaning but its physical form will have to survive the vagaries of changing perceptions and values."[60] Oradour is proving to be no exception to this rule.

AFTERWORD

The sustaining narrative of Oradour was created half a century ago. It has not been revised. The cultural context in which it is embedded, however, has changed radically. The French do not now consider themselves to have been an entirely innocent people in the 1930s and 1940s.

When the memorial at Oradour was built, the French, under de Gaulle's leadership, were engaged in selecting not only what they would remember but what they would forget. Justification was provided in advance by the great French historian Ernest Renan. Writing in 1882, he remarked on the benefits of letting go, of forgetting "ugly or violent deeds" for the sake of national unity:

> It is good for everyone to know how to forget. . . . Forgetting, I would even go so far as to say historical error, is a crucial factor in the creation of a nation, which is why progress in historical studies often constitutes a danger for [the principle of] nationality. . . . The essence of a nation is that all individuals have

many things in common, and also that they have forgotten
many things. No French citizen knows whether he is a Bur-
gundian, an Alan, a Taifale, or a Visigoth, yet every French
citizen has to have forgotten the massacre of Saint
Bartholomew, or the massacres that took place in the Midi in
the thirteenth century.[1]

As Renan observed, telling the story of the nation, whether in
prose or in commemorative ceremony and memorialization, en-
tails choosing to recall certain events publicly and not to speak
about other events. In this sense, commemoration includes not
only the organization of memory but the organization of silences
as well. This dynamic relationship played out broadly in the national commemoration of the experience of the Second World
War, and specifically in the case of Oradour. Just as, according to
Renan, the French citizen needs to have forgotten the massacre
of St. Bartholomew, so the National Assembly in 1953 needed to
forget the participation of Alsatians in the massacre at Oradour.

Those who would evade or suppress the history of the Vichy
period held sway until the upheaval of May 1968. The " '68–ers"
were members of the first generation born after the war. Their
rebellion included demands for truth from their elders about the
war years. The French writer and literary critic Pierre Sollers
evocatively described the moment: "It is only around 1964–1966
that one can consider that memory returned, that one could no
longer truncate it or anesthetize it. . . . And then it was the explosion of May 1968, where real memory, contained for so long,
repressed, came to write itself on the walls, fly with the paving
stones [hurled by the protesters]."[2] The uprising brought about
the political demise of Charles de Gaulle and knocked French
society out of kilter. Then, no longer sheltered by de Gaulle's

presence and his reassuring vision of France as a nation of resisters, faced with the first eruption of the Touvier affair in 1972,
under pressure from filmmakers, writers, and historians, French
legends about the war began to crumble.[3]

In the 1980s the misdeeds of the Vichy regime were being
publicly remembered—yet ambivalence remained. In the many
pronouncements on the Vichy past, one found division and ambivalence on the question of whether the Vichy regime was a
French phenomenon with its roots in France or was entirely imposed from outside. For example, the role of the Vichy regime in
the deportation of Jews from France has been placed on the government's commemorative agenda. In February 1993, President
François Mitterrand declared 16 July, the anniversary of the
1942 roundup of the Jews of Paris by the French police at the
Vélodrome d'Hiver, a "national day to commemorate the racist
and anti-Semitic persecutions committed under the de facto authority of the so-called . . . 'French government' (1940–1944)."
Nonetheless, this statement remained equivocal; it implied that
the Vichy government had been an illegitimate authority, restat-
ing the President's opinion that the current French Republic had
nothing to answer for.[4] But by the early 1990s a significant portion of the French public no longer accepted this interpretation,
and Mitterrand's statement was roundly criticized. Nor have de
Gaulle's efforts to link the experiences of the two world wars survived. Indeed, in recent years, parts of the legacies of the two
world wars have been at cross-purposes. For the post-World
War II generations, Pétain's role as France's betrayer at Vichy
overshadows his reputation as the hero of Verdun. In 1981, Mitterrand instituted the tradition of laying an official wreath at
Pétain's grave on 11 November, Armistice Day; but by 1992,

increasing public disapproval caused the Elysée Palace to end this annual tribute.

In 1995, Jacques Chirac became the first French president to publicly address and deplore the role of the French state in the wartime deportation of Jews from France. In July 1995, at the commemorative ceremony of the roundup at the Vélodrome d'Hiver, the newly elected president spoke forcefully of the French authorities' role in this event. In his speech, Chirac indicated that he was saying something that "everyone knows."[5] Chirac's remark acknowledged the sea change, since the mid-1970s, in public awareness of the misdeeds and injustices of the Vichy period.

As the French come to acknowledge the role of the French state in wartime persecutions, the power of a story of the martyrdom of innocents cannot remain unaffected. The commemorative message of Oradour has remained unchanged from its original formulation. Meanwhile, a new generation of French historians has been excavating French experience of the war and no longer reinforcing its myths, thus promising that the biography of the nation for the years 1940–1944 will soon be thoroughly rewritten. It is still unclear where the tale of the *village martyr* of Oradour will be fitted into the larger story. The ANFM remains vigilant, but its members face inescapable evidence—the deterioration of the ruins—of a threat to the survival of their memorial. The municipal council of Oradour and the survivors and their children have enlisted government support for finding new ways to keep alive the memory of the massacre and to pass it on to future generations.

In 1989, the town council, together with the general council of the Haute-Vienne, decided to create "a cultural companion" to the ruins. They asked a Paris consulting agency that specializes in *l'ingénierie culturelle* (cultural engineering) to prepare a plan for a museum in Oradour. In September 1993, with the approach of the fiftieth anniversary of the massacre, Minister of Culture Jacques Toubon announced that the state would provide half of the 34 million francs needed to create a Memory Center (Centre de la Mémoire) at Oradour. On 10 June 1994, after President François Mitterrand and Prime Minister Edouard Balladur joined in commemorative ceremonies at Oradour on the occasion of the fiftieth anniversary of the massacre, the mayor presented a model of the Memory Center to the Prime Minister. The groundbreaking for the Memory Center took place less than three years later, in April 1997. This renewed commitment from the government to the memorial site of Oradour indicates that, while new stories about the Vichy past are being folded into official commemoration, older stories are not being abandoned.

The museum project for Oradour is consonant with the general evolution of the presentation of twentieth-century history. The desire to perpetuate the memory of the recent past has led to the building of memorial-museums that combine an intense commemorative and moral message with the presentation of historical information. The German concentration camp sites, the Memorial of the Battle of Normandy, the Musée pour la Paix at Caen, the Holocaust Memorial Museum in Washington, D.C., and the museum proposed for Oradour are part of a trend in public history that intentionally blurs distinctions between history and memory. Such museums may have great value in making the viewer conscious of the extent to which history is an interpretation of the past and therefore always represents a certain point of view. But they have been criticized on the grounds that the reverence inspired by memory compromises the critical and analytical reflection of historical investigation.[6]

These memorial-museums also point out the extent to which the state, in providing at least a moral endorsement and often funding them, now considers memory an important form of cultural patrimony. Whereas the long-established *musées nationaux* maintain and display the riches produced by high culture, the new memorial-museums stave off the disappearance of certain memories that are now seen as a threatened national resource. The memorial-museums may come to replace the sites of the Second World War as the focus of commemorative activity. In the case of Oradour, the decision to build a museum reflects the view of the survivors, their children, the town, and the government that the ruins no longer have the power to speak for themselves.

When the wartime generation is gone, historians of the Second World War will be left with four major sources: official records, personal testimonies, physical traces of the events of the war, and the reworking of these events in history, fiction and film. In the case of Oradour, the life of the monument is being prolonged by the efforts to preserve the immediacy of the survivors' testimony; as the physical remains of Oradour erode into the ground, video and voice recordings of survivors' testimony will play an increasingly important role in perpetuating the memory of the massacre and the life of the town before the war. They have a different kind of afterlife than the physical testimony of the ruins and may prove more lasting.

As events of the Second World War recede, public memory of the period is becoming more and more independent of individual recollection. Until now, historians of the Second World

War have been held accountable in their work by people—individuals and associations—who lived through the events they write about. By the turn of the century, most of the survivors of Oradour will be gone. The history of the Second World War will increasingly become the territory of professional storytellers—historians, filmmakers, novelists and writers of historical pot-boilers. In Oradour as elsewhere, they will replace, as the primary interpreters of the recent past, the survivors who have been the historians of their own experience.

NOTES

PREFACE

1. Maurice Halbwachs, *Les Cadres sociaux de la mémoire* (Paris: Librairie Félix Alcan, 1925) and *La Mémoire collective* (Paris: Presses Universitaires de France, 1950). Halbwachs had long been familiar to French historians as one of the original members of the editorial board of the journal *Annales*, founded by Marc Bloch and Lucien Febvre at the University of Strasbourg in 1928.

2. *Cahiers de l'Institut d'histoire du temps présent 4: Questions à l'histoire orale, table ronde du 20 juin 1986* (1986).

3. Particularly useful starting points were: Institut d'histoire du temps présent, *La Mémoire des Français* (Paris: Editions du Centre National de la Recherche Scientifique, 1986); Alfred Wahl, ed., *Mémoire de la seconde guerre mondiale: actes du colloque de Metz, 6–8 octobre 1983* (Metz: Centre de Recherche Histoire et Civilisation de l'Université de Metz, 1984); *History and Anthropology 2: Between Memory and History* (1986); and the general overviews provided by Henry Rousso in *Le Syndrome de Vichy, 1944–198 ...* (Paris: Editions du Seuil, 1987) and Gérard Namer, *Batailles pour la mémoire: la commémoration en France de 1945 à nos jours* (Paris: S.P.A.G./Papyrus, 1983).

4. Pierre Nora, "Between Memory and History: *Les Lieux de Mémoire*," trans. Marc Roudebush, *Representations* 26, *Special Issue: Memory and Counter-Memory* (Spring 1989), 25.

5. Pierre Nora, ed., *Les Lieux de mémoire*, vol. 1, *La République* (Paris: Gallimard, 1984), x. For a trenchant analysis of Nora's project see Steven Englund, "The Ghost of Nation Past," *Journal of Modern History* 64 (1992): 299–320.

6. In particular, David Lowenthal, *The Past Is a Foreign Country* (Cambridge: Cambridge University Press, 1985); J. B. Jackson, *The Necessity for Ruins, and Other Topics* (Amherst: University of Massachusetts Press, 1980); Yi-Fu Tuan, *Space and Place: The Perspective of Experience* (Minneapolis: University of Minnesota Press, 1977); Gaston Bachelard, *The Poetics of Space*, trans. Maria Jolas (New York: The Orion Press, Inc., 1964).

7. See in particular: Primo Levi, *The Drowned and the Saved* (New York: Vintage Books, 1989), chapter one; James E. Young, *Writing and Rewriting the Holocaust: Narrative and the Consequences of Interpretation* (Bloomington: Indiana University Press, 1988); Shoshanna Felman, "A l'âge du témoignage: "*Shoah* de Claude Lanzmann" in *Au sujet de Shoah*, ed. Michel Deguy (Paris: Belin, 1990), 55–145; Lawrence L. Langer, *Holocaust Testimonies: The Ruins of Memory* (New Haven: Yale University Press, 1991).

8. James E. Young, *The Texture of Memory: Holocaust Memorials and Meaning* (New Haven: Yale University Press, 1993).

9. *Oradour. First part, Les Voix de la douleur;* second part, *Aujourd'hui la mémoire (1989; color, 104 min.)*, written by Marc Wilmart and directed by Michel Follin. Produced by FR3 Limousin-Poitou-Charente and the Conseil Général de la Haute-Vienne.

INTRODUCTION

1. The analytic philosopher Ian Hacking offers a tantalizing explanation for the evocative power this term currently holds: "We have learned how to replace the soul with knowledge, with science. Hence

spiritual battles are fought, not on the explicit ground of the soul, but on the terrain of memory, where we suppose that there is such a thing as knowledge to be had." Ian Hacking, *Rewriting the Soul: Multiple Personality and the Sciences of Memory* (Princeton: Princeton University Press, 1995), 5.

2. James E. Young suggests we think of "collected" rather than "collective" memory in order to stress the plural, multiple nature of memory, even when there are efforts to shape these points of view into a unified story. Young, *Texture of Memory*, xi.

3. For a lucid overview of class and group memory, commemoration, and narrative styles in the transmission of social memory, see James Fentress and Chris Wickham, *Social Memory* (Oxford: Blackwell, 1992).

4. Robert Frank, "Bilan d'une enquête," in *La Mémoire des Français*, ed. Institut d'Histoire du Temps Présent (Paris: Edition du Centre National de la Recherche Scientifique, 1986), 377.

5. Antoine Prost, "Les Monuments aux morts: culte républicain? culte civique? culte patriotique?" in *Les Lieux de mémoire*, ed. Pierre Nora (Paris: Gallimard, 1984–1993), vol. 2, pt. 3: 199. The commune is the smallest administrative unit in France. It is run by a mayor, his deputies, and a municipal council.

6. Acquiescing to the desire of French families, the French government agreed to pay for the return of soldiers' remains to their home towns. Parents or widows who agreed to leave their dead in a battlefield cemetery had a yearly visit paid for by the government. For the families of those whose bodies were never found or identified, the name of the loved one, carved on the local *monument aux morts*, substituted for a tombstone. Daniel Sherman, "Art, Commerce, and the Production of Memory in France after World War I" in *Commemorations: The Politics of National Identity*, ed. John R. Gillis (Princeton: Princeton University Press, 1994), 189.

7. For an illuminating discussion of de Gaulle's philosophy and use of history, see François Bédarida, "L'Histoire dans la pensée et dans l'action du général de Gaulle," in *De Gaulle en son siècle, actes des journées*

internationales tenues à l'Unesco, Paris, 19–24 novembre 1990 (Paris: Institut Charles de Gaulle, 1991), vol. 1: 141–49.

8. The date of 11 November carried with it the intense commemorative tradition of the interwar years that honored France's enormous sacrifices during the Great War.

9. He said: "See here these dead returned . . . symbols of so many, many others who chose the same glory with the same humility, grouped around him, whose name is known only to God, underneath the flame that represents the flower of our race cut down in the first battles of this thirty years' war." cited in Namer, *Batailles pour la mémoire*, 137–38.

10. My description of the ceremony is summarized from Namer, *Batailles pour la mémoire*, 127–41.

11. The choice of these particular fifteen avoided reference to those aspects of 1939–1945 that earned these years the name *les années noires*. As Namer notes: "The dead testified to the care taken to represent women fighters and also the care to leave in the shadows prisoners, people sent to work in Germany, and people deported because of their race (*déportés raciaux*). Namer, *Batailles pour la mémoire*, 141.

12. Although the national memorial at Douaumont, near Verdun, was a site of commemoration and pilgrimage for the *anciens combattants* of the First World War, the battlefields were left to grow over. The fact that the visitor can still see scars on the land testifies to the relentless blasting of the earth during the war rather than to any attempt to maintain the site.

13. French military losses for WWI reached a total of 1,397,800. See Jean-Jacques Becker, *The Great War and the French People* (Dover, N.H.: Berg Publishers, 1985), 330. For the Second World War, military losses (*militaires tués au combat ou morts de leurs blessures*) equaled 170,000. In addition, 40,000 prisoners died in Germany. The number of French civilian deaths was 150,000. Jean-Pierre Rioux, *The Fourth Republic, 1944–1945*, trans. Godfrey Rogers (Cambridge, Cambridge University Press), 18.

14. Hans Werner Dannowski et al., *Kirche in der Stadt: Erinnern und Gedenken* (Hamburg: Stienmann and Steinmann, 1991).

15. They were Christ Church, Newgate, and St. Dunstan-in-the-East. The stones of a third, St. Mary Aldermanbury, were shipped to the campus of Westminster College in Fulton, Missouri. It was at this college that Churchill delivered his famous "Iron Curtain" speech in 1946, and the rebuilt ruin is a monument to him. Gerald Cobb, *London City Churches* (London: B. T. Batsford, 1989), 174. See also *Bombed Churches as War Memorials*, with a foreword by Hugh Casson, the Dean of St. Paul's (Cheam, Surrey: The Architectural Press, 1945).

16. The villages around Verdun that were completely destroyed in battle prefigure the martyred villages of the Second World War. For example, at the site of Vaux there stands a simple stone marker inscribed with these words of Poincaré: "Passerby, go tell other peoples that this village died to save Verdun so that Verdun could save the world." In 1919, the city of Verdun had considered maintaining destroyed areas *à l'état de ruine* (in a ruined state). The same year, Churchill proposed that the Imperial War Graves Commission acquire the ruins of Ypres from the Belgian government and preserve them as a monument. Both these plans came to naught.

ONE. THE MASSACRE

1. Direction Régionale des Affaires Culturelles (DRAC), Limoges, Oradour-sur Glane, étude sur la fréquentation du site, note d'analyse, 1992 (Office of the Director, DRAC, Limoges, photocopy).

2. Archives Départementales de la Haute-Vienne (ADHV) 6M 157, Liste nominative du recensement de la population d'Oradour-sur-Glane. Oradour was home to two butchers, two grocers, two bakers, a pastry maker, four hairdressers, three mechanics, two tailors, two masons, a blacksmith, six carpenters, three welldiggers, four electricians, two wheelwrights, seven glovemakers, two clogmakers, and fourteen farmers.

3. As geographers and historians have noted, this was the typical form of settlement in the Limousin; at the time of the war, the majority of the department's 350,000 inhabitants lived in hamlets or isolated villages. The central portion of the department of the Haute-Vienne

(where Oradour was located) was one of the more populated areas, averaging sixty people per square kilometer. The remoter regions of the southeast averaged fewer than thirty-five. Françoise Pastaud, "Contribution à l'étude des maquis F.T.P.F. en Haute-Vienne" (mémoire de maîtrise, Université de Poitiers, 1969), 23.

4. Pierre Vallin, a historian of the rural Limousin, cites the period of 1900–1910 as the time when the bourgs superseded the villages as the centers of social life. Villages suffered irreparably from rural migration, but towns such as Oradour prospered. The Limousin region has long suffered from a poor economy, contributing to a large migration from the department that began after World War I. The population of the department peaked in 1911 at 385,000 inhabitants; by the outbreak of World War II, it had declined to 350,000. "It was thus," writes Vallin, "that the fêtes organized in the *chef-lieu* of the commune took precedence over village festivities." Pierre Vallin, *Paysans rouges du Limousin* (Paris: L'Harmattan, 1985), 266.

5. Albert Hivernaud, *Petite histoire d'Oradour-sur-Glane* (Limoges: Imprimerie A. Bontemps, 1985), 36, says that fourteen men were working in Germany as part of the Service du Travail Obligatoire (STO), and eighty-two were prisoners of war.

6. Marcel Darthout, interview by Marc Wilmart at St-Victurnien, 7 March 1988. M. Darthout was twenty years old in 1944. In 1942, in order to avoid the STO, he found a job near Oradour working at a peat-bog.

7. Camille Bardet, interview by Marc Wilmart at La Grange du Boeil, 8 March 1988.

8. ADHV 187W/199. Fifty Alsatians came to Oradour in September 1939.

9. "Il y a 50 ans, l'évacuation . . . 380,000 Alsaciens hôtes obligés du Sud-Ouest," *Le Monde*, 31 August 1989. This little-known episode in the history of the Second World War was recently the subject of a documentary film: *Les Ya-Ya* (1989; color, 52 minutes), written by Alain Dugrand and Monique Seeman and directed by Alfred Elter. Produced by FR3, Alsace. The history of French-French encounters caused by the

war (both the forced evacuation of 1939 and the exodus of civilians from the northern half of France in June 1940) remains to be written.

10. H. R. Kedward, *Resistance in Vichy France: A Study of Ideas and Motivations in the Southern Zone, 1940–1942* (Oxford: Oxford University Press, 1978), 7. The population of the department tripled. Pastaud, "Contribution à l'étude," 26.

11. ADHV 185W1/49. According to the prefecture of the Haute-Vienne, there were 105 French refugees in Oradour in January 1943.

12. Pierre Poitevin cites 1,680 *cartes d'alimentation* distributed each month to the population of the entire commune in 1944. Poitevin, *Dans l'enfer d'Oradour* (Limoges: Société des Journaux et Publications du Centre, 1945), 18. Statistics compiled from archival material suggest 1,624 in 1943 (1,574 [census 1936] + 105 French and foreign refugees [ADHV 185W 1/49] − 55 prisoners in Germany = 1,624). Comité scientifique, "Dossier pour l'exposition permanente," Centre de la Mémoire du Village Martyr d'Oradour-sur-Glane (Conseil Général de la Haute-Vienne, Limoges, 13 June 1995, photocopy), 5–8.

13. Pierre Poitevin, *Dans l'enfer*, 219.

14. In 1941, Vichy replaced municipal officials considered politically suspect (in 1939 the majority of France's cities were dominated by the socialists [Section Française de l'Internationale Ouvrière, or SFIO] and the communists [PCF] with the *délégations spéciales*, made up of people more sympathetic to the National Revolution). Dr. Desourteaux, a Radical Socialist, represented a small conservative party that had little support in the department and the Limousin in general. On the far left of republicanism at the outset of the Third Republic, the Radicals had grown more moderate in the 1890s. Their outlook remained, nonetheless, egalitarian, positivist, anti-clerical, and patriotic. In the middle years of the Third Republic, as political power shifted from the middle strata of the bourgeoisie to the petite bourgeoisie, the Radicals became the party of small shopkeepers, white-collar workers, schoolteachers, and lesser civil servants. The years 1898 to 1914 marked the height of radicalism in the Limousin and its subsequent dissolution in the face of socialism.

By 1928, the Socialists in turn were facing a forceful challenge from the Communist Party. In 1936 Oradour elected a Socialist mayor, Joseph Beau. The Vichy regime removed him and placed Dr. Desourteaux at the head of the *délégation spéciale*.

15. Roger Godfrin, interview by Marc Wilmart at Bas-Ham (Moselle), 22 March 1988.

16. André Pinède, a nine-year-old Jewish boy, lived with his two older sisters (aged eighteen and twenty-two) and parents at the Hôtel Avril. The parents went to the marketplace and died in the massacre. The three Pinède children hid for hours under the steps of a wing of the hotel. Later in the day, as they made their way through gardens toward the woods, they were stopped by a German sentinel, who then let them pass.

17. Testimonies on this vary. Some accounts speak of five hostages (Poitevin, *Dans l'enfer*), others fifty (Jacques Delarue, *Trafics et crimes sous l'occupation* [Paris: Fayard, 1968]). In *Oradour, ville martyre* (Paris: Editions Mellottée, 1945), Franck Delage says that there is no absolutely precise testimony about the exchange between the SS officer and Mayor Desourteaux. The exact sequence of events is also unclear. It is not known for sure whether the demand for hostages came before or after the questioning about arms. Also, some accounts describe the women and children being led off before the questioning, while others indicate that it happened after.

18. They were Marcel Darthout, Yvon Roby, Robert Hébras, Robert Borie, Clément Broussaudier, and Pierre-Henri Poutaraud. They were all between the ages of eighteen and twenty-two.

19. Darthout interview, 7 March 1988.

20. After the massacre, the delegate mayor listed a total of 328 buildings destroyed: 123 houses, four schools, one tramway station, twenty-six workshops, nineteen garages, thirty-five sheds for farm equipment, forty barns, fifty-eight hangars, and twenty-two stores. Delage, *Oradour, Ville martyre*, 46.

21. The exact number of deaths has never been established due to the state of the bodies. The figure of 642 is the official death toll given by the civil tribunal of Rochechouart on 28 May 1946. Only fifty-two

bodies were identified and declared legally dead. The others, burned beyond recognition, were listed as missing.

22. Those not from Oradour or the region included forty-four refugees from the eastern department of the Moselle, seven Alsatians, nineteen Spaniards, three Poles and seven Italians. This count is an amalgam of figures cited in Hivernaud, *Petite histoire*, 50, and provided by André Desourteaux.

23. This estimate was provided by André Desourteaux, who has made an approximate but detailed list of the survivors. Members of the Mouvements Unis de la Résistance (MUR) who visited Oradour on 12 June located thirty-six survivors. Mouvement de Libération Nationale, *Les Huns à Oradour* (Limoges: La Société P.E.R.F.R.A.C., 25 January 1945), 78, and Delarue, *Trafics et crimes*, 433.

24. Today, people from the region recall that in the years after the massacre some villages had no more children: "You have villages where all the children died. . . . Think about that. Those children who left in the morning for school and who didn't come back. . . . What were the reactions of those people? The woman who left in search of her children and who was made to enter the bourg and who was killed. The man who found himself all alone. Families that . . . found themselves with nothing, villages where there wasn't a child left." André Desourteaux, interview (with Robert Hébras) by Marc Wilmart at Javerdat, 17 March 1988.

25. Albert Valade, interview by Marc Wilmart at Oradour-sur-Glane, 3 June 1988.

26. Desourteaux interview, 17 March 1988.

TWO. FRAMING THE STORY

1. ADHV 993W572, Departmental Review of Civil Defense, notes and reports, Commander Saulnier de Praigney, Departmental Inspector of Civil Defense. Journalist Pierre Poitevin accompanied the rescue squads from Limoges and gives a detailed, first-hand account of their activity in *Dans l'enfer d'Oradour.*

2. Poitevin, *Dans l'enfer*, 97.

3. ADHV 896W/481, Report Renseignements Généraux, 16 June 1944.

4. ADHV 896W/481, report from Regional Prefect Freund-Valade, 15 June 1944.

5. ADHV 896W/481, Déclaration de son Excellence Monseigneur Rastouil, Evêque de Limoges. This undated report was written sometime between late June and December 1944, when it was printed in the appendices of the first books about the atrocity.

6. Poitevin, *Dans l'enfer*, 99.

7. Poitevin, *Dans l'enfer*, 119-20.

8. ADHV 896W/481, letter from the director of the civilian cabinet (Tracou) to the Regional Prefect, 29 June 1944.

9. ADHV 896W/481, tract found 20 June in a mailbox in the neighborhood of the town hall in Limoges, "Le Crime horrible des hitleriens à Oradour-sur-Glane."

10. ADHV 896W/481, "Le Crime horrible des hitlériens à Oradour-sur-Glane." The "Milice" was a French parapolice organization that aided the Nazis in fighting the Resistance. "Boches" is a derogatory French term for the Germans.

11. Delarue, *Trafics et crimes*, 432.

12. Yves Durand and Robert Vivier, *Libération des pays de Loire: Blésois, Orléanais, Touraine* (Paris: Librairie Hachette, 1974), 21.

13. The word *maquis* refers to the scrub land of Corsica, where historically rebels would hide out. In 1941-44, *maquis* came to mean the underground Resistance forces living in isolated areas. Its members were known as *maquisards*.

14. Hoover Institution Archives, World War II Subject Collection, Box 10, #246.

15. Pierre Limagne, *Ephémérides de quatre années tragiques*, 3 vols. (Paris: Bonne Presse, 1987), cited by Henri Amouroux, *La Grande histoire des français sous l'occupation* (Paris: Robert Laffont, 1988), 8:180.

16. Archives Nationales (AN) F4135, Fonds de l'information, conservé en date de 28 juin, communication non datée, dossier bulletin d'écoutes.

17. *Les Lettres françaises* was the newspaper of the Resistance group Comité National des Ecrivains, founded by Jacques Decour (a professor in a *lycée*, member of the PCF, and editor, before the war, of the literary magazine *Commune*), Jean Paulhan, and Jacques Debu-Bridel. Decour was arrested and shot on 30 May 1942. The first issue of *Les Lettres françaises* was published on 20 September 1942.

18. "Sur les ruines de la morale: Oradour-sur-Glane," *Les Lettres françaises*, numéro spécial, 1 August 1944. When Georges Duhamel provided Paillet's testimony to *Les Lettres françaises*, Paul Eluard decided to create a special edition of twenty thousand copies.

19. Marc Bernard, "Oradour-sur-Glane, le bourg exterminé," *Le Centre libre, organe des Comités de Libération*, 24 August 1944.

20. Richard Cobb, *French and Germans, Germans and French: A Personal Interpretation of France under Two Occupations, 1914–1918/1940–1944* (Hanover, N.H.: University Press of New England, 1983) 10.

21. Cobb, *French and Germans*, 54.

22. The Gouvernement Provisoire de la République Française (GPRF) succeeded the Conseil Française de la Libération Nationale on 2 June 1944.

23. "*Français, n'oubliez jamais:* Ascq/Châteaubriant/Oradour-sur Glane," *Ce Soir* (Paris), 22 August 1944. Another example, among many, of this kind of listing of atrocities can be found in the introduction to a small book about the martyred village of Maillé: ". . . bloody acts carried out by fanatics of the regime: the hanged of NIMES, of TULLE, the burned of ORADOUR, the massacred of ASCQ, of MAILLE. . . ." Abbé André Payon, *Un Village martyr, Maillé: récit du massacre du 25 août 1944* (Tours: Arrault et Cie, 1945).

24. Henri Noguères, *Histoire de la Résistance en France* (Paris: Robert Laffont, 1967–1981), 2:148. The sacrifice of the "martyrs" of Châteaubriant became important in the Communists' commemoration of their role in the Resistance. See Fernand Grenier, *Ceux de Châteaubriant* (Paris: Editions Sociales, 1961), published for the twentieth anniversary of the massacre. A detailed account of the massacre is also provided in the memoirs of Bernard Lecornu, prefect of the Loire-Atlantique in 1941:

Un Préfet sous l'occupation allemande (Paris: Editions France-Empire, 1984), 11–96.

25. One has only to look at commemorative plaques in railway stations throughout France to get an impression of the contribution of French railway workers to the Resistance.

26. Noguères, *Histoire*, 4:595.

27. "La Patrie livrée aux fauves," *Le Franc-Tireur* (Edition de Paris) no. 30, 30 April 1944.

28. AN F1cI/227 (Nord). The monument portrayed a blindfolded figure "symbolizing the sacrifice accepted by Frenchmen." In addition, the Comité Commémoratif du Massacre d'Ascq decided to include a public health clinic as part of the memorial complex. "Dispensaire d'hygiène sociale; ensemble du souvenir d'Ascq," Les Frères Arsène-Henry, Architectes. D.P.E.G., *L'Architecture française* 10, no. 87–88 (1949), 5–12.

29. "La Patrie livrée aux fauves," *Le Franc-Tireur* (édition sud), 1 April 1944; *Les Lettres françaises*, no. 16, May 1944. The accounts here are corroborated by the testimony provided by Henri Noguères, who arrived at Nîmes the afternoon of the massacre and saw the bodies where they were left hanging until nightfall. Noguères, *Histoire*, 4:442–43.

30. Xavier Vallat, radio editorial of 27 July 1944, quoted in Noguères, *Histoire*, 5:132.

31. Sarah Farmer, "The Communist Resistance in the Haute-Vienne," *French Historical Studies* 14, no. 1 (Spring 1985): 89–116. Until 1942, Communist resistance in the Limousin, as in the rest of France, took the form of propaganda against Vichy, strikes, and demonstrations. Pastaud, "Contribution à l'étude," 42.

32. For the impact of the STO on the birth of the *maquis* see H. R. Kedward, *In Search of the Maquis: Rural Resistance in Southern France, 1942–1944* (Oxford: Clarendon Press, 1993), chapters 1 and 2.

33. See Laird Boswell, "Rural Communism in France, 1920–1939 (Ithaca: Cornell University Press, 1998).

34. A schoolteacher and secretary to the mayor of the village of St. Gilles-les-Forêts (Haute-Vienne), Guingouin was among the "resisters

from the first." At the end of 1941 he created one of the first *maquis* in France—a little band armed with hunting rifles and guns from the First World War. See Georges Guingouin, *Quatre ans de lutte sur le sol limousin* (Paris: Hachette, 1974); Georges Guingouin and Gérard Mondèdiare, *Georges Guingouin: Premier maquisard de France* (Limoges: Editions L. Souny, 1983). For a scholarly work that focuses on the *maquis* see Kedward, *In Search of the Maquis*.

35. Pastaud, "Contribution à l'étude," 35.

36. It should be noted that Daniel Mayer did revive the Socialist Party on a national level, forming the Comité d'Action Socialiste (CAS), which was primarily a network of Socialist leaders. But CAS never had any control over networks of resisters or *maquis*. John F. Sweets, *The Politics of Resistance in France, 1940–1944: A History of the Mouvements Unis de la Résistance* (Dekalb: Northern Illinois Press, 1976), 157–62.

37. For the *réfractaires* in the countryside, this often meant enlisting in the FTPF, the Communist guerrilla groups. Headed by Charles Tillon, the FTPF was the armed wing of the Communist Resistance movements. In Limoges (Haute-Vienne), Brive (Corrèze), and the large market towns of the Limousin, non-Communists joined a variety of Resistance organizations operating throughout the southern zone. Catholics tended to form regional committees of Combat, while leaders in Libération and Franc-tireur (not to be confused with the FTPF) were often Socialists. By June 1943 these three groups had fused to form MUR, which allied itself to de Gaulle. Socialists organized the second most important *maquis*, the Armée Secrète (AS), the military branch of MUR, linked to the Free French in London. Officers of the defunct French Army organized the third and smallest resistance group, the Organisation de la Résistance Armée (ORA), which was not particularly active until 1944. Members of ORA tended to support Pétain and could not be convinced to join the Free French. See Delarue, *Trafics et crimes*, 334. By 1943, the AS and ORA formed a strong contingent in the Limousin Resistance. Member groups of MUR carried out isolated acts of sabotage, but before the Allied invasion they did not attempt any broad-based anti-German campaign. Following de Gaulle's

policy, their primary concern was to organize and plan for D-Day and to provide London with intelligence information.

38. Stéphane Courtois, *Le PCF dans la guerre: de Gaulle, la Résistance, Staline* (Paris: Ramsay, 1980), 409.

39. Bernard Beuer Nardain, *Les Francs-tireurs et partisans français et l'insurrection nationale (juin 1940–août 1944)* (Paris: Les Editions Internationales de Presse et de Publicité, 1947), 10. For an exposition of Communist strategy see Charles Tillon, *Les F.T.P., la guerilla en France* (Paris: Juillard, 1967). Stéphane Courtois, *Le PCF dans la guerre*, while giving the PCF credit for being the best organized Resistance movement, attributes to the MUR approximately 75 percent of the actions against Vichy and the German Occupation in the southern zone. Nonetheless, in the Limousin, Communists seem to have clearly been in the forefront, due in large part (as already noted) to the force of personality of Georges Guingouin.

40. Charles de Gaulle, *The Complete War Memoirs of Charles de Gaulle* (New York: Simon and Schuster, 1967), 271–72.

41. Henri Michel, *The Shadow War* (London: Deutsch, 1972), 210.

42. Amouroux, *La Grande Histoire*, 7: 487.

43. John F. Sweets has noted, however, the interesting exception of the Auvergne, where "this pattern was reversed in that the Gaullist MUR, with a larger following in the region, was frequently involved in direct encounters with German troops. . . ." *Choices in Vichy France: The French under Nazi Occupation* (New York: Oxford University Press, 1986), 221.

44. Georges Beau and Léopold Gaubusseau, *R. 5: les S.S. en Limousin, Périgord, Quercy* (Paris: Presses de la Cité, 1969), 241. An agreement on 2 April 1943 between René Bousquet (secretary-general to the head of government for police affairs) and SS General Karl Albrecht Oberg (head of security in France) stipulated that "the French police were solely responsible for French citizens charged with all crimes except direct actions against the German forces; German police, however, could intervene wherever they felt their security was threatened." Robert Paxton, *Vichy France: Old Guard New Order, 1940–1944* (New York: Colombia University Press, 1972), 297.

45. Noguères, *Histoire*, 4:437–438. In December 1943, the German authorities forced Vichy to name Joseph Darnand to the cabinet position of secretary-general for the maintenance of order. From this position, Darnand promoted the Milice, formerly the paramilitary wing of the Veterans' Legion, into a parapolice force of volunteers against the Resistance. Paxton, *Vichy France*, 297–98. The most complete book on the history of the Milice is still J. Delperrie de Bayac, *Histoire de la Milice* (Paris: Fayard, 1969).

46. Amouroux, *La Grande Histoire*, 7:483.

47. Archives Départementales de la Corrèze 58W 2168. The Prefect of the Corrèze to the President of the Cabinet, head of government, 15 April 1944.

48. For the perspective of a child, see the memoir of Claude Morhange-Bégué, a Jewish girl whose family took refuge in the Corrèze. On 8 April, in the wake of "the bloody week," Morhange narrowly escaped capture by the SS. Her mother was arrested and deported. Claude Morhange-Bégué, *Chamberet: Recollections from an Ordinary Childhood*, trans. Austryn Wainhouse (Marlboro, Vt.: The Marlboro Press, 1987).

49. Cited in Amouroux, *La Grande Histoire*, 7:487.

50. Sweets, *Choices in Vichy France*.

51. Beau and Gaubusseau, *R.5*, 21. "Here the German army confronted the most direct hostility from the population. It found in these portions of French territory the same poisonous atmosphere as in the vast stretches of Russia." It seems likely that this designation also referred to the prevalence of Communist Resistance groups.

52. Noguères, *Histoire*, 5:118.

53. Cited in Max Hastings, *Das Reich: Resistance and the March of the 2nd Panzer Division through France, June 1944* (London: Michael Joseph, 1981), 77–79.

54. Subunits of Das Reich were given similar tasks in other parts of France. Battalions of the Infantry regiment Deutschland were sent to the Ariège, and battalions of the Infantry regiment Der Führer to the Pyrénées. Guingouin, *Quatre ans*, 181.

55. *"Halbe Erfolge in solche Aktionen nützen nichts."* Cited in Eberhard Jaeckel, *Frankreich in Hitlers Europa: Die Deutsche Frankreichpolitik im Zweiten Weltkrieg* (Stuttgart: Deutsche Verlags-Anstalt, 1966), 324.

56. Cited in Jaeckel, *Frankreich*, 324, and Noguères, *Histoire*, 5:119.

57. Hastings, *Das Reich*, 22. For an excellent study of the fighting conducted by the German Army in Russia, see Omer Bartov, *The Eastern Front, 1941–1945: German Troops and the Barbarisation of Warfare* (London: Macmillan, in association with St. Anthony's College, Oxford, 1985).

58. Hastings, *Das Reich*, 10–14.

59. Hastings, *Das Reich*, 1. The march of Das Reich and its battles with the Resistance have been treated by Hastings, *Das Reich;* Beau and Gaubusseau, *R. 5;* and Gérard Guicheteau, *La "Das Reich" et le coeur de la France* (Paris: Editions Daniel, L'Echo du Centre, 1974).

60. For an insightful discussion of PCF intentions at the Liberation see Maurice Agulhon, "Les Communistes et la Libération de la France," in *La Libération de la France, actes du colloque international tenu à Paris du 28 au 31 octobre 1974* (Paris: Editions du Centre National de la Recherche Scientifique, 1976), 67–90.

61. Guingouin, *Quatre ans*, 175.

62. Jaeckel, *Frankreich*, 325. There have been allegations that some of the dead had been either tortured or mutilated after death. Noguères, *Histoire*, 2:124. Jaeckel casts doubt on these claims and assertions that it was the alleged atrocities that caused the SS to hang civilians. See Hastings, *Das Reich*, 118–21 for a discussion of the debate over these claims.

63. One hundred eleven of these men died in Dachau, raising the total of civilian deaths at Tulle to 210. Noguères, *Histoire*, 2:125. This kind of atrocity, rare in France, had been common procedure in Russia. This is how, according to the prefect, Pierre Trouillé, the German officer in charge of the reprisal responded to Trouillé's exclamation that hanging was too cruel: "I am sorry, in Russia we took the habit of hanging, we killed more than one hundred thousand men at Kharkov and Kiev, this here is nothing for us." Trouillé, *Journal d'un préfet pendant l'Occupation allemande* (Paris: Gallimard, 1964), 134.

64. Mouvement National Contre le Racisme, *Récits d'atrocités nazies, éditions de la clandestinité* (n.p., 1944).

65. Tzvetan Todorov has recently published a study of the town of St-Amand-Montrond in the department of the Cher (bordering the Limousin), where the attempt of the local FTP to take control of the town on 6 June (as in Tulle) unleashed a bloody settling of scores. *Une tragédie française, été 1944: scènes de guerre civile* (Paris: Editions du Seuil, 1994).

66. Serge Barranx, *Mouleydier, village martyr* (Bordeaux: Editions Bière, 1945).

67. AN 4 AG3, letter from the mayor of the city of Mussidan (Dordogne) to President Auriol, 31 May 1947.

68. Madeleine Vincent and Liseron Vincent-Doucet-Bon, *C'était un village de France . . .* (Lyon: Editions de la Belle Cordière, n.d.), 42.

69. G. Cuny, *La Bresse: Cité vosgienne martyre sous l'Occupation allemande, septembre, octobre, novembre, 1944* (Macon: Buguet-Comptour, Imprimeur-Editeur, 1946), 116–117.

70. Historians Yves Durand and Robert Vivier (who was prefect of the Indre-et-Loire from 1944 to 1948) characterized action in the Loire region this way: "The moderation of general opinion left only a restricted place for passionate engagement in geographically limited centers. Likewise, the absence of hilly territory or isolated areas gave only limited shelter to *maquis.* Nothing here resembled the Vercors, or the Limousin, in the Resistance; nothing comparable to the audaciousness of the revolutionary forces of Toulouse, Marseilles, or Lyon." *Libération des pays de Loire,* 15.

71. Durand and Vivier, *Libération des pays de Loire,* 147.

72. Payon, *Un village martyr, Maillé,* 16–18.

73. Fernand Musso, *Après le raz de marée: témoignage du préfet de Corrèze sur le massacre de Maillé* (Treillières [44240]: Pierre Gauthier Editeur, 1980), 17–23.

74. Payon, *Un village martyr, Maillé,* 10.

75. AN F1cI/223.

76. Centre d'Information et de Presse au Mexique du Gouvernement Provisoire de la République Française, *Terreur en France: les atrocités*

allemandes et vichyistes en France, with a preface by Jacques Berthet (Mexico, D. F.: 1944), 13.

77. "Due to the very activity of the Resistance, it was the R5 that suffered the most severe reprisals: 3,378 shot, 1,374 deported, and more than forty places destroyed, the names of which only a few are known to the public, like Oradour-sur-Glane. . . ." Beau and Gaubusseau, *R.5*, 22.

78. That day, members of the Milice disguised as *maquisards* and riding in a truck marked with the cross of Lorraine, the symbol of the FFI, ambushed and killed eleven FTPF *maquisards*. Three *maquisards* were killed in an initial exchange of gunfire. The rest were taken to the local cemetery and shot. After the war, plaques listing their names were mounted on the *monument aux morts* of St-Victurnien and at the cemetery. Comité de la Haute-Vienne de l'Association Nationale des Anciens Combattants de la Résistance, *Mémorial de la Résistance et des victimes du nazisme en Haute-Vienne* (Limoges: A.N.A.C.R., 1988), 181–183.

79. Pauchou and Masfrand, *Oradour-sur-Glane: vision d'épouvante*, 12.

80. Hivernaud, *Petite Histoire*, 51.

81. Delarue, *Trafics et crimes*, 473.

82. Material facts played a role as well; Tulle remained physically intact. As for the geography of commemoration, the ceremonial focus in Tulle lay beyond the periphery of the civic space. The Germans shoveled the bodies of the men they had hanged into a mass grave by the side of the highway near the town dump, five kilometers outside of town. This is the site of the present-day memorial to the hanged and deported of Tulle, inaugurated in 1950. The monument lies low to the ground and would go unnoticed by the passerby but for a small sign, one hundred yards before the site, that reads: "Silence: Champs des Martyrs."

THREE. CREATING THE MONUMENT

1. The history of the French internment camps, relatively little known until recently, is treated in Anne Grynberg, *Les Camps de la honte: les internés juifs des camps français, 1939–1944* (Paris: Editions la Découverte, 1991), as well as in Monique-Lise Cohen and Eric Malo, eds., *Les*

Camps du sud-ouest de la France, 1939–1944 (Toulouse: Editions Privat, 1994).

2. For an illuminating analysis of these statistics and their reliability see Peter Novick, *The Resistance versus Vichy: The Purge of Collaborators in Liberated France* (New York: Columbia University Press, 1968), Appendix C, 202–8.

3. "Nos martyrs," *Le Populaire, organe du Parti Socialiste, édition de la zone nord*, no. 33, May 1944.

4. "Au pilori," *Le Populaire du Bas-Lanquedoc, Aude, Aveyron, Gard, Hérault, Lozère, Pyrénées-O*, No. 1, October 1943. When one takes into account the severe paper shortage and restrictions placed on length of newspapers, the attention to future reprisals seems all the more remarkable.

5. Novick, *The Resistance*, 71. The extent of popular justice has been the subject of exaggeration and extensive debate. Two official inquiries in 1946 and 1948 concluded that there were a total of 9,673 executions: 5,234 before the landings and 4,439 after. A second inquiry in 1952 arrived at a figure of 10,882 executions of persons suspected of collaboration, 5,143 before the Liberation and 3,724 after. There were 1,955 "victims of murders or executions" for which the motive was not established. Novick, *The Resistance*, 204. These are the figures used by General de Gaulle in *The Complete War Memoirs*, 711. Though historians have questioned these statistics, American historian Peter Novick convincingly challenged the more generous estimates offered by others (in particular, Robert Aron in *Histoire de l'épuration*, 3 vols. [Paris: Fayard, 1967–1975]) and concluded that official figures, "while perhaps representing minima rather than mean figures, must provisionally stand." Novick, *The Resistance*, 208. The Comité d'Histoire de la Deuxième Guerre Mondiale launched an extensive survey on the purges (legal and extralegal). The results from the study of seventy-three departments refine and confirm Novick's. See Marcel Baudot, "L'Epuration: bilan chiffré," *Bulletin de l'Institut d'histoire du temps présent* 25 (September 1986): 37–53. For a recent consideration of the purges and an evaluation of statistics see Henry Rousso, "L'Epuration en France: une histoire

inachevée," *Vingtième siècle* 33 (January–March 1992): 78–105. François Rouquet, *L'Epuration dans l'administration française* (Paris: CNRS Editions, 1993) offers a detailed analysis of the purge of the civil service.

6. Jean-Pierre Rioux, "L'Epuration en France, 1944–1945," in *Etudes sur la France de 1939 à nos jours* (Paris: Editions du Seuil, 1985), 162–77.

7. Rousso, "L'Epuration en France," 83.

8. Marcel Ophuls, *The Sorrow and the Pity: Chronicle of a French City under the German Occupation, a Film*. Introduction by Stanley Hoffman. Filmscript translated by Mireille Johnston. (New York: Outerbridge and Lazard, Inc., 1972), 169. Marguerite Duras offers an urban example of settling of accounts in her collection of autobiographical stories, *La Douleur* (Paris: P.O.L., 1985). The story "Albert des Capitales" recounts the capture and beating of an informer.

9. The government established a central purge committee for the magistrature within two weeks of the Liberation of Paris. Almost twenty percent of the judicial corps passed before the commission, and by January 1945 well over half of these—a total of 266 judges—had been suspended. Novick, *The Resistance*, 86.

10. For a comparative analysis see Novick, *The Resistance*, Appendix D, Comparative Purge Legislation and Court Systems.

11. These figures, cited by Novick, *The Resistance*, 186, are official governmental figures produced in January 1951. They pertain to the work of the civil courts only and not to military tribunals. For a discussion of the discrepancies between official sources in 1948 and 1951, see Rousso, "L'Epuration en France," 90–96.

12. The American observer Janet Flanner described the punishment: "National degradation will consist of being deprived of nearly everything the French consider nice—such as the right to wear decorations, the right to be a lawyer, notary, public-schoolteacher, judge, or even a witness, the right to run a publishing, radio or motion-picture company or bank. As time goes on, few collaborationists are going to be shot and more of them, in their national degradation, will be looking for jobs." Janet Flanner, *Paris Journal, 1944–1965*, ed. William Shawn (New York: Atheneum, 1965), 15.

13. De Gaulle, *The Complete War Memoirs*, 791.

14. Rioux, *The Fourth Republic*, 35–36.

15. This notion remains current among the far Right in France today. See, for example, the special issue on the purge of *Le Crapouillot*, April–May 1985.

16. Rioux, *The Fourth Republic*, 40.

17. ADHV 896W/481, proposal concerning the creation of a provisional committee. . . .

18. ADHV 896W/481, letter to the Mayor of Limoges from M. Georges Frugier-Laverine, 2 October 1944.

19. In a meeting on 12 December 1944, the Comité decided that the original title was too limited and formally took the name "Comité du Souvenir d'Oradour-sur-Glane." Comité du Souvenir, "Procès-verbal de la réunion du 12 décembre 1944," *Procès-verbaux des séances du Comité actif de conservation des ruines et création d'un sanctuaire à Oradour-sur-Glane* (Rochechouart: Imprimerie Justin Dupanier, 1945), 19.

20. Marcel Darthout, interview by Sarah Farmer at St-Victurnien, 31 March 1988. Both Darthout and Montazeaud were in their twenties at the time.

21. Its president was Hubert Desourteaux, the only surviving son of Mayor Paul Desourteaux. He was the uncle of André Desourteaux, mentioned above.

22. ADHV 896W/481, letter from Frugier-Laverine to the Prefect of the Haute-Vienne, 27 February 1945. The ANFM held its first meeting in Oradour on 11 March 1945.

23. Membership was open to "people who suffered, in the wake of war, damage to their property, their housing, or their spirit [*des dommages mobiliers, immobiliers ou moraux*] within the territory of the commune of Oradour s/Glane." The spiritually or psychically damaged (*sinistrés moraux*) included "the descendents of these people, that is, people related to a victim in a direct or indirect line (spouses, descendents, brothers or sisters of their spouses). Association Nationale des Familles des Martyrs d'Oradour-sur-Glane, *Statuts, revus et corrigés après la réunion de bureau du 20 janvier 1945* (Limoges: Imprimerie Charles-Lavauzelle et Cie, n.d.).

24. ADHV 1W/150, extrait du Registre des Arrêtés du Préfet du 13 juin 1944.

25. Archives de la Direction du Patrimoine, Dossier de protection d'Oradour-sur-Glane, letter from Pierre Masfrand, Conservator of the Ruins of Oradour-sur-Glane at Rochechouart, to the Prefect of the Haute-Vienne, 10 October 1944.

26. ADHV 896W/481, letter from the Mayor of Oradour to the Prefect of the Haute-Vienne, 2 October 1944.

27. The Fine Arts Administration (responsible for national cultural institutions and in charge of national historic sites and monuments) was under the auspices of the Ministry of National Education until the creation of the Ministry of Culture in 1959.

28. Comité du Souvenir, "Procès-verbal de la réunion du 21 octobre 1944," *Procès-verbaux, 4.*

29. Ibid., 7–8.

30. Comité du Souvenir, "Procès-verbal de la réunion 14 novembre 1944," *Procès-verbaux, 7.*

31. Comité du Souvenir, "Procès-verbal de la réunion du 21 octobre 1944," *Procès-verbaux, 6–7.*

32. Ibid., 5.

33. Gabor Mester de Parajd, architecte en chef des Monuments Historiques, interview by Sarah Farmer, Versailles, 12 February 1988.

34. ADP, Dossier de protection d'Oradour-sur-Glane, Principal Architect to the General Director of the Fine Arts Administration, 24 October 1944.

35. Bibliothèque du Patrimoine, carton 3174, message from the Minister of National Education, 24 November 1944.

36. ADP, Dossier de protection d'Oradour-sur-Glane, Principal Architect to the General Director of the Fine Arts Administration, 24 October 1944.

37. ADP, Dossier de protection d'Oradour-sur-Glane, General Inspector–Director of Classification and Inspection of Sites, Georges Lestel, Report on the classification as a historic site. . . .

38. Bibliothèque du Patrimoine, carton 3174, telegram from the Minister of National Education (M. René Capitan) to Commissioner of the Republic, Limoges, 28 October 1944.

39. Comité du Souvenir, "Procès-verbal de la réunion du 14 novembre 1944," *Procès-verbaux*, 12.

40. Comité du Souvenir, "Procès-verbal de la réunion du 21 octobre 1944," *Procès verbaux*, 9.

41. Bibliothèque du Patrimoine, carton 3174, the Minister of National Education to the Minister of Urban Planning and Reconstruction, 28 December 1944.

42. Archives du Ministère de l'Equipement et du Logement, Mission auprès des Archives Nationales. AFU 10975, dossier 1, chemise du dossier 1, President of the Government of the Provisional French Republic to the Minister of Reconstruction and Urban Planning. Unfortunately for historians, the presidential archives remain in the hands of the de Gaulle family, which has not yet made available the archives of the first cabinet of the GPRF.

43. ADP, Dossier de protection d'Oradour-sur-Glane, General Inspector–Director of Classification and Inspection of Sites, Georges Lestel, report on the classification as a historic site.

44. "N'oubliez-jamais!" *Ce Soir*, 5 September 1944.

45. "Le souvenir des atrocités," *L'Aurore*, 22 September 1944.

46. ADHV 896W/481, note from the Departmental Railway of the Haute-Vienne to the Chief Engineer, 9 July 1945.

47. Comité du Souvenir, "Procès-verbal de la réunion du 12 décembre 1944," *Procès-verbaux*, 16–17.

48. Charles de Gaulle, *The Complete War Memoirs*, trans. Richard Howard (New York: Simon and Schuster, 1955), 3:679.

49. "Par milliers les Limousins ont acclamé le Général de Gaulle," *Le Libérateur*, 10 March 1945.

50. "Après avoir rendu visite à Limoges, ville de la Résistance dont la population l'acclame, le Général de Gaulle se rend en pèlerinage à Oradour," *La Marseillaise (Berry-Marche-Touraine)*, organe quotidien du CDL de l'Indre, 5 March 1945.

51. *Le Travailleur limousin*, bi-hebdomadaire régional du PCF, 7 March 1945.

52. "Par milliers les Limousins ont acclamé le Général de Gaulle," *Le Libérateur*, 10 March 1945.

53. ADHV 896W/744, Subprefect to the Regional Commissioner of the Republic, 12 February 1945.

54. "Accueil triomphal de Limoges au Général de Gaulle, le chef du gouvernement accomplit un pieux pèlerinage à Oradour," *La Nouvelle République du Centre-Ouest*, 5 March 1945.

55. Ibid. This citation is the fullest given in any of the newspapers that quoted de Gaulle's speech.

56. "Par milliers les Limousins ont acclamé le Général de Gaulle," *Le Libérateur*, 10 March 1945.

57. Ibid. De Gaulle's visit was considered a great success, judging from local press coverage. The only sour note came from the Communist paper, which said that the president's visit had suffered from a malaise that had been developing in the region. *Le Travailleur*, bi-hebdomadaire régional du PCF (n.d.).

58. "La France et les états victimes," *L'Aurore*, 14 October 1944.

59. Rioux, *The Fourth Republic*, 42.

60. Bibliothèque du Patrimoine, carton 3174, Oradour-sur-Glane, ruines du village, affaires générales, 1945–1971.

61. Bibliothèque du Patrimoine, carton 3174, letter from the Minister of National Education to the Regional Commission of the Republic at Limoges, 11 April 1945.

62. Archives du Ministère de l'Equipement et du Logement, Mission auprès des Archives Nationales, AFU 10975, dossier 1, chemise de dossier 3, pièce 3.00.14, note for the Director of Research for Urban Planning, Housing and Construction from the Director of Building Projects, Brunot, received 28 April 1945. Minister of Reconstruction René Dautry reasoned: "Once this transfer is accomplished it will be easy to classify the ruins a historic monument. This *classement* would not have been practically possible as long as there was a multiplicity of owners whose agreement was necessary and who, for the most part, have

disappeared and are no longer represented." Bibliothèque du Patrimoine, carton 3174, Minister of National Education to Minister of the Interior, 11 April 1945. The two ministries agreed to have the Ministry of Reconstruction conduct all the land transfers and purchasing concerning the old and new Oradour. The Reconstruction Service, in the name of the Historic Monuments Service, would expropriate the ruined buildings that had made up the old town and would also buy land on which to build the new town. The Ministry of National Education would ultimately become the owner of the ruins. Once built, the houses of the new town would be used to indemnify the proprietors, or, more likely, their closest surviving relatives. It was agreed that, at some future date, the Ministry of National Education would reimburse the Ministry of Reconstruction for the price of purchasing the ruins, plus any compensation or cost paid for dispossession. Bibliothèque du Patrimoine, carton 3174, note with letter from the Minister of Reconstruction, 16 August 1945.

63. Official press release published 5 January 1945, cited in Delage, *Oradour, ville martyre*, 111.

64. Bibliothèque du Patrimoine, carton 3174, Oradour-sur-Glane, ruines du village, affaires générales, 1945–1971, communiqué de presse, 1 November 1945.

65. For the process of episcopal investigation see Thomas A. Kselman, *Miracles and Prophecies in Nineteenth-Century France* (New Brunswick, N.J.: Rutgers University Press, 1983), 147–60.

66. Delage, *Oradour*, 63–64.

67. Delage, *Oradour*, 64.

68. Here in 1858, the Virgin appeared to a young peasant girl, Bernadette Soubirous, and declared, "I am the immaculate conception." Within days, pilgrims were reporting miraculous cures at the grotto and fountain where the Virgin had appeared. In the course of the next decade, a national cult of Notre-Dame de Lourdes developed, drawing from a broader social base and a wider geographical area than the traditional miracle cults. The cult at Lourdes was the first of these to profit from the development of the national railway and the steady increase in

literacy that took place in the second half of the nineteenth century. Kselman, *Miracles and Prophecies*, 57. From 1899 until the outbreak of World War I, more than half a million pilgrims visited Lourdes annually. Kselman, *Miracles and Prophecies*, 162 n.82. These pilgrims were the precursors of the French who would take to the road in the 1950s, when the spread of automotive transport and the institution of yearly vacations for all French employees would initiate the era of mass tourism.

69. Kselman, *Miracles and Prophecies*, 163.

70. Kselman, *Miracles and Prophecies*, 178–79.

71. Kselman, *Miracles and Prophecies*, 114–16.

72. Kselman, *Miracles and Prophecies*, 195.

73. The idea was first proposed by the Jesuit Père de Boylesve of Le Mans in 1870. Three years later, when the National Assembly voted to approve the construction, the public had donated over six hundred thousand francs. Kselman, *Miracles and Prophecies*, 127.

74. Kselman, *Miracles and Prophecies*, 113.

75. *Journal officiel de la République française*, Documents de l'Assemblée Nationale Constituante, annexes aux procès-verbaux des séances, annexe no. 855, Projet de loi relatif à la conservation des ruines et à la reconstruction d'Oradour-sur-Glane, annexe au procès-verbal de la 2e séance du 3 avril 1946.

76. *Journal officiel de la République française*, Documents de l'Assemblée Nationale Constituante, annexe no. 1041. Rapport fait au nom de la Commission de l'Education Nationale et des Beaux-Arts, de la Jeunesse, des Sports et des Loisirs sur le projet de loi relatif à la conservation des ruines et à la reconstruction d'Oradour-sur-Glane, annexe au procès-verbal de la 3e séance du 15 avril 1946.

77. Since the Oradour project entailed preserving the ruins and rebuilding on a new site, two ministries were involved from the very beginning. The Ministry of National Education, which included the Fine Arts Administration and the Office of Historic Monuments, dealt with the ruins. The Ministry of Reconstruction oversaw all work on the new town. The project clearly required close coordination between the two departments.

78. Bibliothèque du Patrimoine, carton 3174, Inspector General Pierre Paquet to the Ministers of National Education, Reconstruction and Urban Planning, 27 March 1945.

79. "For the dignity of the place," he wrote, "it is indispensible to maintain the gardens in good condition—as well kept as the ruins. If one let them lie fallow their appearance would be disastrous and would give the whole necropole a look of neglect that would run counter to the intended goal." Bibliothèque du Patrimoine, carton 3176, vestiges: enceinte du village et jardin, 2ième dossier 1945 à 1949, Report presented by the Principal Architect, J. Creuzot [signed by Paquet], Restoration-maintenance of the Gardens of the old town and maintenance of the Ruins, in the course of fiscal year 1946, 14 April 1946.

80. Bibliothèque du Patrimoine, carton 3174, consolidation of the destroyed bourg, report by Pierre Paquet, 16 July 1945.

81. Bibliothèque du Patrimoine, carton 3174, report by Pierre Paquet, 16 July 1945.

82. Bibliothèque du Patrimoine, carton 3175, restes du village, 1945–1953, letter from François Desourteaux, 8 February 1947.

83. Bibliothèque du Patrimoine, carton 3175, restes du village, dossier 1945–1953, the Minister of National Education to the Minister of Reconstruction and Urban Planning, for the Minister and by authorization of René Perchet, Director of Architecture, 29 December 1949.

84. Bibliothèque du Patrimoine, carton 3175, restes du village, dossier 1945–1953, letter from Jean Creuzot, Principal Architect to the Director of Architecture, Directorate of Historic Monuments, 5 November 1949.

FOUR. THE MEMORIAL LANDSCAPE

1. Sense of place and emotional response to the landscape have often been best explored by artists and writers. Traditionally, reading the landscape has been more a realm of inquiry for geographers or anthropologists than for historians. For example, see Yi-fu Tuan, *Topophilia: A Study of Environmental Perception, Attitudes and Values* (Englewood

Cliffs, N.J.: Prentice-Hall, 1974) and *Space and Place: The Perspective of Experience* (Minneapolis: University of Minnesota Press, 1977). Yet it has also proved a creative avenue into the writing of a *histoire des sensibilités;* Alain Corbin, historian of nineteenth-century France, made an important contribution with *Le Territoire du vide: l'occident et le désir du rivage* (Paris: Aubier, 1988), a history of northern Europeans' responses to the beach. David Lowenthal's study of how we perceive, use, and change the past combines the concerns of historian and cultural geographer in *The Past Is a Foreign Country* (Cambridge: Cambridge University Press, 1985). Simon Schama draws on the work of such scholars in his wide-ranging *Landscape and Memory* (New York: Knopf, 1995).

2. In the introduction to a group of essays by an eclectic group of thinkers and scholars involved in landscape studies, the cultural geographer D. W. Meinig tells us that the term "landscape" is related to but not identical to nature, scenery, environment, or place. For cultural geographers, human perception and interpretation define landscape: "Environment sustains us as creatures; landscape displays us as cultures." D. W. Meinig, introduction to *The Interpretation of Ordinary Landscapes: Geographical Essays,* ed. D. W. Meinig (New York and Oxford: Oxford University Press, 1979), 3.

3. Halbwachs, *La Mémoire collective,* 146.

4. Halbwachs, *La Mémoire collective,* 166.

5. Though Halbwachs acknowledged the existence of "groups with no apparent spatial basis"—these being legal, economic, and religious groups—he nonetheless reasoned that if one reached far enough back into the past, one would find that these groups' status was originally defined by their relationship to the land. Halbwachs explored relationships between geography, history and memory in *La Topographie légendaire des évangiles en terre sainte* (Paris: Presses Universitaires de France, 1941). For an illuminating discussion of the nature of Jewish religious memory, see Yosef Hayim Yerushalmi, *Zakhor: Jewish History and Jewish Memory* (Seattle: University of Washington Press, 1982).

6. Halbwachs, *La Mémoire collective,* 133.

7. Halbwachs, *Les Cadres sociaux,* 279.

8. Halbwachs, *La Mémoire collective*, 133.

9. ADP, Dossier de protection d'Oradour-sur-Glane, the Prefect, Commissioner of the Republic for the Limousin Region and the Department of the Haute-Vienne to the Minister of Culture, 16 June 1983.

10. A system for counting the number of people entering the ruins was first installed in 1991. The profile of summer visitors is based on a poll conducted from 13 July to 14 September by l'Institut BVA. Direction Régionale des Affaires Culturelles, Limoges, Oradour-sur-Glane, étude sur la fréquentation du site, note d'analyse, 1992.

11. Kselman, *Miracles and Prophecies*, 41.

12. When asked if she is a believer, Louise Bardet, the mother of schoolteacher Denise Bardet, who died in the massacre, answered: "Oh, a little. But not like some you'll find. But yes, at bottom I'm a believer. I'm Catholic, so to speak." But when asked if her faith had helped her through the pain of losing her children, she responded, "No, I don't think that it helped me. Because I really didn't deserve that. Oh no, I don't think that it helped me." Bardet, interview, 8 March 1988.

13. The financial records of the ANFM for 1987 indicate 204,698 francs in sales for the official account of the massacre (Pauchou and Masfrand, *Oradour-sur-Glane: vision d'épouvante*) and postcards commemorating the fortieth anniversary. Other books, postcards, and slides are sold under the auspices of the Caisse Nationale des Monuments Historiques et des Sites. The ANFM uses its income for a variety of expenses: purchasing flowers for ceremonial events, maintaining the ossuary in the cemetery, aid for its members over the age of sixty-five, and so forth. Association Nationale des Familles des Martyrs d'Oradour-sur-Glane, "Assemblée Générale du 6 mars 1988, compte-rendu financier," drawn up by Camille Morliéras.

14. Guy Pauchou and Dr. Pierre Masfrand, *Oradour-sur-Glane: vision d'épouvante* (Limoges: Charles-Lavauzelle et Cie, 1945).

15. There are two guides to the ruins, Hyvernaud and Jean Lemaud. All references to the speech given at the ruins refer to Hyvernaud's. Social scientists concerned with memory note this kind of performance as an overlap between individual and collective memory: "Unique features

of individual performance become part of the tradition of presentation. Folklorists' explicit recognition of this collapses the distinction between the individual and social aspects of memory. There is an interdependency between unique performances and a tradition that cannot be inscribed as property of an individual memory even though the performance they may witness and record is one rendered by an individual. It is in any case rendered for an audience, and is designed for that social purpose." David Middleton and Derek Edwards, Introduction to *Collective Remembering*, eds. Middleton and Edwards (Newbury Park and London: Sage Publications, 1990), 4.

16. Tape recording of speech given by Jean-Jaques Hyvernaud at the ruined church, 24 September 1988.

17. Bibliothèque du Patrimoine, carton 3175, Dossier restes du village, 1945–1953, Letter from the President of the Association Nationale des Familles des Martyrs d'Oradour-sur-Glane to the Minister of National Education, 3 August 1948.

18. In the rural Limousin today, one can still find women whose mothers went regularly to a *bonne fontaine* when their children were sick. At the village of Berneuil, ten kilometers from Oradour, there was until 1994 a *bonne fontaine* by an old oak tree just off the side of the highway running from Limoges to Poitiers. One would go in the company of an old woman in the village, who would burn straws from a broom plant (*genêt*) in a bowl. How the ashes fell would indicate the child's chances for recovery. The mother would hang a scrap of the sick child's clothing on a wooden cross beneath the tree. Annie Lajarige, interview by Sarah Farmer at Roussac/Berneuil, March 1988. This *bonne fontaine* disappeared when new owners of the property drained the land. For a scholarly discussion of popular religion in the Limousin, see Louis Perouas, *Les Limousins, leurs saints, leurs prêtres, du XVe au XXe siècle* (Paris: Les Editions du Cerf, 1988), 172–206, as well as Perouas, "Ostentions et cultes des saints en Limousin: une approche ethno-historique," *Ethnologie française* 13, no. 4 (1983):323–36.

19. Dr. Robert Lapuelle, interview by Sarah Farmer at Oradour-sur-Glane, 18 December 1988.

20. Alphonse Dupront, "Tourisme et pèlerinage: réflexions de psychologie collective," *Communications, Ecole pratique des hautes études, Centre d'études des Communications de Masse* 10 (1967): 99. For Dean MacCannell, tourism is a response to the dislocations of modernity: "Sightseeing is a kind of collective striving for a transcendence of the modern totality, of incorporating its fragments into unified experience." MacCanell, *The Tourist: A New Theory of the Leisure Class* (New York: Schocken Books, 1976), 13.

21. The French sociologist Jean Baudrillard has articulated the view that, in the present day, we no longer make the distinction between the real and the imaginary but live in the world of the "hyperreal," where simulations exist without reference to real objects. Baudrillard, "Simulacra and Simulations," in *Selected Writings*, edited and introduced by Mark Poster (Stanford: Stanford University Press, 1990), 166–84.

22. Vanessa R. Schwartz, *Spectacular Realities: Early Mass Culture in Fin-de-Siècle Paris* (Berkeley: University of California Press, 1998). For a discussion of the tourists' search for the authentic, see chapter five of MacCannell, *The Tourist*. For the American case, see Miles Orvell, *The Real Thing: Imitation and Authenticity in American Culture, 1880–1940* (Chapel Hill: University of North Carolina Press, 1989), and the title essay of Umberto Eco, *Travels in Hyperreality: Essays* (New York: Harcourt Brace Jovanovich, 1986).

23. The ANFM observes All Saints' Day, Armistice Day, VE-Day, and Palm Sunday with a procession to the ruins. These ceremonies receive little attention outside the immediate community.

24. Robert Hébras, interview by Marc Wilmart, Javerdat, 17 March 1988.

25. Desourteaux interview, 17 March 1988.

26. André Desourteaux, interview by Sarah Farmer at Limoges, 1 April 1988.

27. Madame Desourteaux, interview by Sarah Farmer at Oradour-sur-Glane, 28 August 1988.

28. André Desourteaux, interview by Michel Follin at Oradour-sur-Glane, 8 June 1988.

29. Desourteaux interview, 8 June 1988.

30. Hébras interview, 17 March 1988.

31. Darthout interview, 7 March 1988.

32. Bachelard, *The Poetics of Space*, 18.

33. Bachelard, *The Poetics of Space*, 27.

34. Desourteaux interview, 8 June 1988.

35. Jeanette Montazeaud, interview by Sarah Farmer at Oradour-sur-Glane, 17 September 1988. On 10 June 1944, she and her mother went to Limoges for the day. Her father, the notary public for Oradour, died in the massacre. She was in the tram that arrived at Oradour on the late afternoon of 10 June. She and the other residents of Oradour were ordered to disembark, held for a few hours, and then released.

36. André Desourteaux, interview and walk with Sarah Farmer at Oradour-sur-Glane, 28 August 1988.

37. Montazeaud interview, 17 September 1988.

38. Lucette Bichaud, interview by Sarah Farmer at Limoges, 14 September 1988.

39. Montazeaud interview, 17 September 1988.

40. Though in his speech Hyvernaud tells visitors that the purpose of keeping the ruins is not to nourish hate or a spirit of revenge, there is evidence that in some places in France anti-German feelings still run high. Citizens from a small town in the department of the Yonne in central France put a marble plaque in the cemetery in 1975: "To the Memory of the Martyrs of Oradour sur Glane, Victims of Nazi Bestiality. To the Memory of all the French Assassinated by the Shameful Invader. On the part of too small a number of the Citizens of the Canton of Charny (89). Shame on Germany, Criminal of the Past. Heed our warning, Germany of today that, alas, permits the rebirth of pro-nazi groups and protects the Old Hitlerian Monsters." It seems most likely that the incident that provoked this outburst was the death of General Lammerding, commander of Das Reich, who died in his bed in Düsseldorf in 1975 without ever having been brought to trial for the atrocities committed at Oradour.

41. The mayor and city council overwhelmingly preferred an ambitious program to renovate the urban center and build modern infrastructures, on the outskirts of town, to attract industry. In the end very little innovative work was done. Only fifteen streets were widened, and plans for expansion and development stagnated. The Verdunnois, in particular the merchants of the main avenue, proved stubborn in their determination to rebuild the town as it had been. Furthermore, plans for modernization and development depended on the acquisition of land belonging to the army—which proved loathe to cede it to the city. "Verdun: les débuts de la reconstruction, 1919-1922," *Connaissance de la Meuse: revue trimestrielle de l'Association connaissance de la Meuse* (Bar-le-Duc) 6 (October 1987): 8-11.

42. Prost, "Verdun," 123-24.

43. Julian Tuwin, cited by James E. Young, "The Biography of a Memorial Icon," *Representations* 26 (Spring 1989): 79.

44. Lowenthal, *The Past Is a Foreign Country*, 243.

45. The assassination had been planned by the Czechoslovak government in exile in London and carried out by Czech partisans who had trained in England and parachuted into Czechoslovakia. For a detailed history of the assassination of Heydrich see Callum MacDonald, *The Killing of Obergrüppenführer Reinhard Heydrich* (New York: Free Press, 1989). Ivan Ciganek, *Lidice* (Prague: Orbis Press Agency, 1982) gives an account of the massacre as well as historical facts about the town, the region, and the commemoration of Lidice. Uwe Naumann, *Lidice: Ein böhmisches Dorf* (Frankfurt-am-Main: Röderberg-Verlag Frankfurt, 1983) devotes three chapters to the international response to the massacre of Lidice and its commemoration.

46. Ivan Ciganek, *Lidice* (Prague: Orbis Press Agency, 1982), 51.

47. They are: Dresden (Germany); Telaväg (Norway); Djistimo (Greece); Kragujevac (Serbia); Warsaw (Poland); Coventry (England); Lidice (Czech Republic); Stalingrad (Russia); Oradour (France); Marzabotto (Italy); Bande (Belgium); Rutten (Holland); Hiroshima (Japan).

FIVE. THE BORDEAUX TRIAL

1. In February 1953, during the trial, a delegation of the French government, on an official visit to London, asked that Lammerding be extradited. The delegation included the head of the cabinet and the Minister of Foreign Affairs. Vincent Auriol, *Journal du septennat*, eds. Pierre Nora and Jacques Ozouf (Paris: Librairie Armand Colin, 1970–71), 7:55. Requests were also made to the British High Commission in Germany, which replied that the case was "under study" and that they were awaiting instructions from London. They added that as of 1 September 1948, the British were extraditing only Germans accused of homicide as defined by German law. In 1985, journalist Jean-Marc Théolleyre added further information: with the onset of the Cold War, the Americans protected Lammerding (as they did many former Nazis, including Klaus Barbie) in exchange for intelligence information. "For them," noted Théolleyre, "the massacres committed at Tulle or at Oradour were ancient history, or more exactly history bypassed. Every hour had its pressing concerns." Jean-Marc Théolleyre, *Procès d'après-guerre* (Paris: Editions La Découverte et Journal *Le Monde*, 1985), 39–40.

2. The trial was referred to in the Alsatian and national press as the Oradour-sur-Glane trial. In the Limousin, it was called the Bordeaux trial, which seems preferable for reasons of clarity. An excellent account of the trial is offered by Pierre Barral, "L'Affaire d'Oradour, affrontement de deux mémoires," in *Mémoire de la Seconde Guerre Mondiale: actes du Colloque de Metz, 6–8 octobre 1983*, ed. Alfred Wahl (Metz: Centre de Recherche "Histoire et Civilisation de l'Europe Occidentale," 1984), 243–52.

3. *Combat*, 20, 25 October 1944; 5, 11 January 1945; and *Le Figaro*, 8 September 1944; 13, 19, 22–23 October 1944; 2, 7–8, 12 January 1945. See also Tony Judt, *Past Imperfect: French Intellectuals, 1944–1956* (Berkeley: University of California Press, 1992), 68–72.

4. Rousso, *Le Syndrome de Vichy*, 62.

5. Ibid.

6. Novick, *The Resistance*, 187–88. See Baudot, "L'Épuration."

7. Novick, *The Resistance*, 188.

8. Novick, *The Resistance*, 188 and Rousso, *Le Syndrome de Vichy*, 64.

9. Théolleyre, *Procès d'après-guerre*, 39.

10. Théolleyre, *Procès d'après-guerre*, 40.

11. Théolleyre, *Procès d'après-guerre*, 125.

12. Josef Bürckel, the *Gauleiter* of Vienna, was named civil adminstrator for Lorraine and the Sarre-Palatinate. Robert Wagner, the *Gauleiter* of Baden, extended his control to Alsace.

13. Though rarely mentioned by the defenders of the *malgré-nous*, the Germans also set up the concentration camp of Struthof in Natzwiller, eleven kilometers from Schirmeck, in the mountains. Whereas Schirmeck was a "re-education" camp for recalcitrant Alsatians, Struthof was a full-fledged concentration camp, complete with a gas chamber and Nazi doctors who performed experiments on prisoners. Although some of the inmates of Schirmeck were sent to their deaths at Struthof, the concentration camp was intended for French resisters and Jews from all over Europe. Whereas those sent to Schirmeck served a sentence and were then released, the people sent to Struthof were worked to death or exterminated. When the sufferings of Alsace and the *malgré-nous* were discussed, almost no mention was made of these people. In portraying their own sufferings, it would seem that the *malgré-nous* had no interest in evoking those who were perhaps greater victims of the Nazis.

14. Marie-Joseph Bopp, "L'Enrôlement de force des Alsaciens dans la Wehrmacht et la S.S.," *Revue d'histoire de la deuxième guerre mondiale* 20 (October 1955): 42. Others cite 130,000 for the number of *incorporés de force*.

15. *Journal officiel de la République française, Lois et Décrets, ordonnance du 28 août 1944 relative à la répression des crimes de guerre*, 780.

16. This does not mean, however, that French citizens were not judged by military tribunals during the purge. Very little is known concerning the activities of these courts; official statistics concerning the purges reflect only judgments of civil courts. See Rousso, "L'Epuration en France," 94–96.

17. These two were Georges René Boos, who admitted to volunteering for the SS, and Paul Graff, who was the only one to confess to having actually killed anyone in Oradour.

18. AN 4 AG 3, relating to the visit of President Vincent Auriol to Oradour-sur-Glane, 10 June 1947, speech of the President of the Republic. "Here there was a village, a sweet French village, a charming oasis of tranquility and labor, where the echoes of the war were heard only faintly; a sweet French village, simple, welcoming, friendly—a big brotherly family—in which nature seemed to want to keep, despite the times, the image of peace [that had been] lost; a sweet French village. . . ."

19. Ibid.

20. AN 4 AG 3, relating to the visit of President Vincent Auriol to Oradour-sur-Glane, 10 June 1947. Telegram report.

21. "For crimes that come under the ordinance of 28 August 1944 on the punishment of war crimes, when these crimes can be attributed to the collective action of a group or military formation that belongs to an organization declared criminal by the international military court [which was the case for the Waffen SS] . . . then all individuals belonging to this formation or this group may be considered coauthors, unless they can bring proof of having been forcibly drafted and also proof that they did not participate in the said crime." *Journal officiel de la République française*, Lois et Décrets, Loi no. 48–1416 du 15 septembre 1948 modifiant et complétant l'ordonnance du 28 août relative à la répression des crimes de guerre, 9138.

22. The Bordeaux trial was not the first time the law had been applied. In 1949, the military court at Metz used the law to convict Germans who had massacred civilians in Ascq on 2 April 1944 (see pp. 38–39 below). "La Loi de 1948 a été appliquée pour la première fois au procès d Ascq," *L'Aurore*, 7 January 1953.

23. AN F7 15431, Commissariat des Renseignements Généraux, Colmar, no. 665/52, 9 December 1952.

24. AN F7 15431, Commissariat des Renseignements Généraux, Mulhouse, no. 5479/52, 23 December 1952; no. 23 1/1042/52, 29 De-

cember 1952; no. 1/1046/52, 30 December 1952. Commissariat des Renseignments Généraux, Colmar, no. 710/52, 30 December 1952.

25. AN F7 15431, Commissariat des Renseignements Généraux, Mulhouse, no. 1/1046/52, 30 December 1952.

26. AN F7 15431, Service des Renseignments Généraux, Strasbourg, No. 2034, 20 December 1952.

27. "Procès d'Oradour," *L'Aurore,* 25 December 1952.

28. AN F7 15431, Service des Renseignements Généraux, Strasbourg, No. 2062, 29 December 1952.

29. *L'Aurore,* 12 December 1952.

30. AN F7 15431, Service des Renseignements Généraux, Colmar, no. 681/52, 16 December 1953.

31. René Hardy, "Langages et dialectes parlés en Alsace-Lorraine" (Rapport au Congrès international des amitiés françaises: Mons, septembre 1911) in *Témoignages pour les Alsaciens-Lorrains* (Paris: Librairie Plon, 1925), 467.

32. Eugen Weber, *Peasants into Frenchmen: The Modernization of Rural France, 1870–1914* (Stanford: Stanford University Press, 1976).

33. Edward Helsey, *Notre Alsace: l'enquête du "Journal" et le procès de Colmar* (Paris: Albin Michel, 1927), 26. Although the term "Alsatian malaise" refers to the interwar years, the Alsatian "question" had existed since 1648 when, by the Treaty of Westphalia, Louis XIV gained Hapsburg holdings in Alsace. Over the course of his reign Louis XIV progressively spread his hold over the rest of the province. Patriotic attachment to France increased under the Revolution and the Napoleonic Wars, to which Alsace contributed an exceptional proportion of generals and marshals. Yet from their earliest days as part of France, the Alsatians made clear that they intended to protect their regional particularities and expected the central government, as promised by Louis XIV, to respect Alsatian rights, customs, and privileges. Emile Baas, *Situation d'Alsace* (Strasbourg: Les Editions de l'Est, 1946).

34. The *Courrier du Haut-Rhin,* a Catholic newspaper, sounded the alarm: "Across the entire region rings the cry against the outrage

committed by the masonic government against the confessional schools in Alsace. It is the first slap in the face. . . . It is the beginning of a systematic repression of the religious institutions and traditions of our homeland, it is the beginning of an outrageous rape committed against the majority of our population." Quoted in *Le Temps*, 8 March 1924.

35. *Le Nouveau Rhin français*, 28–29 December 1952.

36. Georges Lamousse, "Les Alsaciens à Oradour," *Le Populaire du centre*, 5 January 1953.

37. Théolleyre, *Procès d'après-guerre*, 112.

38. Ibid., 115–16.

39. Ibid., 113.

40. Ibid., 119.

41. Ibid., 125.

42. *Journal officiel de la République française*, Débats parlementaires, Assemblée Nationale, 1ᵉ séance du mardi 27 janvier 1953, 464.

43. Ibid., 466.

44. Ibid., 466.

45. Ibid., 474.

46. This debate revealed and exacerbated another regional conflict. The department of the Moselle, part of the Lorraine, had also been annexed and had seen its young men forcibly drafted. But there had been no Mosellans in the company that massacred Oradour. More to the point, forty-four refugees from the Lorraine town of Charly had been killed in Oradour. The ADEIF in the Moselle did not come out in support of the Alsatians being tried in Bordeaux, and Raymond Mondon, the mayor of Metz and a deputy from the department of the Moselle, opposed modifying the law of 15 September 1948. His colleague Jules Thiriet evoked the three hundred thousand Lorrains who were expelled from the department in 1939 and the sufferings of Charly, which had been renamed Charly-Oradour. He too voted against the resolution to exempt the *malgré-nous* from the law of collective responsibility. Yet, as the trial progressed, the Moselle demonstrated an increased sympathy for the *malgré-nous*; on 31 January, the Association Départementale des Anciens Combattants "Malgré-Nous et Réfractaires" adopted a motion of solidarity

with their Alsatian comrades. "Une Motion des 'malgré-nous' de la Moselle," *Le Figaro*, 3 February 1953.

47. *Journal officiel de la République française*, Débats parlementaires, Assemblée Nationale, séance du mercredi 18 février 1953, 1114.

48. AN F7 15431, Commissariat des Renseignements Généraux, Colmar, no. 56/53, 30 January 1953.

49. AN F7 15431, Commissariat des Renseignements Généraux, Strasbourg, No. 132, 30 January 1953. Nonetheless, some Alsatians remained alienated. The Renseignements Généraux noted: "One has also been able to hear this reflection: 'We can do as we like, they treat us nonetheless like krauts [on nous traite tout de même de boches].' "

50. The President recorded his sentiments in his diary: "The trial of Oradour continues. The Chamber is in a panic. It sufficed that there was a groundswell of feeling in Alsace for the deputies who voted for the law of 1948 to immediately want to abrogate it now. It is the most saddening thing to have occurred while I have been in office. In 1948 they passed a law to give satisfaction to the population of Oradour. At that moment, indignation was such that they ceded to it and voted for an absurdity. But see now that it's Alsace that's protesting and immediately the Chamber backtracks. It's enough in this Assembly that someone sneezes for everyone to run for cover. There is no longer any democracy and fear weighs on all these mediocre people. It's saddening. It's obvious that one of these days I'll have to say it. But I can't say it being here [in my current position]." Auriol, *Journal du septennat* 7:38.

51. "Le président Nussy-Saint-Saëns [*sic*] précise la portée exacte de vote de l'Assemblée Nationale sur la responsabilité collective," *Le Figaro*, 29 January 1953.

52. Théolleyre, *Procès d'après-guerre*, 149.

53. "Le président Nussy-Saint-Saëns...," *Le Figaro*, 29 January 1953. President Auriol approved of the judge's cool-headedness: "President Saint-Saëns is a remarkable man, who has proved his independence by twice rejecting motions to sever [i.e., to try the Alsatians and Germans separately], and he appeased the people of Oradour, who wanted to leave, saying that the tribunal would continue to act as it had

in the past; up until now he has ruled in accordance with French laws, normal laws, the good old penal code, which was created by men who knew what they were doing. No one has brought this out, but I have the intention of telling him that he has all my sympathy." Auriol, *Journal du septennat*, 7:38.

54. "Des témoins de l'annexion ont évoqué le martyr de l'Alsace," *Le Monde*, 1–2 February 1953.

55. Théolleyre, *Procès d'après-guerre*, 149.

56. Pierre Scize, "Mme Rouffanche dit ce que fut le martyre des femmes et des enfants dans l'église d'Oradour," *Le Figaro*, 2 February 1953.

57. Théolleyre, *Procès d'après-guerre*, 154.

58. Pierre Scize, "Mme Rouffanche . . . ," *Le Figaro*, 2 February 1953.

59. AN F7 15431, Renseignements Généraux, Guéret, no. 367/C3. "According to [the people of the Creuse, a department of the Limousin], the Alsatians, who invoke mental and physical constraints to justify and camouflage their acts, have done nothing to diminish the barbarity. . . . In addition, reading the proceedings of the trial shows, according to the people of the Creuse, the duplicity of the Alsatians, who pose as victims. . . ."

60. Ibid. The accused Alsatians were often called *les douze* (the twelve). But during the trial they became thirteen when it was established that Paul Graff, the Alsatian soldier who had been in jail since the end of the war, had been also an *incorporé de force*.

61. "Des témoins de l'annexion. . . ," *Le Monde*, 1–2 February 1953.

62. Scize, "Mme Rouffanche. . . ," *Le Figaro*, 2 February 1953.

63. "40,000 Personnes ont célébré à Limoges le sacrifice des martyrs d'Oradour-sur-Glane," *Le Figaro*, 4 February 1953.

64. "Dinge, die gesagt sein müssen," *Le Nouveau Rhin français*, 5 February 1953.

65. "Gedenkkundgebung für die Opfer von Oradour in Bordeaux," *L'Alsace*, 13 February 1953; "Eine eindrucksvolle Kundgebung," Les Dernières Nouvelles d'Alsace, 13 February 1953.

66. "Das Elsass wird dieses Schandurteil nicht annehmen," *Le Nouveau Rhin français*, 13 February 1953.

67. "Après le verdict de Bordeaux," *Le Franc-Tireur*, 14 February 1953.

68. "Ici Mulhouse," *Le Nouveau Rhin français*, 14 February 1953.

69. "L'Alsace, unanime s'élève avec véhémence contre l'arrêt de Bordeaux," *Le Figaro*, 14 February 1953.

70. Ibid.

71. "Die Reaktion im Haut-Rhin," *L'Alsace*, 14 February 1953.

72. "Après le verdict de Bordeaux," *Le Franc-Tireur*, 14 February 1953.

73. "Die Vereinigung der Maires des Haut-Rhin hat eine Reihe von Massnahmen beschlossen," *L'Alsace*, 14 February 1953.

74. Merry Bromberger, "Les Parlementaires alsaciens donnent quatre jours au gouvernement," *Paris-Presse l'Intransigeant*, 15 February 1953.

75. "Après le verdict du procès d'Oradour," *Le Monde*, 15 February 1953.

76. "De Strasbourg à Mulhouse," *Le Figaro*, 14 February 1953.

77. "Après le verdict du procès d'Oradour," *Le Monde*, 15 February 1953.

78. "Manifestations du deuil," *Le Figaro*, 16 February 1953.

79. "Détente en Alsace," *L'Aurore*, 16 February 1953.

80. Paul Ahne, "Le Monument aux morts de Strasbourg," *Archives alsaciennes d'histoire de l'art*, *1936 extrait* (Strasbourg: Libraire Istra, 1936), 167–75.

81. "L'Assemblée discutera ce soir la proposition d'amnistie pleine et entière aux Français incorporés de force," *Le Figaro*, 18 February 1953.

82. Cited in "Les élus socialistes du Limousin reprochent à leurs collègues d'Alsace leur attitude contradictoire," *Le Figaro*, 18 Feburary 1953.

83. *L'Aurore*, 16 February 1953. (*L'Aurore* cited the comment of *Libération*.) For its part, the German government reserved comment on

the verdict until the dossiers and the legal basis for the judgment had been studied. But the ruling Christian Democratic Party gave an overall positive appraisal on account of the fact that the court had not made distinctions in sentencing according to nationality. The party nonetheless added the hope that the Germans and the Alsatians would be accorded a measure of grace, "in the interest of humanity and European cooperation." "Après le verdict de Bordeaux," *Le Franc-Tireur,* 14 February 1953.

84. Auriol, *Journal du septennat,* 7:54–55.

85. Auriol, *Journal du septennat,* 7:707 n. 30.

86. *Journal officiel,* séance du 18 février 1953, 1112–13.

87. *Journal officiel,* séance du 18 février 1953, 1123.

88. Charles de Gaulle, *Discours et messages: dans l'attente, février 1946–avril 1958* (Paris: Librairie Plon, 1970), 563–64.

89. *Journal officiel,* séance du 18 février 1953, 1116.

90. *Journal officiel,* séance du 18 février 1953, 1126.

91. "Wie die Kammer abstimmte," *Le Nouvel Alsacien,* 20 February 1953.

92. "Wie die '13' heim kehrten," *Les Dernières nouvelles d'Alsace,* 24 February 1953; "Die Heimatkehr der '13' ins Elsass," *Le Nouveau Rhin français,* 24 February 1953.

93. *Le Populaire du Centre,* 21 February 1953.

94. AN F7 15341, Renseignements Généraux, 22 February 1953. The veterans' groups that participated were the Fédération Nationale des Déportés et Internés Résistants et Patriotes (FNDIRP), the Amicale des Anciennes Déportées de Ravensbrück, and the Association Nationale des Familles de Résistants et d'Otages Morts pour la France.

95. AN F7 15431, Renseignements Généraux, La Roche-sur-Yon, 16 March 1953.

96. AN F7 15431, Prefect of the Haute-Vienne to the Minister of the Interior, Limoges, 21 February 1953. The regional Socialist Party paper, *Le Populaire du Centre,* ran a statement from the Socialist Federation of the Haute-Vienne asking all municipalities as well as the Limousin population not to join in the demonstrations organized by the PCF.

The Socialist Party had regained the mayoralty of Limoges in 1947 when Betoulle defeated the incumbent, Communist Resistance leader Georges Guingouin. In the early 1950s Guingouin also fell into disfavor within his own party. In 1953, during the Bordeaux trial, he resigned from the municipal council. A few months later, Betoulle and the Socialist press launched an attack on Guingouin accusing him of wartime excesses. This was the beginning of the "Guingouin affair," which has been thoroughly treated by Michel Taubmann, *L'Affaire Guingouin* (Limoges: Lucien Souny, 1994).

97. AN F7 15431, Renseignements Généraux, AY-NI-No. 89, 5 March 1953.

98. "Vichyism, collaboration and Resistance belong to the past; whereas suffering, inverse privileges and the state of 'internal emigration' of the victims of the purge are still, in 1953, something real and present, to which it is time to put an end. . . ." "Pour une amnistie une et indivisible," *Rivarol*, 27 February 1953.

99. Novick, *The Resistance*, 188.

100. Dr. Robert Lapuelle, interview by Sarah Farmer at Oradour-sur-Glane, March 1988.

SIX. THE NEW TOWN

1. Figure for 1945 from Pastaud, "Contribution à l'étude," 92. Figure for 1939 from ADHV 1M 175.

2. Robert Savy, "Recherches sur le personnel politique en Haute-Vienne, 1945–1965" (mémoire pour le D.E.S. de sciences politiques, Université de Poitiers, n.d.), 97.

3. For example, in the legislative elections of 1919 the Socialists in Oradour did substantially better than they did in most other communes in the department, garnering between 62.44 percent and 69.93 percent of the vote, as compared to a mean of 51.16 percent of the vote for the Haute-Vienne. Laird Boswell, "Rural Communism in France, 1920–1939: The Example of the Limousin and the Dordogne" (Ph.D. dissertation, University of California, 1988) 241, map 17.

4. ADHV 896W/482, M. Faugeras, maire communiste d'Oradour. . . .

5. "La Croix d'Oradour," *L'Humanité*, 18 May 1949.

6. ADHV 896W/482. Prefect of the Haute-Vienne to the Minister of the Interior, 27 May 1949.

7. ADHV 896W/482, "La Légion d'honneur d'Oradour-sur-Glane," *Le Populaire*, 3 June 1949.

8. ADHV 896W/482, Renseignements Généraux no. 1708, 13 June 1949.

9. Robert Schmidt, "Oradour, deux fois martyr," *La Liberté du Centre*, 13 June 1949.

10. "11 Juin: Oradour de la Paix," *L'Echo du Centre*, 7 June 1950.

11. ADHV 896W/482, Renseignements Généraux no. 2.034, Limoges, 21 June 1950.

12. ADHV 896W/482, L'Association Nationale des Familles des Martyrs d'Oradour-sur-Glane, communiqué, 30 June 1950.

13. ADHV 896W/482, handwritten note, n.d.; "Des Milliers de personnes font le serment de sauver la paix," *L'Echo du Centre*, 11 June 1951.

14. *L'Echo du Centre*, 9 June 1952.

15. The *liste d'union* has held on in Oradour; since its founding it has been voted nine consecutive mandates, winning between 72 and 82 percent of the vote. Today the *liste d'union* is made up of people who vote Socialist, for the Rassemblement pour la République, or the Union pour la Démocratie Française. This list survived the "union de la gauche" of 1978, when the PCF and PSF made common cause. In 1982, an attempt was made to include Communists to create a single, unified list. The *liste d'union* solicited people who voted Communist but refused to take anyone who held a position in the PCF. The PCF therefore rejected the gesture.

16. Bibliothèque du Patrimoine, carton 3174, report of Inspector General Pierre Paquet, 16 July 1945. The barracks housed the mayor's office, a post office, a tram station, schools, the office of a notary public, a dining hall for construction workers, and the businesses of a few merchants who provided services for the tiny community and the surrounding hamlets.

17. Dr. Robert Lapuelle, interview by Marc Wilmart at Oradour-sur-Glane, 7 March 1988.

18. ADHV 896W/482. In 1953, an exception was made for the prefect of the Haute-Vienne. In a letter to the prefect, Brouillaud singled him out for his "total devotion to our cause and . . . sensitivity to everything that touches Oradour." Letter from the Mayor of Oradour-sur-Glane to the Prefect, 4 June 1953. Still, the prefect was informed that he would be welcome only if he did not come in uniform. For the next twenty years no governmental ministers attended the annual commemoration of the massacre. An exception was made in 1962, when President de Gaulle was invited to Oradour. The next time a president of the Republic visited Oradour was in 1982, when François Mitterrand came.

19. Bibliothèque du Patrimoine, carton 3176, Oradour-sur-Glane, vestiges: tombeaux 1947–1952, engagements de dépenses. Work on the crypt had begun in 1948. When the last work was done in 1952, the total cost for construction had reached 35,400,561 *anciens francs*. While waiting for the crypt to be completed, the remains of the victims who had been identified were temporarily kept in a wooden barrack that had been set up as a rudimentary chapel in a field across from the cemetery. The unidentified remains had been buried in three common graves in the cemetery.

20. ADHV 896W/482, report from M. Mandon-Joly, Architecte des Batîments de France, 17 November 1953.

21. Lapuelle interview, March 1988.

22. ADHV 896W/483, Prefect (Georges Briand) to Monsieur Friol, Director of the Cabinet of the President of the Republic, 1 August 1955.

23. This attitude was reinforced by the Church. While leading a mass on the steps of the ruined church as part of the ceremony of 10 June, the Archbishop of Limoges condemned all festivities in the new town: "We swear that we will maintain the respect due to the country's martyrs. . . . We vow that if once again, a ball is organized here, we will come ourselves, like the ancient prophets, and we will cry: Evil! Evil! . . ." *Le Courrier du Centre*, 11 June 1952.

24. Janique de Catheu, interview by Sarah Farmer at the ruins of Oradour-sur-Glane, 13 February 1988.

25. Lapuelle interview, 7 March 1988.

26. Amélie Lebraud, interview by Marc Wilmart at Oradour-sur-Glane, 14 March 1988.

27. Christiane Jude, interview by Marc Wilmart at Oradour-sur-Glane, 16 March 1988. Madame Jude's mother is considered a *miraculée*. On 10 June 1944, she was among a small group of people stopped by two officers on their way into Oradour. The sixteen-year-old girl did not have her identity papers, but when she told them that she came from Les Bordes, a hamlet that bordered on Oradour, the officers sent her out of town onto the *route nationale*. Moments later, she was stopped again by another group of soldiers; again, when they learned she was not from Oradour, they let her go. The rest of the group was shot in the massacre. Her two brothers, who were attending school in Oradour, also died. A few years later she married a man from Oradour, who had lost his parents, his grandmother, and seven of his eight brothers and sisters. The couple moved into one of the first houses built in the new town and raised a family.

28. Lapuelle interview, March 1988.

29. Jean Thevenet, "Vingt ans après le massacre de la population d'Oradour: Près du bourg martyr ceux de la nouvelle agglomération veulent gagner leur droit au bonheur," *Le Populaire du Centre*, 3 June 1964.

30. Albert Valade, interview by Guy Pouget at Oradour-sur-Glane, March 1988.

31. Lapuelle interview, March 1988.

32. Lebraud interview, 14 March 1988.

33. de Catheu interview, 13 February 1988.

34. Pressure for this change had been building in the community. In 1986 the *comité des fêtes* had planned a party during the month of June and the ANFM asked the municipal council not to allow it. The next year a young woman who belonged to the ANFM requested that she be allowed to marry in Oradour during the month of June. The municipal council refused her request to rent the *salle municipale* for her reception, but in order to put an end to such incidents, the council voted a resolution that limitations on the *salle municipale* would extend only to the five days before and five days after the anniversary of the massacre. The

ANFM then followed the municipal council's initative in revising its statutes. Lapuelle interview, March 1988.

35. Lapuelle interview, March 1988.

36. Jude interview, 16 March 1988.

37. Jean-Francois Beaulieu, interview by Sarah Farmer at Oradour-sur-Glane, 17 September 1988.

38. The screenplay was based on David Hughes's novel *The Pork Butcher* (New York: Schocken Books, 1985).

39. "Michaël Lonsdale, le Jour où j'ai trouvé Dieu," *Télé 7 Jours*, 18 July 1987.

40. "On ne 'joue' pas avec Oradour . . . même pour un film," *Le Populaire du Centre*, 24 July 1987.

41. *Journal officiel de la République française*, Assemblée Nationale, Questions Écrites no. 48, séance du 7 décembre 1987, response of the Ministre de la Coopération to Marcel Rigout on 28 September 1987.

42. Robin Mackness, "The Secret of Oradour," *Sunday Times Magazine*, 6 March 1988.

43. On 29 July 1952, the president of the *Syndicat d'initiative* (tourism office) of Oradour-sur-Glane requested authorization to place signs (one at the lower entrance to the ruins and the other at the intersection near the new town) saying "Touristes—VISITEZ LE NOUVEAU BOURG." The Secretary of State for National Education denied the request. Bibliothèque du Patrimoine, carton 3175, ruines du village. On 13 June 1955, during a visit to Oradour, the principal architect noticed a sign, near the lower entrance to the ruins, advertising the Hotel and Restaurant Milord. He asked that the prefect have the sign removed. Bibliothèque du Patrimoine, carton 3174, Principal Architect to the General Director of Architecture, under the aegis of the Historic Monuments Service, 27 June 1955.

44. ABCD, Etude sur la Fréquentation du Site, 28 November 1991. Forty percent take a meal at one of the restaurants or cafés. Fifty-eight percent eat a picnic. Four percent eat at the house of friends or relatives in the new town.

45. de Catheu interview, 13 February 1988.

46. Lapuelle interview, September 1988.

47. Lapuelle interview, March 1988.

48. See Daniel Milo, "Le nom des rues," in *Lieux de mémoire*, ed. Pierre Nora (Paris: Gallimard, 1984–1993), vol. 2, pt. 3: 281–305.

49. Bibliothèque du Patrimoine, carton 3175, ruines du village, response to the report of Jean Creuzot, Principal Architect, to the General Director of Architecture under the aegis of the Historic Monuments Service, Office of Building Projects and Classification of Historic Monuments, 4 August 1958.

50. Bibliothèque du Patrimoine, carton 3175, ruines du village, report of Pierre Paquet to the State Minister responsible for [*chargé*] Cultural Affairs, 23 March 1961.

51. Bibliothèque du Patrimoine, carton 3174, René Bec, the Regional Conservator of France's Buildings, Clermont-Ferrand, to the Director of Architecture, Office of Building Projects and Classification of Historic Monuments, 18 May 1966.

52. Robert Paxton, *Vichy France: Old Guard and New Order, 1940–1944* (New York: Columbia University Press, 1975) and Jaeckel, *Frankreich*.

53. Rousso, *Le Syndrome de Vichy*, 322.

54. ADP, Jacques Gerard, Prefect, Commissioner of the Republic for the Limousin Region and the Department of the Haute-Vienne, to the Minister of Culture, 16 June 1983.

55. Gabor Mester de Parajd, "Oradour-sur-Glane. Conservation of the Vestiges of the Martyred Village." Study for the Ministry of Culture, August 1983, 1.

56. Mester de Parajd, "Oradour-sur-Glane," 2.

57. Darthout interview, 7 March 1988.

58. Desourteaux interview, 1 April 1988. Photographs taken soon after the massacre show the cars in their original positions. See Poitevin, *Dans l'enfer d'Oradour*, 2–3.

59. "La 202 du docteur Desourteaux restaurée," *Centre-France dimanche*, 4 October 1992.

60. Kurt Forster, "Monument/Memory and the Mortality of Architecture," *Oppositions* 25 (Fall 1982): 6.

AFTERWORD

1. Ernest Renan, "What Is a Nation?" in *Becoming National: A Reader,* ed. Geoff Eley and Ronald Grigor Suny (Oxford: Oxford University Press, 1996), 45.

2. Pierre Sollers, "Littérature: le retour des précieux," *Le Nouvel Observateur* 525 (28 December 1974): 73.

3. Henry Rousso designates 1971–1974 as the years in which "the mirror broke." *Le Syndrome de Vichy,* 111–45. Paul Touvier, a key member of the collaborationist French Milice in the Lyons area, was connected to the murder of important resisters, including Jean Moulin. In 1944 he managed to go underground and was protected for years by right-wing elements in the French Catholic Church. The case of Touvier became an "affair" after President Georges Pompidou granted him a presidential pardon in 1971.

4. He reaffirmed on 12 September 1994, "I am of the opinion that France is not responsible; it is a minority of agitators [*minorités activistes*] who seized the occasion of the defeat to lay hold of power who are accountable for those crimes. Not the Republic, not France! And so I will not make excuses in the name of France." "François Mitterrand ému sans toujours convaincre," *Le Monde,* 14 September 1994.

5. "Yes, the criminal madness of the occupier was, everyone knows it, seconded by French people, seconded by the French State. France, country of the Enlightenment, country of the rights of man, land of welcome, land of asylum, France, that day did the irreparable. Breaking her word, she delivered those under her protection to their executioners. . . . We have, as regards [the Jewish deportees from France], a debt which can never be repaid." Jean-Baptiste de Montvalon, "M. Chirac reconnaît la 'faute collective' commise envers les juifs," *Le Monde,* 18 July 1995.

6. Arno Mayer, "Memory and History: On the Poverty of Remembering and Forgetting the Judeocide," *Radical History Review* 56 (Spring 1993): 7.

BIBLIOGRAPHY

PRIMARY SOURCES

Archival Materials

Archives Départementales Corrèze. 58W 2168.

Archives Départementales Haute-Vienne. 6M157, 185W1/49, 187W/199, 893W/114, 893W/118, 893W/119, 893W/124, 893W/130, 893W/132, 893W/133, 896W/386, 896W/481, 896W/482, 896W/483, 896W/744, 896W/1914, 896W/2414, 993W/387, 993W/388, 993W/572, 996W/389, 998W/284, 1W/150, 1W/151, 1W/152, 119W/1, 1M 175.

Archives de la Direction du Patrimoine. Dossier de protection d'Oradour-sur-Glane.

Archives du Ministère de l'Equipement et du Logement, Mission auprès des Archives Nationales. AFU 10975.

Archives Nationales (Section contemporaine). 4 AG 3, 4 AG 92, F7 15431, F4135, F1cI/223, F1cI/227.

Bibliothèque de Documentation Internationale Contemporaine.

Bibliothèque du Patrimoine. Carton 3174 (Martyrium, 1951–1954; ruines du village, affaires générales, 1945–1971). Carton 3175 (restes du village, 1945–1953; ruines du village, 1948–1961; vestiges de l'ancien village, 1946–1959; vestiges de l'église, 1945–1948). Carton 3176 (vestiges: enceinte du village et jardins, 1945–1950; vestiges: tombeaux 1947–1952).

Hoover Institution Archives. World War II Subject Collection. Box 10, #246.

Interviews

Bardet, Louise, and Camille Bardet. Interview by Marc Wilmart, La Grange du Boeil, 8 March 1988.

Beaulieu, Jean-François. Interview by Sarah Farmer, Oradour-sur-Glane, 17 September 1988.

Bichaud, Lucette. Interview by Sarah Farmer, Limoges, 14 September 1988.

Bonthoux, Louis. Interview by Sarah Farmer, La Chapelle-en-Vercors, 4 September 1989.

de Catheu, Janique. Interview by Sarah Farmer, Oradour-sur-Glane, 13 February 1988.

Darthout, Marcel. Interview by Marc Wilmart, St-Victurnien, 7 March 1988. Interview by Sarah Farmer, St-Victurnien, 31 March 1988.

Desourteaux, André. Interviews by Marc Wilmart, Javerdat, 17 March 1988, with Robert Hébras, Oradour-sur-Glane, 11 June 1988. Interview by Michel Follin, Oradour-sur-Glane, 8 June 1988. Interviews by Sarah Farmer, Limoges, 1 April 1988; Oradour-sur-Glane, 28 August 1988, with Madame Desourteaux.

Godfrin, Roger. Interview by Sarah Farmer, Michel Follin, and Marc Wilmart, Bas-Ham (Moselle), January 1988. Interview by Marc Wilmart, Bas-Ham (Moselle), 22 March 1988.

Hébras, Robert. Interview by Marc Wilmart, Javerdat, 17 March 1988, with André Desourteaux.

Hyvernaud, Jean-Jacques. Tape recording of speech given at the ruined church, Oradour-sur-Glane, 24 September 1988.

Jude, Christiane. Interview by Marc Wilmart, Oradour-sur-Glane, 16 March 1988.

Kremp, Vincenz. Interview by Sarah Farmer, Michel Follin, and Marc Wilmart, Freiburg-im-Breisgau (Germany), January 1988. Interview by Sarah Farmer and Marc Wilmart, Chaptelat, 7 June 1988.

Lajarige, Annie. Interview by Sarah Farmer, Roussac/Berneuil, March 1988.

Lapuelle, Dr. Robert. Interviews by Sarah Farmer, Oradour-sur-Glane, March 1988; 21 May 1988; September 1988; 18 December 1988. Interview by Marc Wilmart, Oradour-sur-Glane, 7 March 1988.

Lebraud, Amélie. Interview by Marc Wilmart, Oradour-sur-Glane, 14 March 1988. Interview by Sarah Farmer, Oradour-sur-Glane, 27 March 1988.

Marguerin, Jean-François. Interviews by Marc Wilmart, Oradour-sur-Glane, 15 March 1988; Limoges, 9 June 1988.

Mester de Parajd, Gabor. Interview by Sarah Farmer, Versailles, 12 February 1988.

Montazeaud, Jeanette. Interview by Sarah Farmer, Oradour-sur-Glane, 17 September 1988.

Picarella, J. L. Interview by Sarah Farmer, Vassieux-en-Vercors, 3 September 1989.

Poncet, Philippe. Interviews by Marc Wilmart, Oradour-sur-Glane, 15 March 1988; Limoges 9 June 1988.

Valade, Albert. Interview by Guy Pouget, Oradour-sur-Glane, March 1988. Interview by Marc Wilmart, Oradour-sur-Glane, 3 June 1988.

Documents

ABCD. "Création d'un Equipement d'Accueil et de Muséographie, Dossier de Consultation des Concepteurs" (document provisoire dans sa forme). January 1993.

———. Etude sur la Fréquentation du Site, 28 November 1991.

Association Nationale des Familles des Martyrs d'Oradour-sur-Glane, Status. "Assemblée Générale du 6 mars 1988, compte-rendu financier." Photocopy.

———. "Project de modification présenté à l'Assemblée Générale du 6 Mars 1988." Photocopy.

———. *Statuts, revus et corrigés après la réunion de bureau du 20 janvier 1945.* Limoges: Imprimerie Charles-Lavauzelle et Cie, n.d.

Bombed Churches as War Memorials. Foreword by Hugh Casson, the Dean of St. Paul's Cheam, Surrey: The Architectural Press, 1945.

Comité Scientifique. "Dossier pour l'exposition permanente," Centre de la Mémoire du Village Martyr d'Oradour-sur-Glane. Conseil général de la Haute-Vienne, Limoges, 13 June 1995. Photocopy.

Comité du Souvenir d'Oradour-sur-Glane. *Procès-Verbaux des séances du Comité actif de conservation des ruines et création d'un sanctuaire à Oradour-sur-Glane.* Rochechouart: Imprimerie Justin Dupanier, 1945.

Direction Régionale des Affaires Culturelles, Limoges. Oradour-sur-Glane, étude sur la fréquentation du site, note d'analyse, 1992. Photocopy.

Front National. *Atrocités nazies.* Preface by Henri Wallon. Paris: 1945.

———. *Nous accusons: les calvaires de la Résistance.* Imprimerie du Front National, n.d.

Français, Françaises debout contre les monstres nazis! Voici comment un ecclésiastique relate le massacre d'Oradour. Limoges: June 1944.

Groc, Léon. *Oradour.* Collection "Patrie Libérée," no. 9. Paris: Rouff, 1945.

Journal officiel de la République française. Documents de l'Assemblée Nationale Constituante, Annexes aux procès-verbaux des séances. Annexe no. 855, Projet de loi relatif à la conservation des ruines et à la reconstruction d'Oradour-sur-Glane, annexe au procès-verbal de la 2e séance du 3 avril 1946. Pp. 825–26.

———. Documents de l'Assemblée Nationale Constituante, Annexes aux procès-verbaux des séances. Annexe no. 1041, Rapport fait au nom de la Commission de l'Education Nationale et des Beaux-Arts, de la Jeunesse, des Sports et des Loisirs, sur le projet de loi relatif à la conservation des ruines et à la reconstruction d'Oradour-sur-Glane, annexe au procès-verbal de la 3e séance du 15 avril 1946. Pp. 1014–15.

———. Débats parlementaires. Assemblée Nationale, séance du mercredi 18 février 1953. Pp. 1109–31.

———. [Alger], Lois et Décrets. Ordonnance du 28 août 1944 relative à la répression des crimes de guerre. Pp. 780.

———. Lois et Décrets. Loi no. 48–1416 du 15 septembre 1948 modifiant et complétant l'ordonnance du 28 août 1944 relative à la répression des crimes de guerre. Pp. 9138.

———. Assemblée Générale, Questions Ecrites, no. 48, séance du 7 décembre 1987.

Le Massacre d'Oradour-sur-Glane par les hordes hitlériennes. Limoges: Imprimerie Brégeras, 1945.

"Le Massacre d'Oradour-sur-Glane." Série "Ordre Nouveau" et Collaboration V-9, no. 9. n.p.: June 1945.

Mester de Parajd, Gabor. "Oradour-sur-Glane. Conservation des vestiges du village martyr." Study for the Ministère de la Culture. Paris, 1983.

Mouvement de Libération Nationale, *Les Huns à Oradour.* Limoges: La Société P.E.R.F.R.A.C., 25 January 1945.

Mouvement National Contre le Racisme. *Récits d'atrocités nazies, éditions de la clandestinité.* N.p., [1944].

Oradour-sur-Glane: souviens-toi = remember. Limoges: Imprimerie Lavauzelle, n.d.

[Pallier, Jean.] "Ma mission des 9, 10, 11, 12 et 13 juin 1944 à Limoges." N.p.: 23 June 1944. Compte-rendu des événements d'Oradour-sur-Glane. Mission effectuée par un ingénieur français les 9/10/11/12/13 juin. Typewritten manuscript. In the Bibliothèque de Documentation Internationale Contemporaine.

Vallière, Claude. *Oradour-sur-Glane, souviens-toi, remember.* Lyon: Imprimerie Hélio-Bellcour, 1953.

Books and Memoirs

Auriol, Vincent. *Journal du septennat, 1947–1954.* Edited by Pierre Nora and Jacques Ozouf. 7 vols. Paris: Librairie Armand Colin, 1970–71.

Barranx, Serge. *Mouleydier, village martyr.* Bordeaux: Editions Bière, 1945.

Brehec, Sophie. *Souviens-toi: Oradour-sur-Glane.* Paris: Encre, 1984.

Carter, Raymond. *Le Scandale d'Oradour.* Les Sables-d'Olonne: Editions le Cercle d'Or, 1975.

Centre d'Information et de Presse au Mexique du Gouvernement Provisoire de la République Française. *Terreur en France: les atrocités allemandes et vichyistes en France.* Preface by Jacques Berthet. Mexico, D.F.: 1944.

Comité de la Haute-Vienne de l'Association Nationale des Anciens Combattants de la Résistance. *Mémorial de la Résistance et des victimes du nazisme en Haute-Vienne.* Limoges: Imprimerie Technique, n.d.

Cuny, G. *La Bresse: cité vosgienne martyre sous l'occupation allemande, septembre, octobre, novembre, 1944.* Macon: Buguet-Comptour, Imprimeur-Editeur, 1946.

de Gaulle, Charles. *The Complete War Memoirs of Charles de Gaulle.* Translated by Richard Howard. New York: Simon and Schuster, 1967.

———. *Discours et messages: dans l'attente, février 1946–avril 1958.* Paris: Librairie Plon, 1970.

Delage, Franck. *Oradour, ville martyre.* Paris: Editions Mellottée, 1945.

Duras, Marguerite. *La Douleur.* Paris: P.O.L., 1985.

Flanner, Janet. *Paris Journal, 1944–1965.* Edited by William Shawn. New York: Atheneum, 1965.

Guingouin, Georges. *Quatre ans de lutte sur le sol limousin.* Paris: Hachette, 1974.

Hébras, Robert, *Comprendre le drame d'Oradour-sur-Glane.* Aérodrome 49400 Saumur: Editions CMD.

Hughes, David. *The Pork Butcher.* New York: Schocken Books, 1985.

Lecornu, Bernard. *Un Préfet sous l'occupation allemande, Châteaubriant, Saint-Nazaire, Tulle.* Paris: Editions France-Empire, 1984.

Malraux, André. *Oraisons funèbres.* Paris: Gallimard, 1971.

Mayran, Camille. *Larmes et lumières à Oradour.* Preface by Gabriel Marcel. Paris: Plon, 1952.

Morhange-Bégué, Claude. *Chamberet: Recollections from an Ordinary Childhood.* Translated by Austryn Wainhouse. Marlboro, Vermont: The Marlboro Press, 1987.

Musso, Fernand. *Après le raz de marée: témoignage du préfet de Corrèze sur le massacre de Maillé*. Treillières (44240): Pierre Gauthier Editeur, 1980.

Nardain, Bernard Beuer. *Les Francs-Tireurs et partisans français et l'insurrection nationale*. Paris, 1947.

Pauchou, Guy, and Dr. Pierre Masfrand. *Oradour-sur-Glane: vision d'épouvante, ouvrage officiel du Comité du Souvenir et de l'Association Nationale des Familles des Martyrs d'Oradour-sur-Glane*. Limoges: Charles-Lavauzelle et Cie, 1945.

Payon, Abbé André. *Un Village martyr, Maillé: récit du massacre du 25 août 1944*. Tours: Arrault et Cie, 1945.

Poitevin, Pierre. *Dans l'enfer d'Oradour*. Limoges: Société des Journaux et Publications du Centre, 1945.

Théolleyre, Jean-Marc. *Procès d'après-guerre*. Paris: Editions La Découverte et Journal *Le Monde*, 1985.

Trouillé, Pierre. *Journal d'un préfet pendant l'occupation allemande*. Paris: Gallimard, 1964.

Vincent, Madeleine, and Liseron Vincent-Doucet-Bon. *C'était un village de France . . .* Lyon: Editions de la Belle Cordière, n.d.

Newspapers and Magazines

L'Alsace
L'Aurore
Aspects de la France
Le Centre libre, organe des Comités de Libération
Centre Ce Soir France dimanche
Combat
Le Courrier du Centre
Courrier du Haut-Rhin
Le Crapouillot
Le Dauphiné libéré
Les Dernières Nouvelles d'Alsace
L'Echo du Centre
Le Figaro

Le Franc-Tireur (Edition sud)
Le Franc-Tireur (Edition de Paris)
France-soir
L'Humanité
Le Journal de Genève
Les Lettres françaises
Le Libérateur
La Liberté du Centre
La Marseillaise (Berry-Marche-Touraine)
Le Monde
Le Nouveau Rhin français
Le Nouvel Alsacien
Le Nouvel observateur
La Nouvelle République du Centre-Ouest
Paris-Presse l'intransigeant
Le Populaire du Bas-Languedoc, Aude, Aveyron, Gard, Hérault, Lozère, Pyrénées-O
Le Populaire du Centre
Le Populaire, organe du Parti Socialiste, édition de la zone nord
Rivarol
Sunday Times Magazine
Télé 7 jours
Le Temps
Le Travailleur Limousin
Die Zeit

Films

Oradour. First part, "Les Voix de la douleur"; second part, "Aujourd'hui la mémoire." Produced by FR3 Limousin-Poitou-Charentes and the Conseil Général de la Haute-Vienne. Directed by Michel Follin. Written by Marc Wilmart. 1989; color, 130 minutes.

Les Ya-Ya. Produced by FR3, Alsace. Directed by Alfred Elter. Written by Alain Dugrand and Monique Seeman. 1989; color, 52 minutes.

SECONDARY SOURCES

Ahne, Paul. "Le Monument aux morts de Strasbourg." *Archives alsaciennes d'histoire de l'art, 1936 extrait.* Strasbourg: Librairie Istra, 1936.

Agulhon, Maurice. "Les Communistes et la Libération de la France." In *La Libération de la France, actes du colloque international tenu à Paris du 28 au 31 octobre 1974.* Pp. 67–90. Paris: Editions du Centre National de la Recherche Scientifique, 1976.

Amouroux, Henri. *La Grande histoire des français sous l'occupation.* 8 vols. Paris: Robert Laffont, 1988. Vol. 8, *Joies et douleurs du peuple libéré,* 159–197.

Aron, Robert. *Histoire de l'épuration.* 3 vols. Paris: Fayard, 1967–1975.

Baas, Emile. *Situation de l'Alsace.* Strasbourg: Les Éditions de l'Est, 1946.

Bachelard, Gaston. *The Poetics of Space.* Translated by Maria Jolas. New York: The Orion Press, Inc., 1964.

Barral, Pierre. "L'Affaire d'Oradour, affrontement de deux mémoires." In *Mémoire de la Seconde Guerre Mondiale: actes du Colloque de Metz, 6–8 octobre 1983.* Edited by Alfred Wahl. Pp. 243–52. Metz: Centre de Recherche "Histoire et Civilisation de l'Europe Occidentale," 1984.

Bartov, Omer. *The Eastern Front, 1941–1945: German Troops and the Barbarisation of Warfare.* London: Macmillan, in association with St. Anthony's College, Oxford, 1985.

Baudot, Marcel. "L'Epuration: bilan chiffré." *Bulletin de l'Institut d'histoire du temps présent* 25 (September 1986).

Baudrillard, Jean. *Selected Writings.* Edited and introduced by Mark Poster. Stanford: Stanford University Press, 1990.

Beau, Georges, and Léopold Gaubusseau. *R.5: les S.S. en Limousin, Périgord, Quercy.* Paris: Presses de la Cité, 1969.

Beck, Philip. *Oradour, Village of the Dead.* London: Leo Cooper, 1979.

Becker, Jean-Jacques. *The Great War and the French People.* Dover, N.H.: Berg Publishers, 1985.

Bédarida, François. "L'Histoire dans la pensée et dans l'action du général de Gaulle." In *De Gaulle en son siècle, actes des journées internationales tenues à l'Unesco. Paris, 19–24 novembre 1990.* Vol. 1, pp. 141–49. Paris: Institut Charles de Gaulle, 1991.

Bellanger, Claude, ed. *Histoire générale de la presse française.* Vol. 4, *De 1940 à 1958.* Paris: Presses Universitaires de France, 1975.

Bopp, Marie-Joseph. "L'Enrôlement de force des Alsaciens dans la Wehrmacht et la S.S.," *Revue d'histoire de la deuxième guerre mondiale* 20 (October 1955): 33–42.

Boswell, Laird. *Rural Communism in France, 1920–1939.* Ithaca: Cornell University Press, 1998.

———. "Rural Communism in France, 1920–1939: The Example of the Limousin and the Dordogne." Ph.D. dissertation, University of California, Berkeley, 1988.

Bourget, Christian. "Entre amnistie et l'imprescriptible." In *Le Pardon: briser la dette et l'oubli.* Edited by Olivier Abel. Série Morales, no 4. Paris: Éditions Autrement, 1991.

Cahiers de l'Insitut d'histoire du temps présent 4: Questions à l'histoire orale, table ronde du 20 juin 1986 (1986).

Case, Malcolm, and Christopher Shaw, eds. *The Imagined Past: History and Nostalgia.* Manchester: Manchester University Press, 1989.

Cobb, Gerald. *London City Churches.* London: B. T. Batsford, 1989.

Ciganek, Ivan. *Lidice.* Prague: Orbis Press Agency, 1982.

Cobb, Richard. *French and Germans, Germans and French: A Personal Interpretation of France under Two Occupations, 1914–1918/1940–1944.* Hanover, N.H.: University Press of New England, 1983.

Cohen, Monique-Lise, and Eric Malo, eds. *Les Camps du sud-ouest de la France, 1939–1944.* Toulouse: Editions Privat, 1994.

Comité de la Haute-Vienne de l'Association Nationale des Anciens Combattants de la Résistance. *Mémorial de la Résistance et des victimes du nazisme en Haute-Vienne.* Limoges: A.N.A.C.R., 1988.

Corbin, Alain. *Le Territoire du vide: l'occident et le désir du rivage.* Paris: Aubier, 1988.

Cosgrove, Denis, and Stephen Daniels, eds. *The Iconography of Landscape: Essays on Symbolic Representation, Design and Use of Past Environments.* Cambridge: Cambridge University Press, 1988.

Courtois, Stéphane. *Le PCF dans la guerre: de Gaulle, la Résistance, Staline.* Paris: Ramsay, 1980.

Dannowski, Hans Werner, et al. *Kirche in der Stadt: Erinnern und Gedenken.* Hamburg: Stienmann and Steinmann, 1991.

Delarue, Jacques. *Trafics et crimes sous l'occupation.* Paris: Fayard, 1968.

Deloffre, Jacqueline. "Manche Hände zittern noch: In Oradour hat niemand vergessen, daß deutsche Soldaten alle Bewohner des Dorfes ermordeten." *Die Zeit,* 29 September 1990.

Delperrie de Bayac, J. *Histoire de la Milice.* Paris: Fayard, 1969.

"Dispensaire d'hygiène sociale; ensemble du souvenir d'Ascq." Les Frères Arsène-Henry, Architectes. D.P.E.G. *L'Architeture française* [Paris: Société et Editions Techniques] 10, no. 87–88 (1949): 5–12.

du Chalard, Roland, Claude Lacan, and Georges-Marc Proux. *Le Limousin de la défaite et de l'occupation. Chronique des années 1940–1944.* Limoges: René Desange, 1978.

Dupront, Alphonse. *Du Sacré: croisades et pèlerinages, images et langages.* Paris: Gallimard, 1987.

"Tourisme et pèlerinage: réflexions de psychologie collective." *Communications, Ecole pratique des hautes études, Centre d'études des communications de masse* 10 (1967): 97–121.

Durand, Yves, and Robert Vivier. *Libération des pays de Loire: Blésois, Orléanais, Touraine.* Paris: Librairie Hachette, 1974.

Duras, Marguerite. *La Douleur.* Paris: P.O.L., 1985.

Eco, Umberto. *Travels in Hyperreality: Essays.* New York: Harcourt Brace Jovanovich, 1986.

Edwards, Derek, and David Middleton, eds. *Collective Remembering.* Introduction. Newbury Park and London: Sage Publications, 1990.

Englund, Steven. "The Ghost of Nation Past." *Journal of Modern History* 64 (1992): 299–320.

Farmer, Sarah. "The Communist Resistance in the Haute-Vienne." *French Historical Studies* 14, no. 1, (Spring 1985): 89–116.

———. "Memorial Landscapes of World War II in France." *French Historical Studies* 19, no. 1 (Spring 1995): 27–47.

Felman, Shoshanna. "A l'âge du témoignage: *Shoah* de Claude Lanzmann." In *Au sujet de Shoah*. Edited by Michel Deguy. Paris: Belin, 1990.

Fentress, James, and Chris Wickham. *Social Memory*. Oxford: Blackwell, 1992.

Forster, Kurt. "Monument/Memory and the Mortality of Architecture." *Oppositions* 25 (Fall 1982): 2–19.

Foulon, Charles-Louis. *Le Pouvoir en province à la Libération: les commissaires de la République, 1943–1946*. Paris: Presses de la Fondation Nationale des sciences politiques, 1975.

Frank, Robert. "Bilan d'une enquête." In *La Mémoire des Français*, ed. Institut d'histoire du temps présent. Pp. 371–93. Paris: Editions du Centre National de la Recherche Scientifique, 1986.

Fussell, Paul. *The Great War and Modern Memory*. London: Oxford University Press, 1975.

Gillis, John, ed. *Commemorations: The Politics of National Identity*. Princeton: Princeton University Press, 1994.

Girard, Bruno. "Les Grands Voyages du général de Gaulle en province après la Libération." Mémoire de maîtrise, l'Université de Paris IV, 1980–1981.

Grenier, Fernand. *Ceux de Châteaubriant*. Paris: Éditions Sociales, 1961.

Grosser, Alfred. *Le Crime et la mémoire*. Paris: Flammarion, 1989.

Grynberg, Anne. *Les Camps de la honte: les internés juifs des camps français, 1939–1944*. Paris: Editions la Découverte, 1991.

Guicheteau, Gérard. *La "Das Reich" et le coeur de la France*. Paris: Editions Daniel, L'Echo du Centre, 1974.

Guingouin, Georges, and Gérard Mondèdiare. *Georges Guingouin: premier maquisard de France*. Limoges: Editions L. Souny, 1983.

Hacking, Ian. *Rewriting the Soul: Multiple Personality and the Sciences of Memory*. Princeton: Princeton University Press, 1995.

Halbwachs, Maurice. *Les Cadres sociaux de la mémoire*. Paris: Librairie Félix Alcan, 1925.

———. *La Mémoire collective*. Paris: Presses Universitaires de France, 1950.

———. *La Topographie légendaire des évangiles en terre sainte*. Paris: Presses Universitaires de France, 1941.

Hardy, René. "Langages et dialectes parlés en Alsace-Lorraine." Rapport au Congrès international des amitiés françaises: Mons, septembre 1911. Cited in *Témoignages pour les Alsaciens-Lorrains.* Paris: Librairie Plon, 1925.

Hastings, Max. *Das Reich: Resistance and the March of the 2nd Panzer Division through France, June 1944.* London: Michael Joseph, 1981.

Helsey, Edouard. *Notre Alsace: l'enquête du "Journal" et le procès de Colmar.* Paris: Albin Michel, 1927.

History and Anthropology 2: Between Memory and History. Edited by Maire-Noelle Bourget, Lucette Valensi, and Nathan Watcher.

Hivernaud, Albert. *Petite histoire d'Oradour-sur-Glane.* Limoges: Imprimerie A. Bontemps, 1985.

Horne, Donald. *The Great Museum: The Re-presentation of the History.* London and Sydney: Pluto Press, 1984.

Hostache, René. *Le Conseil national de la Résistance: les institutions de la clandestinité.* Paris: Presses Universitaires de France, 1958.

Institut d'Histoire du Temps Présent. "Les Commémorations françaises de la Seconde Guerre Mondiale: actes du colloques de Sèvres du 4 et 5 février 1985, Centre International d'études pédagogiques."

———. *La Mémoire des français.* Paris: Editions du Centre National de la Recherche Scientifique, 1986.

Jackson, J. B. *The Necessity for Ruins, and Other Topics.* Amherst: University of Massachusetts Press, 1980.

Jaeckel, Eberhard. *Frankreich in Hitlers Europa: Die Deutsche Frankreichpolitik im Zweiten Weltkrieg.* Stuttgart: Deutsche Verlags-Anhalt, 1966.

Journal of American History 75: Memory and History: A Special Issue. March 1989.

Joutard, Philippe. *Ces voix qui nous viennent du passé.* Paris: Hachette, 1983.

Judt, Tony. *Past Imperfect: French Intellectuals, 1944–1956.* Berkeley: University of California Press, 1992.

Kedward, H. R. *Resistance in Vichy France: A Study of Ideas and Motivation in the Southern Zone, 1940–1942.* Oxford: Oxford University Press, 1978.

————. *In Search of the Maquis: Rural Resistance in Southern France, 1942–1944.* Oxford: Clarendon Press, 1993.

Klarsfeld, Serge. *Le Livre des otages.* Preface by Marie-Claude Vaillant Couturier. Paris: Les Editeurs Français Réunis, 1979.

Kselman, Thomas A. *Miracles and Prophecies in Nineteenth-Century France.* New Brunswick, N.J.: Rutgers University Press, 1983.

Laboratoire Espace Rural et Montagne, Ecole d'Architecture de Grenoble. *La Chapelle-en-Vercors (Drome), village reconstruit, 1944– 1984.* Catalogue for an exhibit in 1985 at the Archives départementales de l'Isère (Grenoble) and the town hall of La Chapelle-en-Vercors.

Langer, Lawrence L. *Holocaust Testimonies: The Ruins of Memory.* New Haven: Yale University Press, 1991.

Larkin, Maurice. *France since the Popular Front: Government and People, 1936–1986.* Oxford: Oxford University Press, 1988.

Levi, Primo. *The Drowned and the Saved.* New York: Vintage Books, 1989.

Lewis, Pierce F. "Axioms for Reading the Landscape: Some Guides to the American Scene." In *The Interpretation of Ordinary Landscapes,* ed. D. W. Meining. New York and Oxford: Oxford University Press, 1979.

Limagne, Pierre. *Ephémérides de quatres années tragiques.* 3 vols. Bonne Presse, 1987.

Lowenthal, David. *The Past Is a Foreign Country.* Cambridge: Cambridge University Press, 1985.

MacCannell, Dean. *The Tourist: A New Theory of the Leisure Class.* New York: Schocken Books, 1976.

MacDonald, Callum. *The Killing of Obergrüppenführer Reinhard Heydrich.* New York: Free Press, 1989.

Mackness, Robin. *Oradour: Massacre and Aftermath.* Introduction by John Fowles. London: Bloomsbury Publishing Ltd., 1988.

Mayer, Arno. "Memory and History: On the Poverty of Remembering and Forgetting the Judeocide." *Radical History Review* 56 (Spring 1993): 5–20.

Mayo, James M. *War Memorials as Political Landscape in the American Experience*. New York: Praeger, 1988.

Meinig, D. W. Introduction to *The Interpretation of Ordinary Landscapes: Geographical Essays*, ed. D. W. Meinig. Pp. 11–32. New York and Oxford: Oxford University Press, 1979.

Michel, Henri. *The Shadow War*. London: Deutsch, 1972.

Middleton, David, and Derek Edwards. Introduction to *Collective Remembering*, eds. Middleton and Edwards. Pp. 1–22. Newbury Park and London: Sage Publications, 1990.

Milo, Daniel. "Le Nom des rues." In *Les Lieux de mémoire*, Pierre Nora. Vol. 2, pt. 3: 281–315. Paris: Gallimard, 1986.

Milton, Sybil. *In Fitting Memory: The Art and Politics of Holocaust Memorials*. Detroit: Wayne State University, 1991.

———. *Collective Remembering*. Newbury Park and London: Sage Publications, 1990.

Namer, Gérard. *Batailles pour la mémoire: la commémoration en France de 1945 à nos jours*. Paris: S.P.A.G/Papyrus, 1983.

Nardain, Bernard Beuer. *Les Francs-tireurs et partisans français et l'insurrection nationale (juin 1940–août 1944)*. Paris: Les Editions Internationales de Presse et de Publicité, 1947.

Naumann, Uwe. *Lidice: Ein böhmisches Dorf*. Frankfurt-am-Main: Röderberg-Verlag Frankfurt, 1983.

Noguères, Henri. *Histoire de la Résistance en France*. 5 vols. Paris: Robert Laffont, 1967–1981.

Nora, Pierre. "Between Memory and History: *Les Lieux de Mémoire*." Trans. Marc Raudebush. *Representations* 26 (Spring 1989): *Special Issue: Memory and Counter-Memory*, 7–25.

Nora, Pierre. Foreword to *Les Lieux de mémoire*. Ed. Pierre Nora. Vol. 1, pt. 1: vii–xlii. Paris: Gallimard, 1984–1993.

Novick, Peter. *The Resistance versus Vichy: The Purge of Collaborators in Liberated France*. New York: Columbia University Press, 1968.

Orvell, Miles. *The Real Thing: Imitation and Authenticity in American Culture, 1880–1940*. Chapel Hill: University of North Carolina Press, 1989.

Ophuls, Marcel. *The Sorrow and the Pity: Chronide of a French City under the German Occupation, a Film*. Introduction by Stanley Hoffman. Filmscript translated by Mireille Johnston. New York: Outerbridge and Lazard, Inc., 1972.

Ozouf, Mona. "Peut-on commémorer la Révolution française?" *Le débat* 26 (September 1983): 161–72.

Pastaud, Françoise. "Contribution à l'étude des maquis F.T.P.F. en Haute-Vienne." Mémoire de maîtrise, Université de Poitiers, 1969.

Paxton, Robert. *Vichy France: Old Guard and New Order, 1940–1944*. New York: Columbia University Press, 1972.

Perouas, Louis. *Les Limousins, leurs saints, leurs prêtres, du XVe au XXe siècle*. Paris: Les Editions du Cerf, 1988.

———. "Ostentions et cultes des saints en Limousin: une approche ethno-historique." *Ethnologie française* 13, no. 4 (1983): *Les Ostentions limousines*, 323–36.

Prost, Antoine. *Les Anciens Combattants*. Paris: Gallimard, 1977.

———. "Verdun." In *Les Lieux de mémoire*. Ed. Pierre Nora. Vol. 2, pt. 3: 111–41. Paris: Gallimard, 1986.

———. "Les Monuments aux morts: culte républicain? culte civique? culte patriotique?" In *Les Lieux de mémoire*. Ed. Pierre Nora. Vol. 1, pt. 1: 195–225. Paris: Gallimard, 1984.

Quantrill, Malcolm. *The Environmental Memory: Man and Architecture in the Landscape of Ideas*. New York: Shocker Books, 1987.

Renan, Ernst. "What Is a Nation?" In *Becoming National: A Reader*, eds. Geoff Eley and Ronald Grigor Suny. Oxford: Oxford University Press, 1996.

Representations 26 (Spring 1989). *Special Issue: Memory and Counter-Memory*.

Rioux, Jean-Pierre. "L'Epuration en France, 1944–1945." In *Etudes sur la France de 1939 à nos jours*, 162–77. Paris: Editions du Seuil, 1985.

———. *The Fourth Republic, 1944–1958*. Trans. Godfrey Rogers. The Cambridge History of Modern France, no. 7. Cambridge University Press, 1987.

Rosch, Lea, and Günther Schwarberg. *Der letze Tag von Oradour.* Göttingen: Steidl Verlag, 1988.

Rouquet, François. *L'Epuration dans l'administration française.* Paris: CNRS Editions, 1993.

Rousso, Henry. *Le Syndrome de Vichy, 1944–198* . . . Paris: Editions du Seuil, 1987.

———. "L'Epuration en France: une histoire inachevée." *Vingtième siècle* 33 (January–March 1992): 78–105.

Santer, Eric L. *Stranded Objects: Mourning and Memory and Film in Postwar Germany.* Ithaca, N.Y.: Cornell University Press, 1990.

Savy, Robert. " Recherches sur le personnel politique en Haute-Vienne, 1945–1965." Mémoire pour le D.E.S. de Sciences Politiques, Université de Poitiers, n.d.

Schama, Simon. *Landscape and Memory.* New York: Knopf, 1995.

Schwartz, Vanessa R. *Spectacular Realities: Early Mass Culture in Fin-de-Siècle Paris.* Berkeley: University of California Press, 1998.

Sherman, Daniel. "Art, Commerce, and the Production of Memory in France after World War I." In *Commemorations: The Politics of National Identity*, ed. John Gillis. Pp. 186–211. Princeton: Princeton University Press, 1994.

Silverman, Dan. *Reluctant Union: Alsace-Lorraine and Imperial Germany, 1871–1919.* University Park and London: University of Pennsylvannia Press, 1972.

Smith, Valene. Introduction to *Hosts and Guests: The Anthropology of Tourism*, ed. Valene Smith. Pp. 1–14. Philadelphia: University of Pennsylvannia Press: 1977.

Sollers, Pierre. "Littérature: le retour des précieux." *Le Nouvel Observateur* 525 (28 December 1974).

Sweets, John F. *Choices in Vichy France: The French under Nazi Occupation.* New York: Oxford University Press, 1986.

———. *The Politics of Resistance in France, 1940–1944: A History of the Mouvements Unis de la Résistance.* Dekalb: Northern Illinois Press, 1976.

Taubmann, Michel. *L'Affaire Guingouin.* Limoges: Lucien Souny, 1994.

Tillon, Charles. *Les. F.T.P., la guérilla en France.* Paris: Juillard, 1967.

Todorov, Tzvetan. *Une Tragédie française, été 1944: scènes de guerre civile.* Paris: Editions du Seuil, 1994.

Troyansky, David G. "Monumental Politics: National History and Local Memory in French *Monuments aux Morts* in the Department of the Aisne since 1870." *French Historical Studies*, 15, no. 1 (Spring 1987): 121–41.

Tuan, Yi-fu. *Topophilia: A Study of Environmental Perception, Attitudes and Values.* Englewood Cliffs, N.J.: Prentice-Hall, 1974.

———. *Space and Place: The Perspective of Experience.* Minneapolis: University of Minnesota Press, 1977.

Vallin, Pierre. *Paysans Rouges du Limousin.* Paris: L'Harmattan, 1985.

Veillon, Dominique. *Vivre et Survivre en France (1939–1947).* Paris: Editions Payot & Rivages, 1995.

"Verdun: les débuts de la reconstruction, 1919–1922." *Connaissance de la Meuse: revue trimestrielle de l'Association Connaissance de la Meuse* (Bar-le-Duc) 6 (October 1987): 8–11.

Wahl, Alfred. Introduction to *Mémoire de la Seconde Guerre Mondiale: Actes du Colloque de Metz, 6–8 octobre 1983,* ed. Alfred Wahl. Pp. 227–42. Metz: Centre de Recherche Histoire et Civilisation de l'Université de Metz, 1984.

Weber, Eugen. *Peasants Into Frenchmen: The Modernization of Rural France, 1870–1914.* Stanford: Stanford University Press, 1976.

Wieviorka, Annette. "Un Lieu de mémoire: le mémorial du martyr juif inconnu." *Revue Pardès* 2 (1985): 80–98.

Wilkinson, James. "Remembering World War II: The Perspective of the Losers." *American Scholar* (Summer 1985): 329–43.

Yerushalmi, Yosef Hayim. *Zakhor: Jewish History and Jewish Memory.* Seattle: University of Washington Press, 1982.

Young, James E. "The Biography of a Memorial Icon." *Representations* 26 (Spring 1989): *Special Issue: Memory and Counter-Memory,* 69–106.

———. *The Texture of Memory: Holocaust Memorials and Meaning.* New Haven: Yale University Press, 1993.

———. *Writing and Rewriting the Holocaust: Narrative and the Consequences of Interpretation.* Bloomington: Indiana University Press, 1988.

PHOTO CREDITS

Endpapers. Map adapted from Robert Hébras, *Comprendre le drame d'Oradour-sur-Glane* (Aérodrome 49400 Saumur: Editions CMD).

Frontispiece. Courtesy of Arno Gisinger, Atelier für Fotographie und Visual History.

1. Vintage postcard, author's collection.

2. Courtesy of the Conseil Général de la Haute-Vienne.

3. Photograph by Lucien Lavaux, courtesy of Archives Documentation Française.

4. Photograph by Lapi, Agence Roger-Viollet.

5. Photograph by Lapi, Agence Roger-Viollet.

6. Photograph by Lucien Lavaux, courtesy of Archives Photothèque Baron.

7. Photograph courtesy of the Institut Charles de Gaulle; rights reserved.

8. Drawn and engraved by René Serres, courtesy of the Service National des Timbres de Poste.

9. Photograph by the author.

10. Photograph by the author.

11. Photograph by the author.

12. Photograph by the author.

13. Photograph by the author.

14. Photograph by the author.

15. Photograph by Lucien Lavaux, courtesy of Archives Photothèque Baron.

16. Photograph by M. Deschamps, Scoop Paris Match.

17. Photograph by M. Deschamps, Scoop Paris Match.

18. Photograph courtesy of Fonds Combier, Musée Nicéphore Niépce, Ville de Chalon-sur-Saône, France.

19. Photograph by the author.

20. Photograph by the author.

21. Photograph by the author.

22. Photograph by the author.

23. Photograph by the author.

24. Photograph by Arch Photo. Paris/S.P.A.D.E.M.

INDEX

Page numbers in italics refer to illustrations.

DESIGNER

Nola Burger

COMPOSITOR

Impressions Book and Journal Services, Inc.

TEXT

10/15 Janson

DISPLAY

Agency; Univers Condensed

PRINTER AND BINDER

Data Reproductions